THE THOUGHT EXCHANGE®

Overcoming Our Resistance to Living a *Sensational* Life

Louise —
Life is SENSATIONAL!
Love,
David Friedman

by
David Friedman

Published By Library Tales Publishing

ISBN: 978-0-578-07790-1

ART: Robert Hicks
EDITOR: Andrew Monroe

Published and Distributed by Library Tales Publishing, Inc.
244 5th Avenue, Suite Q222, New York, NY, 10001
Phone: (347) 394-2629
Fax: (917) 463-0892
www.LibraryTalesPublishing.com

Printed in the United States of America

"Practicing David Friedman's THOUGHT EXCHANGE ideas has been the most fundamentally life-changing, positive experience I've ever had."

LUCIE ARNAZ

****

"I've had the privilege of attending many inspirational and motivational presentations in my years in ministry. Few can parallel the excellence that David Friedman brings to the table. He is a natural and gifted educator and musician with an uncanny capacity to draw out from individuals their inherent gifts and talents. By applying the wisdom found in these pages, you will be able to turn desire into demonstration and realize your inherent magnificence."

REV. RUSSELL HEILAND
FIRST UNITY OF ST. PETERSBURG

****

"David's book was like a miracle dropped in my lap at a time of great need. His concepts helped me to flip my thoughts about a situation and reach for different possibilities about the way I was seeing a painful circumstance. I am now living my dream life instead of the unhappy life that I thought was my future. Thank you, David, for giving us The Thought Exchange!"

TANYA MURPHY

"You brought a lot of class to our program and personally helped me with a road block I could not get around. I am better because I met you, and look forward to our paths crossing again."

ELIZABETH A. JOYNER
PRESIDENT – OKLAHOMA WOMEN'S BAR ASSOCIATION

****

"Thanks for taking the time to address your own issues so that you're now able to explain these concepts so clearly that we can actually understand and use them."

JOHN LOCHNER
UNITY OF DALLAS

****

"It was as if something unlocked within me at The Thought Exchange Wednesday night. I've read countless books, and all roads have lead to your door. What you give, share and teach with such clarity and simplicity all pulls together on a personal level and the professional, creative level. It is, for me, like a giant piece of a puzzle that kept eluding me, and now I've found it."

DORA RUBIN
NEW YORK CITY

"There isn't a way for me to express my gratitude for you or for your work. I have a renewed way of looking at the world since I began studying with you. I never truly believed that I could walk through my feelings. I have now done it, and I know that this new ability is a direct result of going to your classes. The moment when things "clicked" was just astonishing."

MELISSA GARNO
NEW YORK CITY

****

"Everyone was stunned by the emotional impact of the music and I believe forever changed by the experience."

"Yesterday was superb... totally beyond my expectations!"

"Such talent and many of the songs had "brilliant' written all over them. So many tears in the audience."

WORKSHOP & CONCERT ATTENDEES
UNITY OF SAN FRANCISCO

****

"I can't think of any experience like this, where the level of heartfelt consciousness is so active and trusting, and inspiring for us to continue working on our most creative project, ourselves... and to have someone like you who really gets it all and makes it happen is a gift. I feel very lucky to have landed in this space. It's an incredible experience which requires work, hard work, in allowing feelings to take center stage."

ARJE SHAW
AUTHOR OF "THE FIX"

ACKNOWLEDGEMENTS

I would like to express my gratitude to Paul Tenaglia, Founding Minister of Unity of New York, for giving me the opportunity to take over The Artists' Circle, where I was first able to develop the principles of Thought Exchange; to Susan Hasho, Augie Hasho, Jaye Restivo and Robert Yarnall, for being my "guinea pigs" and participating in my experimental workshop, where we explored resistance and how to move through it; to Susan Hasho for generously editing my first manuscript; to Pat Brody, whose constant suggestions to look at how feelings figure into the equation added important depth and relevance to The Thought Exchange; to Arje Shaw for being such an enthusiastic supporter of my work and for generously introducing me to Usher Morgan, CEO of Library Tales, who by agreeing to publish this book, has given me the opportunity to spread the wealth of my discoveries and teachings to a wider audience; to Shawn Moninger for reasons too numerous and complex to list; and most of all, to the thousands of people who have participated with me in Thought Exchange Workshops in New York and around the country. Your willingness to trust me with your deepest thoughts and feelings has not only allowed this work to develop and thrive, but has allowed me to personally develop and thrive as well."

And most importantly....

No matter how specific the method of working, no matter how "controlled" or "in the mind" it may seem, let us never forget that all that we do operates within a system that is much greater than we are and that is essentially unknowable. Call it Spirit, call it God, call it Source, I give thanks for the reliable, unswerving, omnipresence whose laws cannot fail and within which our possibilities are truly unlimited.

TABLE OF CONTENTS

PART 5: STAYING WITH SENSATIONS   *157*

Chapter 19: AFFECT TOLERANCE

PART6: APPLYING THOUGHT EXCHANGE   *175*

Chapter 20: LOVE, RELATIONSHIP, HEALTH, MONEY AND DIETING   177

Chapter 21: FOR PEOPLE IN THE CREATIVE ARTS   203

Chapter 22: APPLYING THOUGHT EXCHANGE PRINCIPLES TO CORPORATE COACHING   217

PART 8: STORIES, METAPHORS AND POINTS OF INFORMATION

AUTHOR'S FOREWARD

"Our thoughts create our reality. What we think appears before us in the world. Change your thoughts and you change your life."

We all know this. Why don't we do it?

With the recent mainstream popularity of *The Secret* and so many other wonderful books and seminars on New Thought, people are, more than ever, thinking that all you have to do is think a thought and whatever you want will appear.

In my experience, this is actually true. A new thought does create a new reality. But why is it that when most of us try it, we soon become discouraged and don't follow through? We're not stupid. We're not lazy. We're not just missing the point. There must be something else to it, something we're not taking into account. There must be something that frightens us, some perceived danger that kicks in when we take on a new thought, that causes us to drop the thought and go back to our old thought.

I began writing this book because, in my own life and in my teaching, I had stumbled upon a way of working with new thought that was producing amazing results in helping people to manifest what they wanted to see in their lives. People were very excited about this, and would jump in, exchange thoughts, and immediately see changes in their lives. But then, for inexplicable reasons, resistance would suddenly come up, people would go back to their old thoughts, and their old patterns of not achieving what they desired would reappear.

I knew I was on to something with "The Thought Exchange," but I also knew that unless I tackled the resistance, and was able to help people to "stay on the horse" of their new thought through any difficulties that might arise, I would only be telling half the story.

In this book, I tell the whole story. As happens in many New Thought books, you may become very excited as you read the first few chapters and realize that you have in your hands, a way to see all your dreams appear effortlessly in the world before you. But should you, as also often happens, hit that wall of resistance, I promise you, this book will not drop you, but will give you the tools to move through that to a real and true mastery of healing and manifestation.

So join me on a ride that perhaps you have begun many times, and know that this time, I'll stay with you until you get to where you want to go.

INTRODUCTION

Look in a mirror. What do you see there? You see yourself. You see what you're wearing. You see what you look like. Right? But what's really in the mirror? Is there anything real in the mirror? If there was a smudge on the nose of the image in the mirror, could you take Windex and wipe it off? If you didn't like what the image in the mirror was wearing, could you reach into the mirror and change the outfit? Of course not. It would be ridiculous to try, and no one in their right mind would even think of doing that.

And yet, in our lives, we try to do just that every day. We try to get others to behave differently. We think we'll be happier if we can get a raise, find the right partner, or win some personal battle we're fighting. Time and again, we look at the circumstances in our world as though they're "out there," and try to change them, "out there."

What if the world is not where real life takes place, but merely a mirror of our thoughts, an outward reflection designed purely to show us and reflect back to us what we are thinking? Without a mirror, you have no way of knowing what your own face looks like, yet any change you might make to your face as a result of what you see in the mirror would be made on your face, not in the mirror.

Like many people I know, I got into spiritual work for, shall we say, non-spiritual reasons. Although I claimed I was seeking "inner peace," communion with God, a deeper understanding, if truth be told, I was really seeking all these things so that I could have the "stuff" I wanted. Somehow, I thought that the source of my happiness would be a lot of money, a great home (or two or three) the right relationship, massive success in my work, etc. If I paid attention, I noticed that people who had those things were not necessarily happier than I was, but I tended to ignore that. Whatever it took, prayer, meditation, EST, The Forum, Primal Scream, therapy, retreats, I was going to do those things so that I could have "stuff." I actually thought of inner peace and harmony as the booby prize, things I would have to try to settle for if I was unsuccessful at achieving the REAL purpose in life, having success, money and "a relationship." I would hear a statement like, "Seek ye first the Kingdom" and silently add, "So I can have a new car." Sound familiar?

So I set out on my journey to try to find a way to get "stuff." I figured that if I could uncover the secret to manifesting what I wanted in the REAL world, I could control my life, have whatever I wanted whenever I wanted it, and "Be Happy."

So many systems, so many new thought institutions, so many books, offer the promise that if you follow their method, you will manifest whatever you want, and thus lead a fulfilled and happy life. I've read most of those books, participated in many of those seminars, but somehow I always ended up frustrated and disappointed. I began to wonder why, so I made up my mind to explore that very question.

I decided I would do this by observing life in general, and specifically my experience of it, and asking the question, "What is irrefutably true?" The answers I found were very surprising, and in fact, the opposite of what I'd expected. Not only that, they were the opposite of what I'd hoped to find. But in the end (and of course there's no such thing as the end, just where we are right now) I found everything I'd been looking for, but in surprising and different ways.

This book is the story of that journey, the steps I took along the way, and how each piece of progress led to the next wall, the next blockage, the next question which had to be addressed and answered in order to progress. Each step seemed to be "the answer," until I ran into another question, another "loophole" which led to the next step. But suddenly, without realizing how far I'd travelled, I found myself in a life that looked and felt completely different, because my life was being lived in a completely different context, in a completely different place. In this place, it didn't matter what events occurred. It didn't matter what "happened." Because in the place I lived, none of that had any effect on my happiness.

Now that idea may seem disappointing to some. "Where's the success? Where's the striving? Where's the excitement?" But think of it like this. Imagine being in the stock market, and having a system where you make money whether the stock market goes up or down? Doesn't matter. You make money.

A great deal of my journey was made using the stock market as a laboratory, as money had always been something by which I'd measured my success. I don't know about you, but I'd rather make money all the time, not just when conditions are a certain way. And I'd rather know that I'm happy and successful all the time, no matter what's happening.

I won't tell you right away what that surprising and different place is. I think the only way to truly get there is to take the journey and go through all the steps of discovery as I did (and as I, of course, continue to do.)

The first section of this book is my personal story, which led up to the discoveries and revelations that changed my life. The facts and events are particular to me, but hopefully they will resonate with what you have experienced in your earlier life.

If you want to go right to the Thought Exchange Method without the story, simply skip to Section 2 and begin reading there.

At any rate, hopefully you'll recognize your own journey as you walk through mine with me.

HOW TO USE THIS BOOK

This book has been written and rewritten many times. My original goal in writing it was to give the public a succinct description of the Thought Exchange process and how it could be used to "get what you want" in the world. But as I wrote the book, and continued to teach and practice Thought Exchange, I began to discover that there was so much more to it than that. Not only did I keep uncovering new applications, new areas in which Thought Exchange could be used effectively, but I also eventually had a complete turn-around in the way I saw life and in my understanding of what's important and where we really live.

My goal in writing the book now became twofold. One, to take the reader on the entire transformational journey that I have traveled up to now-with Thought Exchange, and two, to provide a complete reference guide where people could find the information they needed to apply Thought Exchange to whatever areas of their life and work they wished.

Hence, this book is divided into sections which can be read together or separately. The only sections you must read in order to understand everything else are Sections 2, 3 and 4, which describe the basic Thought Exchange® principles as they unfolded to me over time. If you want a complete history of my journey from living on the "outside" to living on the "inside," by all means read the entire book.

Once you've read Sections 2, 3 and 4, if you're having trouble staying with your sensations, read Section 5. If you have a particular area of interest, such as Singing, Corporate Work, Health, Forgiveness or numerous others, you can go to the specific sections or chapters that address those. If you want a group of inspirational stories, revelatory experiences and ideas pertaining to Thought Exchange, there's a chapter full of those. And if you want examples of "new thoughts" or definitions of terms as we use them in Thought Exchange, those can be found in the Appendix at the back of the book.

Sometimes, in order to make sure that each section can stand alone as well as be part of this book, I will repeat information from one section in another section. If you are reading the book in its entirety, do not skip these repeats, but simply use them to strengthen your insights or give you new ones.

One thing I must point out is that although these individual sections stand on their own, none of them gives the whole story. The information in each section can be applied without reading the other sections (as long as you've read sections 2, 3 and 4 to get the basic Thought Exchange® principles) but remember that the conclusions and revelations that we come to at the end of each section are only steps on a continuing path to complete transformation. Only by reading the whole book will you get the whole story.

However you use this book, I hope it brings you to new levels of understanding that enhance your experience of your life and its possibilities. As the title promises, it is my fervent goal that all who read it come away knowing that life is *sensational*, all the time.

PART I
LIFE BEFORE THE THOUGHT EXCHANGE

CHAPTER 1
"THE PURPOSE OF LIFE"
(ACCORDING TO DAVID FRIEDMAN – AGE 5-20)

I spent the first several decades of my life learning, and trying to live, the same things that so many of us were taught. Life was about the physical world. The object of life was to be successful in obtaining the "things" that made one happy. And those things were money, success and "love."

Money could buy you anything you wanted, give you comfort, give you power, provide you with safety, and keep you away from experiencing many of life's more disturbing challenges.

Success would mean not only that you were fulfilled in your work, but that you would have a constant sense of joy and contentment, the respect of others, and yes, all the money you would need to buy the things which would make you happy (like homes, cars, trips and even glamorous partners) and avoid the things that would make you unhappy (like flying coach, not being able to pay your bills, having to work at a job you didn't care for.)

And "love." Love meant having "a relationship," a marriage to someone who always understood you, who supported you and whom you supported, whom you could count on to give you a feeling of security and happiness and safety at all times. Love also meant a family that was always there for you, and friends on whom you could always depend and with whom you could always have a wonderful time.

This was the object of life. The "things" you needed in order to be happy, were money, success and "love."

Movie stars were happy. Why? Because they had money, success and "love." It didn't matter if they married and divorced several times, or periodically ended up in rehab. They were always with someone glamorous, they were always starring in movies for which they were getting paid a fortune, so as my grandma Gussie used to say (with Jewish inflection) "What's not to be happy?"

Business tycoons were happy. They could afford all the luxuries in life, had unlimited financial resources, and could buy their way out of anything unpleasant.

Grandma Gussie (clearly, and perhaps unfortunately, one of the greatest influences on my early philosophy of life) once told my older brother that she "only wanted to see him married." My brother felt compelled to ask her, "What's so wonderful about marriage? Is your marriage so great?" to which she replied, "Never mind that. First get married. Then we'll discuss it!" Marriage made you happy. So you needed to get married as quickly as possible. It didn't really matter to whom, as long as she was Jewish, though her coming from a rich family would definitely be a plus, since that way you could kill two birds with one stone. Love and money.

So having money, success and love were the goal in life. But they were not really considered an end in themselves, but rather a means to an end. They were the way to find "inner peace," and "happiness. By getting things on the outside, you could achieve inner peace and happiness on the inside.

Behind all this was some concept of "God." God ran everything. So if we wanted to be happy, we had to go to God. The purpose of connecting with, or at least "believing in" God was so that God (whoever and wherever He was – it was so annoying that He always seemed to be invisible) would be more inclined to allow us to have the things that would make us happy. Money, success and love.

Oh yes, you had to be a "good person" too. But the reason you needed to be a good person was so that God would like you and allow you to have the money, success and love that would make you happy.

So to review:

- Life was about being happy.
- The way to be happy was to have money, success and "love."
- If you were a "good person" and believed in God, God would help you to get those things.

Sound familiar?

All this seemed pretty straightforward and clear to me, so very early on, I started down the prescribed path to "happiness." I set goals, tried to figure out what I would "be" when I grew up (based not only on whether I liked to do it, but on how much money I could make and how much prestige and admiration I might receive.)

I constantly viewed my life as working toward some goal which, when achieved, would mean I had arrived and would live "happily ever after." The achievement of this goal would determine my value as a person. In other words, I identified myself as those achievements. My life in the present was not important. It was just a path to that future time when I would "have it all."

I worked hard. I got good grades. I went to college. I was a "good boy." I met the "love of my life" at age 14 and we were engaged when I was 19." Young, I know, but I felt I was getting ahead of most people, moving more quickly toward happiness than most of my friends who were floundering as to what they wanted to do or whom they wanted to be with. I wasn't wasting time by trying different things or questioning what I wanted or making "unnecessary" mistakes. I was flying along, checking off the requisite achievements and on the path to the job I wanted (concert pianist) the money I wanted (which would be brought in by the job) and the success and recognition I wanted (after all, I'd be on the stage playing beautifully for people, traveling, being written up in magazines and newspapers, on T.V.) I had the love in place, I was about to marry a beautiful girl who, in fact, was the only woman I had ever been with, giving me an added sense of the purity and perfection of our love. (My parents had had a similar history, which I was emulating.)

In the background, somewhere inside of me, I had a constant sense of anxiety and tension. It could be said that I felt "disconnected," as though my life was not real. But I just assumed that that was because I hadn't yet put all the elements of happiness together. I figured if I kept working at it, kept moving forward, the anxiety would go away.

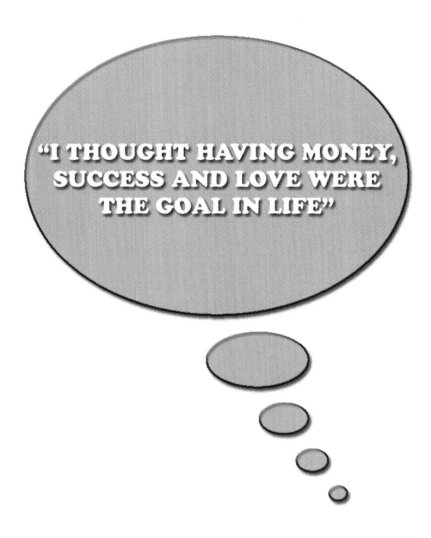

CHAPTER 2
OR MAYBE NOT

At the age of 20, I got married. I had looked forward to marriage as the most significant step to achieving lasting happiness. Once that was in place, I would never have to worry about love again, and even if other things didn't go well, I would know that the power of our love would sustain me while I was working toward success and money. I had one element of happiness "in the bag," and given how hard I was working in school (I was still in college) the others couldn't be far behind.

We had a big wedding, lots of friends, lots of presents, and drove off into the sunset to go on our honeymoon.

Three days later I had a complete nervous breakdown.

What happened?!?!

I had just achieved a goal that I had thought would give me a sense of fulfillment and safety, yet all I felt inside was a yawning emptiness and a sense of panic. I found it impossible to practice the piano. All my goals suddenly seemed unachievable, and even if I did achieve them, happiness suddenly seemed to have nothing to do with those goals. I just couldn't be "happy." And on top of that, I began to become painfully aware that I was going to die some day, something from which no achievement could save me. In fact, when I died, all the money, success and love I'd have accumulated, not to mention my body, would disappear. Or at least I wouldn't be there to see them. There was no safety, no way to get control of life or to feel comfortable. Suddenly all the things I thought I could do to ensure happiness seemed meaningless.

Over the next few months, I developed a severe case of agoraphobia, more commonly known as panic attacks. I couldn't go out of the house. The room always seemed to be spinning, my heart pounding, my breathing shallow. I would get dizzy. I would panic.

My life essentially stopped.

Things got so bad that I ended up spending a few months in a psychiatric hospital. Basically, they just gave me drugs that made me crazier than before, but no matter what they did, life seemed totally pointless, and I couldn't seem to move forward.

At a certain point, just because there was nothing else to do, I checked out of the hospital, came home, and began to painstakingly try to rebuild some sort of life. I managed to finish my senior year of college, and began doing some limited private piano teaching for little kids in the suburbs.

At the time, it seemed like this "breakdown" had ruined my life, derailed me from my purpose, and made me unhappy. But in looking back, it's clear that when my life "fell apart," what was actually happening was that a path was being cleared for me to move in a direction that was my only chance for true happiness. It was as if something in me was saying "I'm not going to let you continue on this path of working for 'love,' success and money, because there's nothing down that path."

The most important thing about this "breakdown" was that it showed me that there had to be "something else," some part of the "success formula" that I had overlooked. I had always regarded life as something to be worked on, with goals to be achieved and places that had to be gotten to. (From where I sit today, that seems so effortful and painful, but at the time it was all I knew.) At any rate, I had worked very hard, but somehow all the work had not brought me the happiness, fulfillment and sense of purpose I had sought.

Until this point, I had been working on my life entirely from the outside, but now that that had not worked, I was, in a sense, forced to explore the invisible world of feelings, sensations, and thoughts.

I began writing songs for the first time. These early efforts were not so much about music as about digging into my own feelings and trying to heal myself. When I look back on them now, they seem so self-indulgent and naïve as to be embarrassing, but they were actually one of the most important steps in bridging the huge gap I had created between my life on the "outside" and my life on the "inside."

I went into therapy and spent a lot of time working on my childhood. I spent many years being furious at my parents, trying to figure out what they had "done to me" to cause me to feel like this. Although I did a lot of exploring of my feelings, in my mind the object of therapy was to "get rid of" those things that were standing in the way of my achieving the goals I'd set so that I could be happy. Obviously there was something preventing me from succeeding in life, so I was going to find out what that was, get it out of the way, and then I could resume my quest for money, success and "love."

A lot changed over the next few years. I began to explore what I "really" wanted, who I "really" was, and found that I'd been living a very inauthentic life. I had been studying to be a concert pianist, but in fact, discovered I had much more interest in pop music and theater. My marriage ended, and although it took another long relationship for me to really figure out who I was, I gradually came to the understanding that I was gay.

I moved back to New York and began to pursue a career in something I felt I really loved, something that I thought would bring me what I really wanted. Theater.

CHAPTER 3
"SUCCESS"

Over the next few years, in conjunction with pursuing my career, I participated in almost every modality of psychology, spirituality and personal growth known to man, and read every self-help book I could get my hands on. In addition to constantly being in therapy, I took EST, one of the first mass-market new thought break-through workshops, attended a Chareeva weekend (a primal scream experiential workshop) meditated, visualized, kept diaries, did The Artist's Way, went on retreats, studied various religions, did body work, massage, Rolfing, chiropractic, took megavitamins, in short, tried everything that offered some promise of breakthrough. I would usually get involved with each of these things because they promised to be THE ANSWER.

But the moment I would finish one of these workshops or courses or healing methods, I would be told that in order to REALLY GET THE ANSWER, I would have to move on to the next step. I never did get THE ANSWER from any of these pursuits, but the important thing was that I was acknowledging, for the first time, that there might be more to the world than what I could see. Perhaps there was something in the world I <u>couldn't</u> see that would make it possible for me to get what I wanted in the world that I <u>could</u> see.

I had a great breakthrough in terms of my agoraphobia. With the help of a book called "Hope and Help For Your Nerves" by Dr. Claire Weeks (a book which I had stumbled upon in the library) I came to understand that the only way through panic disorder was to simply experience the sensations involved with it and not try to get rid of them.

One fortuitous Christmas eve (one of the busiest and most frenetic shopping days of the year) I asked my father to drive me down to Macy's in Herald Square in New York City. I got out of the car, stepped into the store, walked through the entire length of the store, head spinning, heart pounding, and had my father meet me at the other end. I had done it! I had experienced my sensations while doing something frightening, and I hadn't died. At that point, I asked myself, "What if I feel these sensations for the rest of my life?" And my answer was, "So be it."

I now set about doing my life, sensations or no sensations.

I had no idea at the time how important this decision to experience my sensations, rather than trying to make them go away, would be in my later life. But for now, this willingness allowed me to continue my pursuit of the things that I thought would make me happy, albeit trembling and shaking, but at least I could resume going after my dreams.

I achieved a lot. I began to teach, and developed a large private vocal-coaching practice. As time went on, I got jobs playing piano and music-directing shows, Off-Off Broadway, Off-Broadway, and in cabarets around town. A Children's show for which I had written the music got produced at a tiny theater in Greenwich Village.

After a few years, I conducted my first Broadway show. Now imagine how challenging it would be for an agoraphobic to conduct on Broadway. Someone who, for years, couldn't even sit in a theater without wanting to run out screaming, was now standing in a confined orchestra pit, committing to conduct for 2-1/2 hours straight without stopping, with well over a thousand people watching. I certainly was still trembling and shaking, but I put a sign on my podium that said "SO DIE!" By this I meant, "Drop dead if you must, but DO NOT WALK OFF THE PODIUM!" And for thousands of performances, I conducted, no matter how I felt, and gradually I began to get used to it and it ceased to be a problem.

I went on to do 5 more shows on Broadway, and this led to my going to Hollywood where I conducted and vocal arranged many of the classic Disney animated movies, including Beauty and the Beast, Aladdin, Pocahontas, The Hunchback of Notre Dame and numerous others.

Gradually, I began writing songs that were more, shall we say, suitable for public consumption. I wrote songs about emotion, and about a hopefulness that I didn't always feel, but people began singing them and listening to them, and I became well known as a songwriter.

During this time I also met "the love of my life," (This one I KNEW was the real thing. The other "love of my life" had obviously been a mistake) and settled into a serious, long-term, committed relationship with a man.

My songwriting led to my meeting singer Nancy LaMott, for whom I produced 5 gorgeous CD's. I also began composing music for the movies.

The interesting thing about this was that just as had happened in college, although I was achieving a great deal, there was still this nagging feeling that it wasn't enough, that something was missing. I also noticed that certain "really big" achievements always eluded me. I was making good money but wasn't wildly rich. I wasn't winning Oscars or Tony Awards (as some friends I had started out with were). Things often seemed to move forward, but then not get anywhere.

In fact, whenever I would begin to get really successful at something, I would decide that that wasn't really it, and change careers. I had wanted to be a vocal coach, but when my coaching practice became firmly established, I decided I didn't want to do that, but rather I wanted to conduct on Broadway. And just as I was becoming a successful Broadway conductor, I decided that I wanted to go to Hollywood. And just when I was becoming a successful Hollywood arranger and conductor, I decided that that was meaningless, and what I really needed to do was write. And as my writing became successful, I decided that I needed to lecture and teach.

Now, from the outside this might look like a career naturally progressing, but my inner experience was that I was not successful and that I had to do something else to get successful. Except I could never stay with anything long enough to be successful. I would always get that nagging feeling and move on. It seemed to me, at the time, that the feeling of emptiness was appearing because I wasn't successful, but in retrospect, the only time that empty sensation would appear was when I WAS getting successful. This would seem paradoxical, although understanding this would prove to be a major key to breaking through to true enlightenment. But I'm getting ahead of myself.

It would take about 20 more years before I would realize that and have that breakthrough. More about that later.

Suffice to say, beneath the apparent success and creativity, there was still some sense that this was leading nowhere and that I couldn't really have the big things I wanted. And though I would be happy when I achieved something, I always quickly returned to a state where there was something missing, something more I needed in order to be happy. I used to joke that no matter how much money I make, I always make $200 a week less than I need.

I also noticed that there was always some situation in my life that was creating tremendous upset. The situations would change, but the upset would be the same. Sometimes it would be about money, sometimes about relationship, about a lawsuit or an apartment I couldn't sell, or fear of being sick. As each situation would arise, I would grip, stop off my life, and say, "If I could just solve this I would be totally happy." And then I would solve it and the next situation would arrive and generate the exact same sensations and thoughts.

I stayed in therapy and did a lot of other work in pursuit of that "big breakthrough," that method or that understanding that would allow me to push past my obstacles to manifesting what I wanted to see in the world, and finally get what I wanted and achieve the big dreams that I had.

Even with all I had learned about my inner world, the bottom line was that I still thought that it was all about manifesting. Even though no matter what I manifested, I still ended up with the same empty feeling and desire for more, I continued to think that there was some amount of money, some achievement, some relationship that would finally, once and for all, make me happy.

I was determined to find a foolproof way to insure that I could manifest anything I wanted, when I wanted it.

After years of searching, I had a huge breakthrough, and was sure that I had found what I was looking for.

In fact, it was not at all what I was looking for, because ultimately it would not lead me to where I thought I wanted to go. Instead, it would lead me to where I TRULY wanted to go. But I didn't know that at the time, so I was excited at the thought that I had finally found a way to make all my dreams come true.

But again, I'm getting ahead of myself. Before I tell you what that huge breakthrough was, I need to tell you some of the events that led up to it. These events, like my "nervous breakdown" when I was 20, seemed awful at the time but were actually part of a powerful compass that was guiding me to my greatest good.

"THE ONLY TIME THAT EMPTY SENSATION WOULD APPEAR WAS WHEN I WAS GETTING SUCCESSFUL"

CHAPTER 4
"DISASTER" STRIKES
AGAIN......AND AGAIN

It was 1995 and I was flying high. I had conducted 5 Broadway shows, was the Music Supervisor of Beauty & The Beast Broadway, and I was on my fourth major Disney movie. I had become an award-winning cabaret songwriter, had had a near-hit pop song with Diana Ross, and most gratifying of all, had produced 5 wonderful CDs for perhaps the most extraordinary cabaret singer who had ever lived, Nancy LaMott, and was actually seeing Nancy moving out of the cabaret world and onto the precipice of national stardom. On top of all that, on a personal level, my partner and I had just celebrated our 10th anniversary.

Even with all this, that nagging emptiness still persisted, but I assumed that all I had to do was find a way to have a #1 hit pop song, write my own Broadway musical and get Nancy to stardom, and I would be "home." After all, what more was there to do? What more was there to life?

Nancy had had Crohn's disease for nearly her entire life. Although she had amazing powers to triumph and get herself onto the stage no matter what, this disease had always seriously impeded her career. In 1993 she had a surgery that changed all that, and she was finally well. Now nothing could stop her. Or so we thought.

In May of 1995 Nancy came over to my house one afternoon and announced that she had just been to the doctor and that she had Uterine Cancer. She assured me that the doctor had said that it was totally operable and that, in fact, she could wait a few months and finish her latest CD before having the surgery. I was skeptical, but she insisted, so that's what we did, producing by far the most lavish and most popular or her CDs. The CD came out in November. Nancy died on December 13th.

The world fell apart for me, but since everyone around me who had been associated with Nancy truly fell apart, I had to keep going. I had promised her on her deathbed that everyone in the world would hear her sing, and I was going to do that. My assistant couldn't function and quit a few days after her death. My partner, for whom I had secured the job of manager and director for Nancy, had been appointed executor of Nancy's will, but it soon became clear that he too was non-functional. Even with all this disfunction around me, I had the incredibly good fortune to find a great business manager to run the company. Together, we started to promote Nancy's CDs in a way that led to exponentially greater sales than ever before.

Then, out of the blue, Nancy's family came after us, demanding money and control of the record company. They had never participated in Nancy's career in any way, but being her family, they wanted a say in what happened now that she was gone.

Lawsuits ensued which caused the company to fold. A dream I'd been working on for 8 years was turning to dust. All the money we had made was lost in the legal battle and we had to close up shop.

A few years later, my partner fell in love with a singer I had introduced him to, and left me. I spent the next 3 years alone, unable to get so much as a decent date. It was as if all my deepest fears were coming home to roost.

Why was all this happening? As I said at the end of the previous chapter, only years later, in hindsight, would I realize that like my nervous breakdown when I was 20, these seemingly-disastrous events were not disasters at all, but rather my unerring inner guidance system moving me in the direction I needed to go.

I can hear you asking, "How could these 'outer' events have had anything to do with my 'inner' guidance system? Good question. You'll have to read on to find the answer to that one.

CHAPTER 5
A BREAK IN THE CLOUDS

Within a few years, I was in the midst of perhaps the biggest depression I had experienced since my "breakdown" when I was 20. I had been alone for 3 years, Nancy was dead, the record company was defunct, I had given up conducting and arranging the Disney movies to write my own music, and although I'd had some successes, I'd had several disappointments where I had done wonderful work and for some reason it had not led my career anywhere.

One day, a friend who was performing on Broadway, and who had sung my song "We Can Be Kind" at an annual charity benefit we always did together, asked me if I had the piano music to the song in his key. He had been invited to sing at Unity of New York, a well-known New-Thought church that often invited Broadway performers to sing at Sunday services, and he wanted to sing my song there. I, in fact, didn't have the piano part handy in his key because we had performed it with an orchestra at the benefit and I had played for him. But for some reason I heard myself say, "I'll come down and play for you." I'd heard about Unity for years and was curious as to what it was like, so down I went.

To my surprise, when they announced my name, I got a standing ovation. Apparently, unbeknownst to me, they had been singing my music there for years and I was well-known to the congregation. We performed the song, it went over beautifully, and I decided that as long as I was there I would stay for the minister's talk.

That day changed my life. Something about the new thought principles, about hearing Jesus referred to for the first time in a way that made sense to me (I was Jewish) as someone who was an example rather than a God who was to be worshipped, and hearing about a world of unlimited possibilities based on the way we think, was just what I needed to hear at the time.

I began riding my bike down to the church every Sunday and quietly sitting on the side to hear the weekly sermons. (There was a lot of hugging going on and I felt uncomfortable participating in it.)

A few weeks later, I got a phone call from out of the blue. The message on my machine said, "Hi, This is Britt Hall, the music director of Unity of New York. I'm sticking my neck out here, because we don't know you very well, but we do know you've been coming to church every week, and we were wondering if we could hire you to sing and play at a 5 day retreat we're doing called "Healing Your Heart."

Well I didn't know these people very well either, but I couldn't resist the synchronicity of that particular subject being brought up, so I took a leap of faith and said "Yes."

They say that if you say yes, you will always come away with either a good time or a good story. I came away with both.

When I arrived at the retreat, I thought that although, in my head, I wanted to move on, I couldn't, because my heart was broken. But during the 5 days of the retreat, I learned that your heart can never be broken, because unlimited possibilities always exist, no matter what has happened. I began to realize that it was my head that was broken, filled with thoughts of impossibility and disaster, and in this context, the "outer" world could do nothing but reflect those thoughts.

I didn't know why, and didn't know that I was about to have an experience that would set me on the path to my true healing and to my true life's work, but I could definitely see that my life had turned into an outer picture of what I was thinking inside.

On one of the last days of the retreat, I was sitting in a small chapel by myself, when I suddenly had a change of thought. I found myself thinking, "Wait a minute. Patti LuPone must have auditioned for Cats, but she didn't get it because Betty Buckley got it. Patti didn't make the decision, based on that one audition, that she can't do a Broadway show. She went on to do many Broadway shows.

Why am I making the decision, based on one guy dumping me, that I can't have a boyfriend? I would make someone a wonderful boyfriend. I have a tremendous amount to offer. I'm kind and smart and talented and good-looking."

And at the very moment I had that thought, the door opened, and Shawn Moninger walked in. Shawn was part of the staff of the retreat, a licensed Unity teacher who also was running the sound. I knew him peripherally because he had been the lighting and sound designer at Don't Tell Mama, a club which I had attended from time to time to hear various cabaret singers perform. (I had, in fact, first heard Nancy LaMott sing in that club many years before.) Shawn had not known I was in the chapel when he walked in, and had a look of surprise on his face as he said, "Hello."

Shawn sat down to talk with me, and after about 10 minutes I looked across at him and thought, "This guy is hitting on me. I haven't seen that in years!"

And we've been together ever since.

Shawn later told me that he had been interested in me for the past 5 years, but of course, with the thoughts I was holding, I couldn't see it.

So I had a new boyfriend, and I began to attend Unity regularly and participate in classes and events they had to offer.

I still didn't have the success or money I wanted (and in fact spent my first several years with Shawn deeply questioning the love) but life seemed to be moving in the right direction.

More importantly, the experience of exchanging my thought ("I'm un-date-able" for "I deserve to have a boyfriend") and the immediate appearance of that boyfriend, paved the way for the work and the transformation that would truly change my life in ways I'd never even imagined.

PART 2 THE THOUGHT EXCHANGE

CHAPTER 6
THE THOUGHT EXCHANGE
CREATING THE LIFE YOU WANT
BY SIMPLY CHOOSING A NEW THOUGHT

In 2002, I attended a meeting of the Artists' Support Group at Unity of New York. This was a group that met every Tuesday for the purpose of offering Spiritual Support to Artists. In the group, they would go around the room and each person would state an affirmation about their work or their career.

I was struck by the fact that most affirmations seemed to be more about wishes, hopes and even delusion than about truth or about spirit. People were saying things like, "I am a famous, successful artist and millions of people pay me a fortune to see my work." And I would think, "No you're not. That's not what's happening. That's not true." It seemed as though people were thinking that if they said something strongly enough and frequently enough, and in exactly the right way, that whoever it was who was "out there" giving out such things would hear them and give them what they wanted. I thought to myself, "That's ridiculous. This can't be the way the world works.

In my own "quest for success" I had used affirmations many times. Sometimes they worked. Sometimes they didn't. I had always thought that maybe I wasn't doing them correctly, wasn't repeating them often enough, but as I listened to this group affirming, it became clearer to me that affirmations were, at best, unreliable and unpredictable.

This led me to wonder if there might be some way to go deeper into the truth and find a more practical and reliable way to tap into the infinite resources of the universe and bring about not only results, but an understanding of how and why those results occurred. I wanted to understand what actually went on when we were affirming, to know more about the truth of why affirmation did or didn't work. In short, I wanted to take it from the area of wishing and hoping into the area of living and working with the Truth.

A few months later, I got the chance to explore these possibilities. The leader of the Artists' Circle decided to leave, and in an impulsive leap of faith, not knowing exactly what I was going to do, I asked if I might take over leadership of the group.

I decided that in my exploration, I would only refer to and use what I KNEW to be true, not what I wished was true or what I hoped would be true. Only FACTS. So I set out to examine what I knew to be FACTS.

In the physical world, I know that when I drop a pencil it falls to the floor. So, it could be said that gravity is a fact. I know that in order to be physically alive, people have to breathe, and when they stop breathing they are physically dead. So, "You need oxygen for your body to survive" could also be said to be a fact.

When it comes to things that are less apparently physical, or which have a physical component but also involve processes that we would not consider to be physical, our method of determining what's true may become a little less obvious. For instance, if I really look at the process of how I pick up a piece of paper from the table, I can see that I have to, in some way, have the thought (conscious or not) that I want to pick it up, or the impetus to pick it up, before my body will actually act and do it. I don't know exactly how that thought or impetus gets translated into my picking it up, but I can see the result, so I can see that somehow it does.

Walking across the room would be preceded by wanting to walk across the room (whether I know it or not) or thinking about walking across the room, or being stimulated by something that makes me walk across the room. I don't know why or how, but again, I can infer the truth from the result that I see. So it could be said to be a fact that picking something up or walking across the room is a result of a desire, a thought, or some other stimulus.

There are other things I just know through observation. For instance, in my work as a conductor of orchestras, I notice that when I hear something, my arms move in a certain way, and the orchestra does what I hear.

When I hear the same passage of music differently, my arms move in a different way and the orchestra plays the passage differently. So it could be said that there is a definite cause and effect relationship between what I hear, how my body moves and what the orchestra plays.

There's a very difficult puzzle called the Double Crostic that comes out in the New York Sunday Times every two weeks. I had never been able to come close to finishing one, but one day, about fifteen years ago, a close friend of mine said (in a reprimanding tone) "David, you're a bright guy, there's no reason in the world you can't finish the Double Crostic if you just stick to it." Since that time, I have done every Double Crostic in the New York Times, and have never failed to finish one. For some reason, I KNOW I can do that puzzle, so I always do.

So KNOWING the truth seems to be tantamount to knowing "The Law." There seems to be a certain way the universe works — Certain laws about how things act — Gravity — Breathing — A relationship between thinking, desire and action — How an orchestra gets conducted — How a Double Crostic puzzle gets done. We can't always know how, or why something happens, but we can see, through observation, that certain things are the Law of the universe, "The Way It Is."

The question now became, "what can we KNOW, by observation, to be the truth about affirmation?" Since I was teaching this class at a church, Unity of New York, it seemed doubly interesting to include a spiritual perspective in my "scientific" exploration of how things move from being thoughts, ideas and sensations in the inner world to appearing in the outer world.

When people talk about praying, they often refer to a God who is "out there" somewhere and who is deciding, like a person, whether to give them things or not. But the bible also talks about how everything has already been given. It's all here for us. "Ask and you shall receive." "Seek ye first the kingdom and all will be given." What does this mean?

If we think about it, everything that could possibly exist already exists in the realm of possibility. We just don't see it yet. Another way of saying this is that everything already exists in the Un-Manifested, waiting to be revealed. So in spiritual or religious terms, God already made everything, and God has already made it all available to all of us. Some of it we see. and the vast majority of it is waiting to be revealed.

Let me give you a few examples. Penicillin was "discovered" in the twentieth century as a way to cure infections. Now what does the word dis - covered actually mean? "Dis" means "un" and covered means hidden. So essentially, we "un-hid" penicillin, or revealed what was already there but unseen. Can you see that penicillin has always existed? It was created at the beginning of time. In the time of dinosaurs, penicillin was already in existence and able to kill infections— it just hadn't been revealed yet. Even if penicillin wasn't actually around at that time, the elements that would eventually make up penicillin, the possibility of penicillin, the "cause" of penicillin, had to exist, or penicillin couldn't be here today.

I'm a songwriter, and when I write a song, am I creating something new? No. That combination of notes and words already exists in the Un-Manifested, I'm just going in there, sorting through the infinite combinations of notes and words that already exist (in possibility) and pulling out that particular combination. When someone's singing my song, it's in the Manifested (it has physical form.) As soon as it's over, it goes back into the Un-Manifested. But now that I've "written" it and we've heard and seen it appear, we remember that particular combination of notes, and every time someone sings it, it's re-manifested. In the song *I Write The Songs,* Barry Manilow is not narcissistically talking about himself when he says "I am music. I write the songs." He's talking about the original writer of all songs, or God if you will. "I Am Music, and I write the songs." It's all written already. In the Un-Manifested. We have the choice about which part of it we want to experience in the Manifested, but it's all in Un-Manifested all the time.

So everything has already been created, including us, and we all live in, and are, in fact, part of, the same Great Un-Manifested, filled with all possibilities, every possible thing we could want and not want, every condition, every item, including us. Some of the items are temporarily showing, and the rest are there but unseen. We are among the items that are temporarily showing. At some point, like everything else that arises, we return to the Un-Manifested, still there in possibility, like a song that has been sung (and perhaps may be sung again) but is just not showing at the moment.

Whether or not you believe in reincarnation, there was a confluence of events that came out of the infinite possibilities that are always present, that caused you to appear, and that confluence could happen again, in a year, or in ten billion years and you would appear again.

So everything is ALWAYS in the invisible, and the parts of that "everything" that we see are TEMPORARILY in the manifested world.

An image I like to use is that of invisible ink. When you write in invisible ink, you can't see the writing, but it's there. As soon as you shine a special kind of light on it, you see it, it's revealed, it's there. So I began to think, "What is the light that we shine on the Un-manifested to reveal it?" The answer that came to me was.... Thought.

With that answer in mind, I set out to find a way to set up an experiment to see what part thought might play in revealing the life we desire.

THE CIRCLE OF EXPERIENCE

I began by listing the areas of experience present in every human life. I listed them as:

- Thought
- Physical Sensation
- Belief
- Manifestation (the event in the physical world)

That seemed to about cover it. Then I began to explore how they interacted, looking to see what caused what.

You may have noticed that I used the words "physical sensations" rather than the word "feelings." Some might think that the two are synonymous, or that I'm leaving out the important area of feelings, but the difference between physical sensations and feelings is one of the most crucial distinctions of this work. In fact, this distinction is the break-through that allows us access to complete freedom of thought, which in turn allows us access to complete freedom of experience.

When I say physical sensations, I mean physical experiences such as tightness, hotness, coldness, shaking, sweating, dizziness, weakness. Most of us are not used to describing things that way, but immediately go to what we call feelings. Angry, sad, in love, jealous. But in thinking about this, I realized that what we call feelings are actually interpretations of sensations, or put another way, thoughts about sensations.

When someone says "I'm angry" I often ask them, "How do you know you're angry?" When they explore this, they usually say, "Because I feel a hotness in my face and a tightness in my throat." But why does that mean you're angry? That's just an interpretation of those sensations.

Almost all performers who goes on stage experience "butterflies" in their stomach. Some would call the experience terror. Others might call it excitement. Same sensation, different interpretation.

One of my favorite examples of this is; If you told me that you were hot and cold all over, shaking, having trouble catching your breath, your heart was pounding and you felt dizzy, I might ask, "Are you having an orgasm?" This question usually generates a laugh, because most of us sitting in a classroom together would not associate these sensations with an orgasm. We'd be more likely to call them "a panic attack," which is how we would interpret them if we were experiencing them while speaking in front of a group of people. But the fact is, the sensations involved with an orgasm are exactly the same as those of a panic attack, but in the situation of an orgasm we call them pleasurable, while in the situation of a panic attack we call them dangerous and upsetting.

(It has occurred to me that it might be useful for me to say, "Every time I go on stage I have an orgasm!) But more about that later.

At any rate, the importance of this distinction, between sensations and feelings, will become clearer as we explore how things move from the invisible world of thought to the visible physical world.

So back to the basics of experience

- Thought
- Physical Sensations
- Belief
- Manifestation

Even though Thoughts are the first thing on the list, l began my exploration by looking at Sensations, since I tend to first become aware of my experiences through sensations. In other words, usually what I notice first is a sensation. This sensation tells me that something is going on, and that's when I begin paying attention. I'm not saying that sensation is the first thing that actually happens. In fact, there are many people for whom sensations are the last thing they notice. As we will find out later, we will often do almost anything to not experience a sensation, if that sensation is associated, in our minds, with something that was painful early in life. But for me, sensations tend to be the first thing I notice.

In thinking about sensations, the first thing I realized was that I have never been able to change a sensation by going at it directly. I have never been able to say, "I won't have my heart pound, I'll have it beat slowly. I won't be short of breath, I'll be able to breathe easily." Although many of us have spent our lives saying "I don't want to feel this sensation, I've got to find a way to get rid of it," in truth a sensation is a sensation is a sensation. However, I have noticed that when I change the thought behind a sensation, the sensation changes.

So, for instance, if I'm feeling a sensation which I'm interpreting as being angry at someone, and some explanation or new fact comes into the picture, my sensation, and thus my thought of anger, may suddenly disappear. If I'm feeling a sensation that I'm interpreting as being frightened of something, a new piece of information about that thing can immediately transform the sensation, and thus the fear.

Think about that "love of your life" who left you, and how physically miserable you felt. Why? Because you had the thought you couldn't live without him or her, that your life was over, that you were humiliated. Years later, or even months or weeks later, as you received more information, about how perhaps they were a creep, about how much better another relationship could be, about how you didn't need them, or about how they actually cramped your style, the sensations associated with them changed. That's because the sensations were a result of the thoughts you were holding about the person or the circumstance. When the thoughts changed, the sensations changed. (And for those of you who are still feeling those sensations years and years after being left, or hurt, it's not the leaving or the incident that's causing your sensations, it's the thoughts you're still holding.)

So, if thought has the ability to generate and alter sensations, then we can say, for the purpose of this exploration, that thought is "cause" and sensation is "effect."

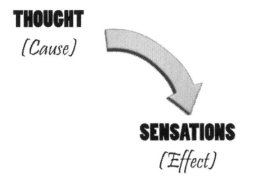

THOUGHT
(Cause)

SENSATIONS
(Effect)

We have a thought, and it generates sensations. An important thing to notice here, is that the sensations will not always "match" the thought. What I mean by this is that you will not necessarily feel "good" when you have a thought that you think of as "positive." This is another crucial distinction in this work.

You choose a thought, and the sensation simply comes with it, whatever that sensation is.

One of the greatest and most misleading misconceptions in New Thought is that when you are on the right track you will "feel good." An even greater misconception is that when you get what you want you will "feel good." The fact is, the way you "feel" (the sensations you experience) relates completely to your history with whatever thought you're taking on.

For example, if you were a child and you said, "I can do it" and someone slapped you across the face when you said that, any time you think, "I can do it" you are most likely going to feel the sensation you felt when you were about to be slapped across the face years ago. If this is a sensation that you think you can't tolerate (because it was emotionally and physically intolerable when you were a child with no recourse or ability to escape) the only way you can get away from that sensation, or at least ensure that you will not be in a situation where that sensation might arise, is to exchange the thought behind it ("I can do it") for a thought that will keep you "safe." That thought would be, "I can't do it." You will now feel "safe" but of course you won't "do it" since, as we will see, thoughts are the source of all we do and all we see before us.

So thoughts are choose-able and sensations are not. I'm sure it makes sense to you that we have the choice to think any thought we please. We don't necessarily believe that thought (I'll get to belief in a minute) but we certainly can think anything we choose. And each thing we think will come with a sensation that may or may not seem to make sense, but which none-the-less, is there.

For instance. I often ask everyone in a Thought Exchange group to take on the thought "I am the most beautiful person in the room." Even the thought of thinking this thought makes many people squirm, giggle and roll their eyes. But eventually everyone agrees to take it on.

I then ask, "What sensations arise, and what other thoughts arise when you take on this thought?" Some people say they feel wonderful. Some people say they immediately have the thought, "That's ridiculous. I'm lying." When I ask them if they noticed a sensation between the first thought, "I am the most beautiful person in the room" and the second thought, "I'm lying," they always report something like a tight chest, constricted throat or pounding heart. Since these are sensations that they have spent their lives protecting themselves from, it's interesting to observe that most of the time they don't even notice them until they're pointed out. They go right to the thought, "That's ridiculous." Can you see that a thought that we might call "negative" actually protects them from experiencing a "disturbing" sensation that is associated, for them, with "I'm the most beautiful person in the room?" It's in some way perceived as dangerous for them to have that thought, so they immediately exchange it for one that, although seemingly "negative," is actually safer for them because it keeps them from the sensation that comes with the thought "I am the most beautiful person in the room."

At this point, there's almost always someone who asks, "Why on earth would it be dangerous to take on the thought, "I'm the most beautiful person in the room?" Well, let's think about it. Suppose you were a child who was criticized or even punished for being too "full of yourself." Or you had a mother or parental figure who was in competition with you. (Remember Snow White and to what lengths her wicked stepmother went to get rid of the competition?) In extreme cases, say, if someone had been molested as a child, the thought "I am the most beautiful person in the room" might actually send them into a panic, because it might come with the idea that it would draw attention to them, and they might associate being noticed or being attractive with being open to molestation. The thought in itself cannot possibly hold any danger, but the physical sensations it creates are deemed dangerous and the person immediately exchanges the thought for a "safer" one, even if the safer thought limits their possibilities.

So we choose a thought, and sensations arise.

We now have come to another point of choice, perhaps the most crucial, and yet the most overlooked one of all. We can choose to either be with the sensations, or try to get rid of them. Now remember, we can't change sensations directly, so the only way we can attempt to "get rid of them" is to take on a different thought.

This point, right here, is the secret to being able to stay with a thought.

As I said in the introduction to this book, almost everybody knows that when we hold a thought, that thought manifests, but so many of us choose a thought and then become frustrated because we don't see it manifesting. Why? Because we can't seem to stay with that thought and we exchange it away for another. It seems to us that things "happen" that cause the thought "not to work," but in fact, all that happens is that when we take on the thought, we have sensations, and if we don't think we can tolerate those sensations, we exchange the thought away to try to get rid of the sensations. Then, we're living inside the new thought we've taken on, not the original thought that would have gotten us what we'd wanted. And if thoughts cause results, we're seeing the results of the "protective" thought rather than the original thought we took on.

So when we take on a thought and experience a sensation, we are now at a crucial point of choice. To either stay with the experience of that sensation, or try to get rid of it in the only way possible; by exchanging our thought for one that will not produce that sensation. And that thought will always be, "I can't, I won't," etc.

So first let's talk about what happens when we stay with the sensation. When we stay with the sensation, we are able to stay with the thought. And when we stay with the thought, that thought becomes a belief.

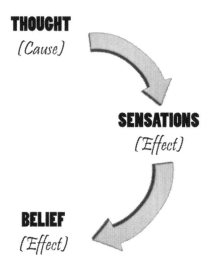

THOUGHT
(Cause)

SENSATIONS
(Effect)

BELIEF
(Effect)

Many new thought disciplines use the words thought and belief inter-changeably, but in Thought Exchange they have very distinct meanings. In Thought Exchange, we define a Belief as "a thought that you think is true."

When we take on any thought, we know that there is also another, contrasting thought. In fact, we usually know that there many other possible thoughts which are just as available to us. For instance, if I have the thought "It's impossible for me to have money," I also know that there is a thought, "I can have money." Neither thought is true. They are just two of the infinite possibilities that exist in the Great Un-Manifested at the same time.

But if I hold the belief that I can't have any money, I forget that there are other possibilities, and think that it's a fact that I can't have any money.

Can you see that by definition, a belief is a lie? A belief is not true because it slices out a small piece of the pie of infinite possibility and says that that piece is the only possibility that exists. When we hold the belief, rather than the thought, that we can't have any money, we really think that there's no possibility whatsoever that we could have money.

And this just can't be true. Every possibility ALWAYS exists in the Great Un-Manifested, and no thought, belief or occurrence can change that.

So why do we hold beliefs? Why do our thoughts transform into beliefs? And what is it that determines what we believe?

What determines what we believe are our thoughts, our sensations and our willingness or unwillingness to stay with them!

Since, in this section, we're exploring how our thoughts appear in physical manifestation, let's first look at what happens when we think a thought, are willing and able to be with the sensation it generates, and thus allow the combination to generate a belief that matches the thought. For example, I have the thought that I can do something, I experience a sensation which I am able to stay with, and this generates the belief that I can do it.

Belief could be said to be our point of focus. When we choose a thought, we know it's a thought among many thoughts so the other possible thoughts are still in our awareness. When we experience the sensation associated with that thought, we then have to make a decision as to whether to stay with the thought or jump away from it to another one in order to avoid the sensation. When we decide to stay with the thought and the sensation it generates, there is nothing to distract us from that thought (since sensation is the only thing that can distract us from a thought) so that thought becomes the only one we think, and hence automatically turns into a belief, which is a thought that we think is true.

If we follow the path we've been on a little further, we could hypothesize that out of thought, sensation and belief comes event or manifestation. We think something, sensations are generated, and when we can stay with the sensations, that thought turns into a belief, the thought that this is the only outcome available in the universe, and lo and behold, we see whatever it is we believe appear before us in the physical universe. Since, as we said before, beliefs are nothing more than thoughts that we think are true, it could be said that when our thought has generated a belief, the particular slice of the unlimited possibilities in the Great Un-Manifested which that belief represents is what we see show up in our lives.

The place between belief and manifestation is another crucial turning point, in that this is the point at which things from the invisible or as we call it, the Un-Manifested World (thoughts, sensations, beliefs) appear as things in the visible or Manifested World. How this happens is anybody's guess, but like everything else in this book, and in fact, in life, we know it does happen because the results are observable.

Sometimes manifestation seems to occur as a result of actions we've taken based on our thoughts, sensations and beliefs. Sometimes things seem to just show up from nowhere, or from "outside" of us.

But however things appear, it could be said that what we see in the manifested world is simply a mirror of the belief that has formed as a result of a thought we are holding.

Is this true? Is this the way the universe actually works? These are the questions I set out to answer when I began doing this work. It began as just a hypothesis, but over the course or time, as I began to look at the world in a different way and test the theory, it became clearer that this is, indeed, the way things work.

MIRROR, MIRROR

My own observations in conducting orchestras, examining my own life from this point of view, and exploring the relationship between what people are thinking, feeling and believing and what's showing up in their lives, has proven to be strong evidence that there is a definite cause and effect relationship between what goes on inside us and what appears before us. This is, of course, for each of us to explore within our own lives, but based on the evidence I have personally seen and experienced, it could be said that what we see in our lives is merely a mirror of what we are thinking, feeling and believing.

You don't have to "believe" this. I'm not saying that it's a "fact." I'm not saying it's true or false. It is merely a hypothesis.

I only ask that for the purpose of this book, you be willing to look at your own life and explore the possibility that what you're seeing in it is merely a reflection of your own thoughts, sensations and beliefs. After you've read the book, done the exercises, and looked at the results, you're then free to draw your own conclusions.

But for now, let's hold our own lives up as though we're looking at them in a mirror, and see what it is we see reflected there.

The word mirror is very important. If you stand in front of a mirror and really look, you will observe several very interesting things. First of all, a mirror is the only way you can see what your face looks like. Think about that for a minute. You can NEVER see your face — you could have a huge scar on it, it could be what you call attractive or ugly, it could be dirty or clean and you wouldn't even know it. You have no idea what you look like. You MUST have the mirror to see it. But, and this is very important, THE MIRROR IS NOT YOU. It looks EXACTLY like you, but there is really nothing there. You'd have to be nuts to see an outfit in the mirror and start trying to change it by reaching into the mirror, or to see your face in the mirror and start putting makeup on the mirror. That could NEVER work because what you're seeing in the mirror isn't there. Or to be more precise, it's not what it appears to be. It's only a REFLECTION of reality.

The other important property of a mirror is that it doesn't think, it has no power to do anything on its own, and it MUST reflect EXACTLY what is before it. You would never step in front of a mirror and hear it say, "Forget it. I'm not reflecting that! You look awful." You would never look in the mirror, see a red shirt, and say, "I'm not wearing a red shirt. I don't know why it's in there." You would never look in a mirror, see your arm moving to the left, and say "I don't know why that arm is moving to the left. I didn't move to the left." We all laugh when we hear the quote from *The Madwoman of Chaillot*, who says, "I never look in the mirror. That old woman is in there!" IF YOU SEE IT IN THE MIRROR, IT MUST BE GOING ON IN FRONT OF THE MIRROR.

A mirror cannot reflect something that's not in front of it, and a mirror cannot NOT reflect what IS in front of it.

And yet, as I said in the introduction to this book, time and again, we look out into the world and try to fix what we see there, when all it is is a reflection of our thoughts.

So in our hypothesis, thought is "cause," sensation and belief are "effect" and what we see appearing in the world is "mirror." If we made a chart of it, it would look like this:

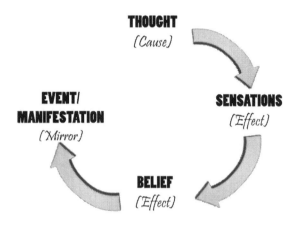

Now here's where most of us make our mistake. We take what we see in the mirror and we choose our next thought based on it. So if we see failure, we take on the thought, "I cannot succeed." Now, if thought is what's generating manifestation, can you see how taking on this next thought would immediately lead to more failure? The thoughts were mirrored in "The Manifested" as the original failure, we take on another failure thought which will again be mirrored as failure, and before long we're in a whirling hurricane generating more and more failure over and over again, thinking that the reason this is happening is because of our original failure.

But what if that's not true? What if our original thought generated our original failure, and each new thought of failure is generating new failure?

Most of us can think of places in our lives where we have repeated and repeated the same self-defeating pattern, and the harder we try to fight circumstances the more they seem to take hold. After a while, we begin to think that we're cursed, that that's "just the way things are," or that the world is against us.

But that would be like saying "The mirror is against me." It's not possible. But when we fail to realize that it is our own thoughts that are being reflected by the manifestations we see, what else are we to think?

To show how this pattern works, I added a line to the diagram above, connecting event back to the next thought, causing it to become a continuous circle, like a whirlwind, with Thought (cause) at the top, Sensation (effect) on the right side, Belief (effect) at the bottom, Manifestation (mirror) on the left side, leading back to the next thought. The chart now looked like this.

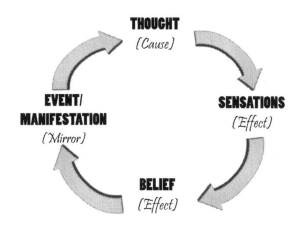

BREAKING INTO THE SYSTEM

As I looked at this self-perpetuating system, I wondered, "Where can I break into this system and effect a change?"

I can't choose or change my sensations, so if I start the circle at the point of sensations, I will just have to take whatever sensations I'm having, which will automatically generate a belief, which will automatically appear as manifestation out of which I will form another thought based on the results of those sensations which will cause those sensations, beliefs and events to continue.

If I start with my beliefs, I have the same problem. Since beliefs are the result of thoughts combined with sensations, and since, by definition, a belief is a thought that I think is TRUE, I cannot exchange a belief for another belief, because the ability to change a belief would belie its very definition.

So if I begin with a belief, whatever belief I'm currently holding will manifest, and out of that manifestation I will generate my next thought, which will create sensations based on that thought, which will generate more of the same belief and hence more of the same events.

I can't start with manifestation, because manifestation is just a mirror and has no power to cause anything by itself. If I start with manifestation, I will take whatever just happened and create my next thought based on it, which will create sensations and belief and recreate what just happened over and over again, so I'm always a prisoner of what just happened. Since, as we've explored, what just happened is merely a mirror of the thoughts, sensations and beliefs that preceded it, it would follow that there's no way to change what's happening by going to what's happening itself. I must find and go to the source of it.

And so, as you may have already guessed, there was only one place left to look, and that place was Thought. And as I looked into it, I realized that the only place I have a choice is, in fact, in Thought.

Now let's look at Thought for a moment.

CHOOSING OUR THOUGHTS

Do we have the power to choose a thought? Any thought? Try it. Think "I am intelligent." Again, as before, I'm not asking you to feel it. I'm not asking you to believe it, I'm not asking you whether it's true. I'm just asking, can you think the thought "I am intelligent?" I think you'll agree, the answer is, "yes."

OK, now think the thought "I am stupid." That thought is just as easy to think. (People are often unwilling to even admit that they can think this thought because it seems so "negative," but remember, I'm not asking you to feel it or believe that it's true. I'm just asking you to think it.)

From this little exercise, I think you can see that, unlike sensations, beliefs and manifestations, thoughts are something that can be chosen. All thoughts exist all the time. We never change them, but rather exchange them for another thought. The old thought still exists and might be used by someone else, or by you, at any time.

I often like to use the image of thoughts being all the things you find in a kitchen when you're cooking. Many, many ingredients exist in a kitchen, and for each recipe, you use some and don't use others. It doesn't irritate you, while baking a cake, that pepper exists and is, in fact, in the kitchen. You don't have to change the pepper into something else or put it in another room. You simply don't pick it up and put it in the cake. It's still there should you want to use it later, in some other dish. Also, anyone can come into the kitchen and use it. It's there for everyone, and each of us chooses to pick it up for a while when we want it, and put it down or not use it when we don't want it.

Another useful analogy is that of radio waves. Are you aware that many, many radio stations are in the room with you right now and at all times? They're all invisible, and without the proper receiver, you don't hear any of them. But they're all here. You only hear the one you choose, by having a receiver (radio) that you set to vibrate at a particular frequency which matches the frequency of the radio station you're trying to receive (manifest). Someone else could be in the same room and be listening to a different station at the same time.

All the stations are all here all the time. What you listen to is your choice.

So it is with thoughts. They all exist, they are all available to all of us, to be taken on or discarded as we see fit. If we are having a thought and want to take on another one, we do not have to fight with the thought we're having, we don't have to wrestle with it or try to have it go away or be something different. As I said above, we don't have to change it, we merely have to ex-change it for another thought. The old thought still exists. We're just not taking it on at the moment.

So, we have discovered that of all the parts of the circle of experience — thought, sensation, belief and manifestation — thought is the one area in which we can make a change by ex-changing one thought for another. The first key to doing this would be to break the circle between the most recent event that has occurred, and the next thought we take on. I represented this in my circle with a large double slash through the line that connected our most recent manifestation with our next thought.

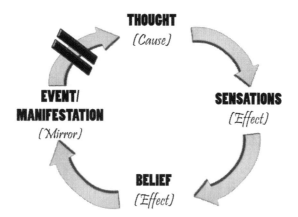

Once we know that we have a choice of any thought, when we notice that we have taken on a thought that is based on the last manifestation, we can go to what I call "The Invisible Source of All Thoughts" and exchange our thought for another thought that is more likely to produce the result we desire.

That chart would look like this:

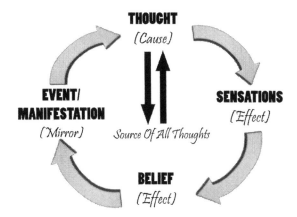

With this in mind, I set out to do the work of exploring how these principles might be put into a practical form that could be used by anyone to transform their lives. Over a period of time, through a lot of trial an error and much feedback and contribution from the members of the original Artists' Support Circle, the group transformed into what I called The Thought Exchange Workshop.

CHAPTER 7
THE ORIGINAL THOUGHT EXCHANGE WORKSHOP
HOW OUR FIRST GROUP WORKED

Sitting in a circle, we usually begin the group by closing our eyes and doing a brief, guided meditation in which we acknowledge and remind ourselves that everything and anything we could ever want (and not want) has already been created, exists in the Un-Manifested and is there to be revealed. We further acknowledge that all possible thoughts already exist and are here for us to choose to think. We take a moment to form a picture, in our own minds, of The Great Un-Manifested, that place where EVERYTHING already is. That picture can look different for different people. Some see it as a big circle, some see it as a room, some see it as the size of the whole universe. Some see it as being inside them, some see it as being around them, with them being a part of it. But at any rate, it's a place where everything exists in the invisible, in the imagination if you will. When we've got a picture of that in our minds, I ask everyone to locate certain objects. Find a baboon (in your mind's eye) and say "Got it" when you've found it. People, of course, say "Got it" immediately. How long does it take to "imagine" a baboon?" See yourself standing on your head on the moon. Easy, in the Un-Manifested. There are no restrictions like "how would I get there?" or "I need air." You're just on the moon, immediately. See a one dollar bill in your hand. Easy. See yourself depositing a check for a billion dollars, written out to you, in your bank account. Just as easy, in the Un-Manifested. So it's all here, right now, in the invisible world.

After acknowledging our essential one-ness and connectedness in the fact that we are all part of this great, infinite Un-manifested in which some things, including us, are showing and some things are not, we open our eyes and bring our attention back to the room.

Whoever wishes to speak first, begins with some life issue, problem or situation that is uncomfortable or that they desire to change. They describe it in whatever way they wish, talking about how it feels, how it frustrates them, how they've tried to change it, saying whatever they want to say about it, until we get a clear idea of what the situation is and how they feel about it. It's very important that there be no restriction on how they describe it. They don't have to use spiritual words, they don't have to be "positive," they don't have to think about solutions or see where they might be misguided. They simply have to describe the situation with all the details, all the complaints, all the frustrations, all the sensations, all the thoughts, all the feelings, all the beliefs, all of whatever is in there for them. We want a clear picture of exactly what they're seeing in the mirror.

In many workshops, and certainly in ordinary conversations, people often hear about a situation and respond by giving advice as to what a person can do about it or how they can feel better. We don't do that. Since, in our original premise, we are postulating that situations or manifestations are nothing more than a mirror of our thoughts, we ask the question, "Given that you're seeing this situation in the mirror before you, what might you be thinking that would reflect in the mirror as this situation?" It's sort of like asking, "Given that you see a yellow shirt in the mirror, what might you be wearing that would reflect as a yellow shirt in the mirror?" In that case, the answer is obvious, and nobody would ever say that they are not wearing the yellow shirt they see in the mirror before them. Even if they didn't realize they had it on, the fact that they saw it in the mirror would be proof positive that they were indeed wearing it.

In the case of our looks or our weight or our clothes, we often delude ourselves, saying that we don't look a certain way, that we're not overweight, that we're not aging, that an outfit looks great on us, but when we look in the mirror we see the truth reflected. Most of us would agree: THE MIRROR DOESN'T LIE.

However, when it comes to complex life situations, it's sometimes a little more difficult to pinpoint what thought you might be "wearing" that is appearing as the situation reflected in the mirror.

This is made more complicated by the fact that so often people do not know about, or want to admit, that they have what they would call "negative thoughts." So you have to remind people that you cannot possibly see something in a mirror that is not standing in front of the mirror.

Often things that have been said (in the initial description of the situation) give us clues as to what the thought might be. If not, we ask more questions.

Once we have clarity on what the "negative" thought is that is appearing in the mirror (negative simply meaning a thought that is reflecting in the world as something we don't wish to see there) we then ask the question, "What thought might you choose in exchange for that thought that might be reflected in the Manifested as what you would like to see there?"

An exploration follows in which we locate a thought that feels right (you can always see it on the person's face when they've hit it.) When we come upon the thought, the whole group turns toward the person, puts their hands up toward them and states the thought out loud, in the second person (you). Then each group member writes it down for him or herself in the first person (I.)

Perhaps providing a few examples would be the best way to demonstrate how this works.

CHAPTER 8
EXAMPLES FROM THOUGHT EXCHANGE WORKSHOPS

MAKING "IMPOSSIBLE" CAREER CHOICES

Joanne (not her real name) is an actress who had achieved quite a measure of success in Dallas, but had not really worked much since she'd moved to New York. She was holding down a day job in the office of a large toy store, and not really auditioning very much, though she said it was her desire to be a full time actress. The quandary she presented was that she felt it would be necessary to quit her day job in order to be a full time actress, but that were she to do that, she would not be able to support herself. Looking at this situation, we could see that she was in an untenable position; the only choices that seemed to be available to her were to work at a job she didn't like in order to support herself, or leave that job and do what she really wanted to do, and starve. Working backwards around the circle of experience, from situation (manifestation) through belief (the thought she was thinking was true) and sensations (what was going on in her body) to find the thoughts that might be being mirrored in this situation, we came across "I can't support myself doing what I want to do." This seemed like the right thought, because the situation as Joanne was living it completely reflected it. The two choices she saw, doing a job she didn't enjoy to make money, or doing a job she loved and starving, both fulfilled the thought that she could not support herself doing what she wanted to do.

Now, if we look at Joanne's thought as a thought among all possible thoughts, we realize that there is also somewhere in the vast, unlimited Un-Manifested, the thought, "I can support myself doing what I want to do." Holding that thought might allow something different to happen, so we asked Joanne if she would be willing to take that thought on. Joanne considered it and said that it didn't feel quite right, so we continued to explore and go deeper.

When questioned about what thought might be reflecting in the mirror as her not getting recognized at auditions, or, in fact, not even getting auditions, she suddenly came upon the core thought, "I don't matter." This one struck a resonant chord with her. It felt like something that felt "true" for her (core thoughts always feel true until they are revealed to be just thoughts) and she sat with it for a few moments, realizing how it played out in her life — giving her an insignificant job at the toy store and no visibility or success as an actress. Sensations went along with this thought, and she took a few minutes to simply sit and feel the sensations she was having. She realized that they were quite familiar, and even though some would call them upsetting and uncomfortable, she was so used to them that she had no trouble staying with them. In fact, in some ways they felt like an old shoe that fit.

The next question to ask was, "What thought, when reflected in the mirror of life, might give you the possibility of having what you want?" And what she decided to take on was, "I matter." Although this thought brought on uncomfortable sensations (as holding the thought of what we want often does, if it's a thought we've been avoiding) Joanne decided to stay with the sensations, no matter how uncomfortable they were.

It was fascinating to watch what began to happen next in Joanne's life. She began to matter, both at work and at auditions. It suddenly was not her job or her station in life that made her important, but rather just her very existence. She could do nice things for people at work, make a difference, take acting classes and workshops with important people in the industry, go to auditions, and whatever happened, she walked through it with the thought that she mattered. Her life and career began opening up in all areas as she moved through it contextualized by a different thought. As a person who mattered, she somehow began to approach everything with a confidence and a sense that no matter what happened she was important. Before long she began getting auditions, and in not too much time was booking films. In a matter of months she had quit her day job and was pursuing acting on a full time basis.

It's extraordinary to uncover that there is often a simple, basic, almost clichéd thought that we're holding that is completely dictating the outcome of our lives. Often it's thoughts like, "I'm not good enough; I don't deserve anything; Things always get taken away from me at the last minute," that are underlying the way we live our lives and the decisions we make. In this workshop, we explored what happened when we simply took on a different thought. The results were amazing.

WE'RE ALL "THE BEST SINGER IN THE ROOM"

In one group, there were 5 singers, and all of them decided to take on the thought "I am the best singer in the room" at the same time. This was a fascinating experience. It didn't matter who really was the best singer (in fact it's never possible to prove who is the best singer because singing is such a qualitative thing) but it was amazing to see the results that holding that thought produced for each of the singers. Over the next few weeks, each of them made great strides, not only in their self-confidence, but in their actual careers. Since thoughts are not us, are non-exclusive and are exchangeable, each thought is available to anyone who wants to hold it. That point is beautifully illustrated by the fact that five people held the same thought of being the best and there was no conflict in them all holding that thought at the same time.

"I CAN'T WRITE A BOOK"

Joe (not his real name) a successful entrepreneur, knew that he had a book he wanted to write, but noticed that he wasn't writing it. When we explored what thought might be being reflected as his inability to write a book, he immediately came across the most obvious thought, "I can't write a book." Just as obvious was the answer to the question, "What thought might you take on that might reflect as your being able to write a book?" Simply removing a little "apostrophe t" brought him to the thought "I can write a book." He decided to take on that thought for a week and see what happened.

He came back the next week and said he felt completely different about the idea of writing a book, and knew, in his heart, that he could do it.

However, he noticed he still wasn't writing. So we explored further. When I asked the question, "What thought might be being reflected as knowing you could write a book and not writing it?" he said, "If I write a book, I might be in the public eye." When I asked what thought he had about being in the public eye, he said, "People in the public eye get criticized." When I asked him what his thought about getting criticized was, he said, "Criticism is impossible to tolerate."

Interesting thought among all possible thoughts. Is it a fact? Or just a thought? I asked him to think of someone very famous and very successful who got criticized a lot and was successful nonetheless. He thought for a minute and came up with Madonna. I asked him what he thought Madonna might think about criticism. (Mind you, we have no idea what Madonna actually thinks about criticism, but this was Joe's thoughts we were dealing with.) After pausing for a moment, Joe said, "Madonna probably thinks, 'who gives a shit!'" This got a big laugh out of the group, and Joe decided to take on that thought.

He began writing his book.

"LIFE IS A VACATION"

The Thought Exchange is not only about problems, but about noticing what's working in your life and being able to find and identify the thought behind it so you can keep accessing it. Luke (not his real name) came in and shared that he had just been to an important audition for admission to a lyric-writing workshop he wanted to join, and had had a wonderful time there. For the first time, instead of viewing the audition as a life and death situation in which he had to achieve a certain result, he found that he could view it as just another experience, to be lived and to be enjoyed. Throughout the process, he had a strong connection to a sense that he didn't have to know what the result of any experience would be; that if he didn't get this one, there would always be another one, and that life was simply a safe and enjoyable unfolding of experiences. When he thought about it, he compared it to a vacation. When you're on vacation, you just go from one thing to another, you don't have to have an agenda, you enjoy a restaurant, visit some site, enjoy it, don't enjoy it so much, go on to the next thing, but there's this sense of freedom and exploring and enjoyment.

As we discussed it, Luke realized that he traditionally approached work-related events inside the thought, "This is life and death and I have to get what I want." That approach usually led to desperation, very little enjoyment, and in fact, often seemed to generate a situation in which Luke would not get what he wanted. As he thought about the feeling he'd had at this particular audition, he realized that the thought reflected in it was, "Life is an all-expense-paid vacation." The thought brought a smile to his face, and he looked forward to what work situations would be like when he carried this thought.

By the way, he was accepted into the workshop two days later.

"I Can Be Forgiven"

Joanne also came in with a positive story. If you'll remember from earlier in this chapter, Joanne was the one who was wrestling with leaving her day job but felt she couldn't make it as an actress. After exchanging her limiting thoughts for, "I am worthy of prosperous acting jobs" and later for, "I matter," Joanne came back from the summer to report that she had shot two movies, turned down a third because the conditions weren't right, and had made a big splash in the acting class of an important television casting director. Clearly Joanne was in a totally different place — her new thoughts were reflected in the mirror of her life.

Joanne had also taken Edwene Gaines' prosperity workshop, and had taken Edwene's suggestions about the importance of forgiveness, to heart. Joanne reported that she had been keeping a forgiveness list, and had been actively forgiving, on a daily basis, the people and situations with which she'd had the most problems throughout her life. She noticed that the more she forgave, the more her life expanded.

Forgiveness is one of those principles that many spiritual teachings subscribe to, but like so many other things of that nature, people often attribute some magical or superstitious beliefs to it, thinking, "They'd better forgive" because otherwise they won't get what they want.

Since, like Luke, Joanne was in good shape and was noticing that something was working for her, we decided to see if we could get some insight into how forgiveness actually works and why it seemed to be producing the results it was clearly producing.

As we discussed forgiveness, we came to the realization that if you are able to forgive someone for something, that means that whatever that person did is forgivable — by forgiving them, you have just created a world in which that forgiveness exists. Since you live in that world, that same forgiveness also must exist for you. It follows that anything for which you could not forgive someone else would then be something for which you could not be forgiven yourself. With this understanding, Joanne realized that as she forgave other people, anything she might have done that was similar, automatically became forgivable. She now had, in her hands, the power to heal and let go of anything and everything from her past that might have made her uncomfortable, and with this realization, she took on the thought, "I am completely forgivable."

The smile on her face and the relieved glow in her eyes were enough to show the group that Joanne was now ready to realize her success, free of anything in the past that might be holding her back.

"I Can Have It All"

Judy (not her real name) had come to The Thought Exchange Workshop with the complaint that she was a talented actress and performer but had a lucrative day-job and a husband, and could not figure out how to satisfy her artistic self, make a living, and spend time with her husband. All attempts to logistically put these three together failed — if she went out and acted, she would have to leave her job and risk having no money. If she performed at night, she would not see her husband. If she stayed at her job, she could not possibly act, and would be unfulfilled artistically. When we looked at the thought that might be being reflected as this situation in the mirror of her life, she realized she was thinking, "It is not possible to have it all."

She exchanged that for, "It is possible to have it all" and immediately began working on her nightclub act.

Several weeks later, she came in and said that everything had seemed to come to a halt....she was unable to work on her club act, she was discouraged, she didn't know what to do. Her first thought was, "This thought isn't working." But what's interesting about thought is that it ALWAYS works. When we take on a thought, the mirror of the world immediately begins to reflect it, but often the path to the manifestation of that thought contains things that we are afraid of or don't want to do — that's why we were reluctant to take on that thought in the first place.

So, what we could deduce from Judy's current situation, was that the thought, "It is possible to have it all," brought up the next obstacle. Upon exploration, we discovered that Judy's mother had told her, "Actors are selfish; be safe; you need a job to fall back on," and all sorts of "negative" statements like that. Now the important thing to realize is that even if someone tells us something, it is we who take it on for ourselves and make it powerful. Since this is often unconscious, we don't know we're doing it, but if you're seeing it in the mirror of your life, you MUST be thinking it. So when she examined these thoughts and got to the root of them, Judy realized that she was thinking, "I am bad," as she was moving toward actualizing her dreams. As soon as she realized this, she decided to exchange the thought for, "I am good."

We broke for the summer, and when Judy came back, a lot had happened. She had taken a 3-week workshop in acting, and it had gone so well that she had applied for a full-time program. She was terrified that she might get it (which would mean she might have to take the leap of giving up her job) and terrified she wouldn't get it (because she really wanted it.) We talked about the fact that she didn't have to make that decision, and didn't even have to know if she would take it if she were accepted. All she had to do was move along inside the thought she was holding.

"I am good."

We also talked about the fact that the thought, "I can have it all" was clearly at work, and that her life as she knew it was coming apart, but that this was naturally what would have to happen in order for her life to be rearranged to include all she wanted to see in it. She didn't have to know "how" it would happen, she just had to stay with the thought and it would be reflected in her life.

Her issue was, however, that the whole thing made her very anxious, and when we discussed it further, she realized that she was still holding the thoughts her mother had expressed to her, especially the thought that "actors are selfish," and this thought was impeding her ability to move forward, trust the process, and see what happened.

As soon as she voiced, "Actors are selfish," and we asked the question, "Is that a fact or is that a thought?" she realized it was just a thought. When I asked her to look and see what thought would be more likely to allow her to see all that she wanted in her life without hurting anyone or being selfish, she came up with, "My success as an artist improves the lives of EVERYONE around me." With that, she was able to joyfully jump into the fray.

The next week, Judy came back, excited and frightened. She had auditioned for the acting program and been accepted, and was now debating about whether to take the big step of leaving her job. She had gone to her mother and told her about being accepted, and her mother, shockingly, said, "Life is short, you need to do what you love doing. Why don't you let me support you financially!" We couldn't fail to notice that this was the same mother who had said, "Actors are selfish;" so we realized we were seeing the immediate results of two thoughts — the original thought, "It is possible to have it all," combined with the thought, "My success as an artist improves the lives of EVERYONE around me."

It was amazing to note that the seemingly insoluble problem of how Judy was going to find a way to both support herself and be artistically fulfilled, was solved by the universe in a way that Judy never would have dreamed of, namely by her mother putting up the money. This was a great example of "someone else" changing based on your exchanging a thought. But remember, there is no "someone else." There's only the mirror. This can be difficult to wrap our minds around, but it stands at the core of this work and of how we experience life.

We will go into this in much greater detail later, but for now, back to Judy's story.

In addition to now having the financing from her mother, Judy remembered that a certain organization she had worked for had just lost their part-time assistant, and when she called to ask if they needed anyone, they offered her the job immediately. This job, unlike her other one, was part time, with flexible hours, and would in no way interfere with her classes.

You would think that Judy would be ecstatic about all this, but when she related all these seemingly fantastic events, events which clearly were leading her directly toward the fulfillment of her thoughts, she seemed to be anxious and apprehensive. As I've said over and over, one of the main reasons we are often reluctant to think the thought that we know will reflect in our lives as the things we want, is that it forces us to move through places that we are afraid to move through, and sensations that we are afraid to experience..

So we set out to explore just what the "fly in the ointment" was for Judy.

Two more thoughts came up. One was "acting is playful and fun and if I just play I will go down the drain," and the other was, "I will not be taken care of. I am making the decision to leap and I'm going to run out of money and be destitute." Looking further into that, we realized that Judy was living inside a common thought, "There is a limited supply of what I need in the world."

As Judy looked at this, she made the first crucial transition of realizing that these, rather than being "the truth," were merely thoughts. As we began to explore what thought might be more likely to reflect in the mirror of life as what she wanted to see there, we realized that her thought had to somehow encompass two ideas; one, that it was alright for her to play, and two, that there was an unlimited abundance in the world. In the unlimited possibilities available in the Great Un-Manifested, both of these are clearly there. After batting around different possibilities, Judy chose, "When I play, I'm taken care of."

This was a very satisfying thought for her to hold, in that it not only covered permission to play and the notion of being taken care of, but it linked them together and had the added meaning of interpreting the word "play" as meaning "to participate, to go for something, to get into the game."

Inside of that thought, Judy made the decision to leave her job, sign up for the two-year acting program, accept her mother's financial help and take the part-time, flexible job she'd been offered.

Her original thought, "It is possible to have it all," was clearly appearing in the mirror of her life in ways she'd never dreamed possible.

"THERE'S A WAY!"

Bill (not his real name) had definitely become our most frustrating group member. Week after week, he would come in with tales of how he couldn't get a job, how his teachers were treating him unfairly, and how even though he had a masters degree and was a gifted writer, nobody would give him the time of day. He developed sciatica and foot trouble so he could not take a job that required standing on his feet. He sent out hundreds of resumes but never heard back from anyone. His computer wasn't working properly and it was too expensive to go to an Internet café. He was out of money. He was being thrown out of his apartment. When he went to apply for public assistance, they told him he needed an apartment. When he went to find an apartment, they told him he couldn't get an apartment if he was applying for public assistance.

Any suggestion you gave Bill was immediately countered by the reasons it couldn't work.

On one particular occasion, when he started telling his story in a Thought Exchange Workshop, some people actually left the room, while others shrank into their chairs in frustration. You could literally feel the air being sucked out of the room.

As I looked at Bill and listened to him drone on about his woes, I suddenly realized that Bill was completely living inside the thought "There's no way!" And it struck me that inside this thought, Bill was extremely powerful. I pointed out that it was amazing that no matter what situation was given to him, he could turn it into a failure. I told him I was not making fun of him, but that I wouldn't dream of offering any suggestions, because I so completely realized that he could take ANYTHING I offered and turn it into disaster.

At first, Bill was nonplussed, but then he began to realize the power he'd been exerting over his life through his thought. It's something I've stated over and over again, but it bears repeating — you must not be afraid to discover your "negative" thought, because in discovering that, and realizing that it is that thought that is appearing in the mirror of your life, you put your hands on the steering wheel and get in touch with the idea that it is your thought, not something outside you, that is powering the appearances in your life. Armed with that knowledge, you can then exchange the thought and watch your life change. Without that knowledge, you have no idea why things are happening, and no power to affect them.

So Bill had his "aha!" and decided to take on the thought, "There's a Way!" He didn't have to know how, he didn't have to know what to do, but I told him that considering how strongly the other thought had been embedded, he would probably find himself thinking, "There's no Way" about every 10 seconds and have to exchange it for, "There's a Way." He left the room saying, "There's a way, there's a way, there's a way" under his breath.

The group couldn't wait to see what would happen next.

Although the group was very excited by Bill's shift in thought, they were also very activated by his share, because it touched on something that they all feared. I got many calls and e-mails after the session from people who admitted that they had been upset, but had realized that there was a real opportunity here. If Bill could get through this, it meant that anything they might face could also be changed just by an exchange of thought.

The next week, Bill came in and his whole demeanor was different. He had had two job interviews, and one of the people had offered him a job. He hadn't taken it because the prospective employer seemed to be a bit shady and had lied in several areas, but nonetheless, Bill saw that it was possible to be offered a job…"There was a Way." He related the same troubles in all areas, but his reaction was different. He described, in each case, how when he hit a snag, it moved him to take a different action. He realized that faxing his resumes wasn't working, so he began e-mailing them and began to get responses. He began asking around to find out if people he knew personally had leads on jobs. His father sent him some money. He found a back brace that helped his back to feel better. We could see he was on his way to making a shift, and that the thought "There's a way" was beginning to do its work. It was clear that he should continue to hold that thought…it was simple, easy to remember, and right to the point. He left the group committed to continuing to exchange the thought "There's No Way" for "There Is a Way" every time it came up.

The next week, Bill sent an e-mail apologizing for not being able to attend The Thought Exchange. He was working!

CAN'T ACCEPT A DOLLAR

It's very important to remember that what we see appearing in the mirror of the world in front of us is an EXACT reflection of EVERY thought we're having. When you look in the mirror, it doesn't reflect just your shirt and not the shoes you're wearing. It doesn't reflect your facial expression but not the color of your skin. It reflects EVERYTHING down to the tiniest detail.

Many times, we'll take on an affirmation and wonder why what we are affirming is not appearing in front of us. In these cases, we must look at what's actually appearing, and determine what thoughts we are having that are being reflected as exactly that.

For example, in a Thought Exchange Workshop, one of the participants was affirming that she was wealthy, prosperous, and open to receiving unlimited financial abundance.

I was sitting next to her, and in response to her affirmation, I reached into my wallet and handed her a dollar, saying, "Here, this is yours."

She looked at me anxiously, and then tried to hand it back to me. I said, "No, it's yours." She looked around the room, said, "What am I supposed to do with this?" and tried to throw it in the offering basket. "No, it's yours," I said. She then tried to hand it to the person on her right, who refused to take it, saying, "It's yours."

I pointed out that it was very interesting that someone who was affirming that infinite abundance was available to her could not even let herself take a dollar! When we explored what she must be thinking in order to be seeing this reflected in the world, we came across all sorts of thoughts like, "I'm not allowed to have anything I didn't earn, I can't take contributions without retaliation" and "You can't trust money that comes from nowhere."

She exchanged all those thoughts, and thus became more available to allowing herself to receive the abundance she had been affirming, from wherever it might appear. And she took the dollar, and put it in her pocket.

"ONE OF THE GREATEST AND MOST MISLEADING MISCONCEPTIONS IN NEW THOUGHT IS THAT WHEN YOU ARE ON THE RIGHT TRACK YOU WILL 'FEEL GOOD'"

CHAPTER 9
THE THOUGHT EXCHANGE STORE
A WONDERFUL PLACE TO SHOP

To aid us in being able to take on a new thought, we created a "store" which we called The Thought Exchange. At The Thought Exchange, you can exchange any thought for any other thought. Remember, you're not changing a thought, you're ex-changing it. Now most of you have probably heard of Nordstrom, the store that is famous for its "the customer is always right" service. Among their other wonderful services, Nordstrom has a no-questions-asked return policy. Well, with even better service than Nordstrom, The Thought Exchange will allow you to return any thought (even if you've had it for fifty years and have completely worn it out) and exchange it for any other thought. It's open 24 hours a day, always has everything in stock, and has sales help to guide you if you're not sure what you're looking for.

You can go there (in your mind) to exchange a specific thought and pick up a specific new one, or, if you're not sure what you're looking for, look around until something catches your eye. You can go there 100 times a day and still receive the same open, friendly service. The thoughts you exchange are kept there in the likely event that others will want to use them. You can hook up an "online" system or a button inside you (however you can best visualize it) to allow yourself to exchange thoughts any time, day or night.

Different people have come up with creative ideas about what The Thought Exchange contains and the services it offers. In discussing it in our original group (which was at Unity of New York, where the work was done with a definite spiritual component) we decided that although, of course, there were no preferred customers (all services are always completely available to everyone) there were many special services that you needed to request in order for them to be made available. One person always saw herself pulling up in a super-stretch limo and being greeted by a doorman who addressed her as "Your Grace."

89

Another member of the group, who was working with a particularly challenging situation involving the exchange of long-term, deeply held thoughts, decided to check into the Ritz Carlton® Thought Exchange, a 5-star hotel that is attached to the Thought Exchange, for people who have to constantly shop during a particular period of time. Others imagined different products that were offered, like miners' hats with lights which could reveal anything that was in the "invisible ink" of the Great Un-Manifested by just shining the light of Thought on it. Personal shoppers, home service, private thought consultants, were just a few of the other services they came up with to aid them in the imaginative process of knowing that they could exchange any thought for any other thought, easily and any time they chose.

One actress in the group loved to play "Thought Exchange Sales Clerk." She would get up and say, "Welcome to the Thought Exchange. What thought can I exchange for you today? Oh, you'd like to exchange 'I'm a piece of crap' for 'I can do it?' Wonderful. We can do that. Here's 'I can do it,' and I'll take the thought 'I'm a piece of crap' and put it right here in the front counter display case. It's one of our most popular thoughts and people come in for it all the time, because it prevents them from doing so many things that might cause upsetting sensations."

Because the process of Thought Exchange was so successful in allowing people to change their lives, we decided to rename the Artists' Group "The Thought Exchange."

CHAPTER 10
THE ORIGINAL THOUGHT EXCHANGE GROUP PROCESS
A STEP BY STEP

The process evolved, and the next form the group took on was as follows:

INTRODUCTION - If this is the first time a group is meeting or if there are new members, I explain the basics of The Thought Exchange, as explained in Chapter 6 of this book.

MEDITATION - I then lead a brief meditation to center and remind ourselves that every possible thought and every possible thing already exists in the Great Un-Manifested, and that we are sitting in and are, in fact, part of that great Un-Manifested. A look around the Un-Manifested to locate those things one is interested in revealing can serve to strengthen the awareness that they are already there.

The meditation might go something like this:*

"Now everyone close your eyes, take a deep breath, get comfortable, and settle in to knowing that you are in and a part of the Great Un-Manifested, where every thought, every thing you could want and not want, every success, every failure, every romance, every friendship, every amount of money, every project, every possession, every thought, every feeling, every sensation, already exists. Some of them are temporarily showing, like yourselves, like the furniture in this room, like the building itself, and others are there in un-manifested form, but just as much there as the things that are showing.

FOR A RECORDED VERSION OF THIS MEDITATION, GO TO DAVID'S THOUGHT EXCHANGE MEDITATION CD, AT WWW.THETHOUGHTEXCHANGE.COM

Now, think about the things that you would like to see manifest in your life, and staying in the eyes-closed place, look around and actually see them there in the Great Un-Manifested. There's that million dollars sitting right over there in the corner. There's the love of my life. There's the successful outcome of my project. You can also see: There's the failure. There's the unhappy relationship. There's the poverty. They are there too, along with everything else, and it's OK for them to be there. You're free to leave them there, you don't have to fight with them. Just as when you go shopping in a store there are many items you see but don't pick up because they're not items you're looking for, let everything be there, and just notice the things you're looking for. If you don't know what you're looking for, just gaze around the Great Un-Manifested and see what you see there. Let's take a minute and do that.

(Pause for a minute of silence.)

Now, whatever it is you've spotted or whatever it is that has called to you, walk over to it (in your mind) or bring it toward you until you are standing in front of it. Now, step into the same space as it, so that you and it are occupying the same location. You can do this in the Great Un-Manifested because nothing is physical here.

Take a few moments to notice what that feels like, what thoughts you have, what looking out from the same space as the object or thought you desire feels like.

(Pause for a few moments.)

And now, knowing that even when your eyes are open, you are living in, and a part of, the Great Un-Manifested, since there's no way you or anything else, whether showing or not showing, can be outside it, slowly come back to the room and open your eyes, still sitting here in the same space as what you desire, and still sitting with everything else that the Un-Manifested contains (which is EVERYTHING) around you."

DISCUSS WHAT PEOPLE SAW IN THE GREAT UN-MANIFEST-ED - We often take a few moments for people to share what they saw in The Great Un-Manifested, just to get an idea of the scope and variation of people's dreams, and to stimulate people to allow themselves to see and talk about what they want out of life.

PRESENT AN ISSUE - Someone in the group shares an issue in his or her life, and describes it, until that person as well as the group are clear on what the issue is.

IF YOUR LIFE WERE A MIRROR OF YOUR THOUGHT, WHAT THOUGHT MIGHT THIS BE REFLECTING? - We ask this question, and discuss it until the person with the story feels that they have the thought that is being reflected. It's sometimes a very mundane, trite thought, but it often has great power and a sweeping ability to thwart the person's deepest desires.

WHAT WOULD YOU LIKE TO SEE HAPPEN? - The person discusses what they would like to see happen in the physical, manifested world.

WHAT THOUGHT, WHEN REFLECTED IN THE MIRROR OF YOUR LIFE, MIGHT ALLOW ROOM FOR THAT TO HAPPEN? - We work with the person until they come up with a thought, from all possible thoughts, that might be reflected as what they want to see.

AFFIRM - When they have the thought, we all hold our hands up toward them and say the thought to them in the second person. So it might be something like, "You Can Write A Book," or "The Love of Your Life is Available to You Now."

WRITE IT DOWN - Then we each write down the thought on our own piece of paper, in the first person, so we can carry it for and with the person, and also so that we can have it as our own thought. Since the thought came out of the consciousness of the group, on some level it's our own thought as well as the person's who spoke it. We can change it slightly if the person was very specific and it doesn't apply to us. For instance, "I can have success as an actress" might be changed to "I can have success as an accountant."

READ ALL THE THOUGHTS - At the end of the session, we read all the thoughts aloud. More often than not we find that they are all very much related, which to me is a sign of our one-ness and the fact that we're all really working on the same things in a larger group consciousness. (Whatever the thoughts, I invariably find, when I run Thought Exchange workshops, that the issues that come before me in "other people" are issues that I myself am working on.)

CLOSING MEDITATION - We close with a brief meditation or prayer acknowledging our oneness and our gratitude for the fact that all possible thoughts and outcomes have already been created and we are free to take on, explore and use, at any time and no matter what is going on, any and all of the infinite richness of ideas and experiences that are here for us all.

DURING THE WEEK - During the week, we keep track of the issue we worked on in The Thought Exchange, and every time we notice a problem, or notice that we're having a thought that is counter to what we desire to see appear in the reflection of the mirror of life, we exchange that thought for the thought we took on in the workshop, and see what happens. The results are often astounding.

PART 3

WE'VE GOT THE TOOLS

WHAT STOPS US FROM USING THEM?

CHAPTER 11
A SENSATIONAL DISCOVERY

So there we had it! A simple, concise method for changing our lives and manifesting anything we wanted!

Week after week, people would come in with issues, pinpoint the thoughts that those issues were reflecting, exchange those thoughts, and the appearance of those issues in the physical world would change.

This is the point at which most books would stop. We have the method, we know it works, so just use it and change your life!

But somehow, as the weeks went by, I began to notice that the change wasn't always holding. Sometimes, people would simply backslide into holding the old thoughts. At other times, the issue would seem to be solved, only to be replaced by another issue that appeared to be different but actually was just a different form of the same issue.

Why couldn't people hold the change? Why did they keep backsliding?

Something was missing.

My first hypothesis was that since issues often had many thoughts attached to them, perhaps by dealing with only one thought per session we weren't covering the whole thing.

So I decided to create a special "Exploratory Thought Exchange Workshop." Inviting four of my most experienced Thought Exchange members to participate, I asked each of them to pick one issue to work on. Over the next four weeks, our mission was to exchange every single thought that had to do with that issue. In this way, we assumed that we would be able to clear up one big issue once and for all. Having done this, we would then have a template for how to truly clear up lifelong challenges we'd been having.

The group started out great. Through various worksheets and processes, we mined every thought we were having and found thoughts to exchange them for. Things began to move in people's lives. Everyone was excited. Everyone reported breakthroughs.

And then, suddenly, in the fourth week, for no explainable reason, everything stopped. It was as though we had all simultaneously slammed on the brakes. Suddenly everyone was doubting, everyone was frustrated, nothing seemed to be working, and everyone was backsliding.

What could be the problem? What was it that was stopping everybody?

It was at this juncture that we decided to extend the workshop beyond the four weeks. (It actually lasted three years.) During this time, we began to explore the important question that lies beyond affirmations, beyond "The Secret," beyond most metaphysical methods that deal with manifestation.

IT'S ONE THING TO CHOOSE A NEW THOUGHT. IT'S ANOTHER THING TO STAY WITH IT.

Why would we not want to stay with a thought that would bring us what we want?

That seemed ridiculous, yet here was the evidence, right in front of us, in the mirror. No matter how hard we tried to push through, to renew our efforts, we ultimately kept stopping ourselves.

What was it that was holding us back?

We went back to the circle of experience (Thought generates Sensation which generates Belief which generates Manifestation) and very carefully and meticulously began to look at everything that was going on with us when we took on our new thought.

What we discovered was that when we took on a new thought, especially a thought of something life-long that we had wanted but had not achieved, the sensations that arose were perceived as extremely uncomfortable and frightening. This might seem counterintuitive. Why would the "positive" thought bring on the "negative" sensations? But upon observation, this was clearly what was happening.

Furthermore, since you can't change sensations by going directly to the sensations and trying to make them be different, we were doing the only thing we could do to get away from them; exchanging the thought that was producing them for a thought that wouldn't produce them. If the thought that was producing the sensations was, for example, "I can do this," then the thought that wouldn't produce the sensations was, "I can't do this." Simple enough. If a thought is producing a disturbing sensation, take on the opposite thought, and then you won't have the sensation.

Of course, as I think must be obvious by now, the only fly in the ointment is that when you do this you won't see what you want appear in the world! But nevertheless, this is what we were doing.

This process was often unconscious, and most of us were not even aware that we were having these sensations. The thought would exchange so quickly that we would not even notice a sensation. Perhaps the purpose of these 'negative" thoughts was to protect us from experiencing the sensations? Why?

We began by taking on our new thoughts and looking very carefully at the sensations that arose when we thought them. People immediately described those sensations as horrible, intolerable and painful. In fact, it was even difficult for people to describe them as sensations. Rather, they would move immediately to their thoughts about them, their fears about what the sensations meant or what might happen if they didn't get rid of them.

People would say things like, "It feels as though my head is going to explode." Now, since I've never actually seen someone's head explode, and it's unlikely that I ever will, I realized that that was just a thought taken on in fear of the sensation. What exactly WAS the sensation.?

When the person zeroed in, they realized they had a pounding or a tightness or a tingling or a hotness or a coldness or an 'empty' feeling. All of them were run-of-the-mill, normal sensations that people have all the time and don't think twice about. Could they tolerate them? Of course. So why were they so afraid of them in these particular situations?

Our exploration led us back to our childhoods. Somehow, the thoughts we were trying to take on now, had been dangerous or threatening to us in our childhoods. Someone punished, threatened, reprimanded or ignored us when we dared to think, "I am great" or "I can do this" or "I'm pretty" or "I'm going to be a star." When we're little children, the thought that we will either lose our parents or be attacked by them is intolerable. We have no recourse. We can't leave. We can't fight back. We can't argue. Our whole survival depends on our parents. We have this "awful" sensation and there's nothing we can do about it. We have no support in being with that sensation, no validation that what we're feeling is appropriate, so all we can do is take on a thought that will make sure we never go near that sensation again. And that thought is always an "I can't, I won't, I'll never, I don't have" thought.

So we actually took on these thoughts to protect ourselves from sensations that signaled real danger to us when we were children. We're not in the same danger now, because as adults we can tolerate that sensation, and we have the tools to deal with whatever situation might arise. But we don't know it.

Can you see how challenging and confusing this can be? As we move toward what we want, we get more and more uncomfortable. And this is the key.

THE ONLY WAY TO HOLD A NEW THOUGHT AND SEE IT MANIFEST IS TO BE ABLE TO BE WITH THE SENSATIONS THAT COME WITH IT.

As I said at the beginning of this book, one of the biggest fallacies in New Thought is thinking that you're going to feel good when you get what you want. What you are going to feel is the sensations you've been avoiding your whole life by not taking on the thought you wanted to take on.

When people hear this, they often say, "Oh no. You mean I'm going to feel like this for the rest of my life?"

The answer is, "Yes, you are most likely going to feel this sensation for the rest of your life. But what this sensation means to you will radically change as you become able to be with it."

For instance, as I described in section One of this book, when I was 20 years old I had severe panic disorder. Without warning, for no apparent reason, I would experience physical sensations that terrified me. I thought I couldn't go out of the house. I thought I couldn't go on the subway. I thought I couldn't sit in a theater. Actually, what was happening was that when I did those things, I had a sensation which I thought I couldn't tolerate, so I would avoid those places.

When I looked closely at those sensations, I realized that they were nothing more than a coolness in my wrists, a tightness in my chest and a "funny feeling" around my eyes. That was it! A complete panic attack was actually nothing more than that. Was I capable of tolerating slightly cool wrists a tightness in my chest and a "funny feeling" around my eyes? Of course I was. So I made the decision that even if I felt these sensations for the rest of my life, I would still go to the theater, get on the subway, and do what I wanted to do. I was very uncomfortable, but I was beginning to live again.

Over time, it's not that these sensations went away, but they so ceased to mean anything that I hardly noticed them. If I had them, I had them. Gradually, my experience began to be that I was completely undisturbed at being in situations in which I'd formerly been terrified, because it didn't matter whether or not I had the sensations. Eventually I stopped noticing them altogether.

Think about it. As a little child, if you had to stand on a long line, you might scream and cry and throw a tantrum. You couldn't tolerate the sensations that went with waiting that long for something. As adults we don't like long lines either, and we might say, "Oh no, I hate this" or "I don't have time for this," but we have the ability to stand on the line because there's something we want at the other end of it.

So we realized that we had left out a crucial step in our Thought Exchange Process.

After you choose your new thought, you must stop and ask yourself, "What sensations am I feeling when I take on this thought?" And to your surprise, you will often find that the more exciting, the more new, the more revolutionary your new thought is, the more breakthroughs it offers you, the more UNCOMFORTABLE your sensations will be.

Holding the new thought and seeing its fulfillment in the manifested world is totally dependent on whether or not we can BE WITH the sensations that arise with that thought.

There are those who will give you the advice, "You'll know you're on the right track when you feel good." Nothing could be further from the truth, and if you wait until you feel good, you will most likely never achieve your dreams. As a performer, I often have to go on the stage, and it's extremely rare that I feel anything other than a pounding heart, a queasy stomach and tingling all over my body. Someone once said to me, "Imagine how fantastic you're going to feel when you're out there on opening night on Broadway!" Well I've done that, numerous times, and frankly, I feel like I'm going to throw up. But I want to be out there on Broadway, so I'm willing to feel that way.

So once again, thoughts do manifest in the mirror of the physical world, but in order to have them manifest, we have to stay with them. And the only way to stay with them is to be able to stay with the physical sensations that come with them.

THE UPDATED TEMPLATE FOR THE THOUGHT EXCHANGE PROCESS

So the new template for doing thought exchange became this:

BEGIN WITH A MEDITATION ON THE EXISTENCE OF THE GREAT UN-MANIFESTED.

DESCRIBE AN ISSUE YOU'RE HAVING IN YOUR LIFE, EXACTLY AS YOU SEE IT.

ASK YOURSELF, "IF MY LIFE WERE A MIRROR OF MY THOUGHT, WHAT THOUGHT MIGHT THIS BE REFLECTING?"

WHAT WOULD YOU LIKE TO SEE HAPPEN?

WHAT THOUGHT, WHEN REFLECTED IN THE MIRROR OF YOUR LIFE, MIGHT ALLOW ROOM FOR THAT TO HAPPEN?

EXCHANGE THE THOUGHT YOU'RE THINKING FOR THE NEW THOUGHT.

SIT STILL AND NOTICE THE PHYSICAL SENSATIONS YOU'RE HAVING. DON'T ANALYZE THEM, IF YOU NOTICE YOU'RE HAVING ANY THOUGHTS, SIMPLY GO BACK TO THE SENSATIONS.

WHEN YOU CAN SIMPLY BE WITH THE SENSATIONS, THE INFINITE UNIVERSE OF ALL POSSIBLE THOUGHTS OPENS TO YOU.

CHAPTER 12
PHYSICAL SENSATIONS
THE DOORWAY TO THE GREAT UN-MANIFESTED

So we noticed that when we could be with our sensations, infinite possibilities opened up. We didn't even seem to have to do anything, take conscious action or try to make anything happen. When we could stay with the sensations that arose when we took on a thought, things just seemed to happen naturally. Ideas would pop into our heads, actions would be taken spontaneously and automatically, and even things that seemed like they were outside of us would begin happening. People would call, offers would come in, we'd run into just the right person, or get something in the mail.

Why did it work this way? What was the explanation for why simply being able to be with the sensations that a thought generated caused the thought to manifest?

As we explored what we already knew about Thought Exchange, and the work we'd done on why and how we resist staying with our sensations, we began to come up with answers.

As I've said earlier, when we have a trauma in our childhood, it is always associated with sensations that we think we can't tolerate. Sometimes the trauma is tremendous and obvious, like sexual or physical abuse, but sometimes it may be as simple as your mother walked out of the room for a half hour when you were two months old and you panicked.

We must remember that as children, we are totally helpless and dependent on our parents. We have no recourse, we are smaller than they are, they give us our food, we cannot choose to leave or fight back or go out and earn our own living. That's a difficult sensation for us to recreate as adults.

Think of it like this. Suppose you were on life support and the person operating your life support let you know that if you didn't treat them a certain way, they would die. You would have to treat them that way, because otherwise they would die and, since they're operating your life support, you would die too. Or suppose they said that unless you let them sexually abuse you they would turn off the life support. Or they told you that if you told anyone about the sexual abuse, they would turn off the life support.

This is the level of dependence that children have on parents. So no matter how mean, how insane parents are, their children must find a way to cope with them.

Now think for a moment about the sensations that might arise in you if you were on life support and someone told you that unless you let them sexually abuse you they were going to turn of the machine and end your life. Imagine how "impossible" it might be to stay with those sensations. Whatever choice you make, there are devastating consequences.

To a child, their life is always in the hands of their caretakers, and any threat to their life generates devastating sensations. A child doesn't have the mental capacity or the physical independence to make some of the choices that an adult can make, so the child must find a way to get away from those "awful" and "intolerable" sensations.

The only way to do that is to take on a thought that not only doesn't produce those sensations, but more importantly, makes sure that the child will never again be put in a situation where those sensations might occur.

Those thoughts are always, "I can't, I won't, I'll never" kinds of thoughts.

So if you were threatened by your caretaker when you tried to be independent, in order to get away from the sensations that threat produced, you will make sure that you take on a thought that does not allow you to ever try to be independent.

If you were threatened by your caretaker when you began to become successful, you will take on thoughts that will make sure you never go near success.

What happens when we do this, is the thoughts usually become so well-oiled that we don't even know we're having a sensation. The second we think, "I can do this," we will think, "No I can't." There's a sensation that happens right before we exchange the thought, but since the thought is designed to keep us away from that sensation, we usually don't even notice the sensation until we slow the process down and develop the ability to be with the sensation.

Now here's where we get fooled. Because this whole process is designed to get us away from a sensation, we actually begin to believe the new thought we've taken on, the thought "I can't, I won't, I'll never." We then think that our problem is that we're afraid of success, or afraid of independence or afraid of being powerful. This often causes us to go into therapy to try and find out why we're afraid of these things, to express our feelings, to try to take bold actions, etc.

But it never works, because WE ARE NOT AFRAID OF SUCCESS. WE ARE NOT AFRAID OF INDEPENDENCE. WE ARE NOT AFRAID OF BEING POWERFUL.

WE ARE AFRAID OF THE <u>SENSATIONS</u> THAT THOSE SITUATIONS GENERATE.

These sensations are not intrinsically dangerous. In fact, sometimes they're as simple as a little stomach ache or a runny nose or a tight throat. But because those sensations have come to be associated with danger, we run from them, and in some sense, would rather think we're afraid of these things than experience the sensations.

The more trauma we have had, the more sensations we run from.

And since sensations are generated by thoughts, the more trauma we have had, the more areas of thought we are afraid to go to.

And since the world is nothing more than a mirror of our thoughts, we cannot see what we want in the world if we cannot hold the thought of it on the inside, in the invisible world of the Great Un-Manifested.

So our lives become more and more constricted, and we think its because we're afraid of things. But all we're afraid of is the sensation that goes with even thinking those things.

When we do this work, we consistently find that the thoughts that bring on the most challenging sensations are thoughts like, "I can, I'm powerful," even "It's possible."

So think about it. Over the course of our lives, in our effort to avoid sensations that we associated with upsetting things, there became more and more places where we couldn't go. As adults, we're fully capable of experiencing these sensations, but because we've unconsciously associated them with unbearable experiences (to a child) we refuse to go there. All we have to do to be able to go there is to be willing to experience those sensations as we think the thoughts we want to think. This is totally possible, but we've been duping ourselves into thinking that the sensations mean something.

Take the example of invisible fencing for dogs. Invisible fencing is a very efficient way of keeping a dog within the bounds of your yard. The way it works is, there is a wire laid around the edge of the property that sends out an electrical signal. The dog wears a collar, and as the dog approaches the wire, the collar gives it a shock, first mild, and then stronger and stronger as it gets closer to the fence. The shock is never dangerous, it could never really injure the dog, but the dog feels the discomfort and shies away from the perimeter of the property and stays within its bounds.

But some dogs experience the discomfort and decide that freedom is more important than the fear of a shock. The dogs who do this, break through the invisible fence. They feel the shock, but the shock is not actually dangerous to them. Once they've done this, the invisible fence can't hold them. They want to be on the outside, and are willing to experience the harmless tingling sensation that comes with it.

We have built an invisible fence around our lives in the areas where we don't want to feel certain sensations. And the invisible fence is an illusion. All we have to do to break out of it is to experience the sensations it generates.

This is obviously easier said than done, because the sensations seem truly threatening in that at one time they were designed to keep us out of danger. So we have taken on protective thoughts to keep us away from those sensations and the perceived danger that we think goes with them. But what they end up protecting us from is the experience of sensations from which we don't need protection, and in doing so, they are keeping us from living our dreams.

Think about people who go on the stage for a living. People who don't do this think that the reason people can do this is because they are unafraid. Nothing could be further from the truth. As I said before, I rarely go on the stage without feeling a pounding heart, a coldness in my hands, a numbness, a rushing of my blood. That being so, I can only go on the stage if I'm willing to feel those things. Stage fright is not a fear of going on the stage. Everybody in their right mind has a fear of going on the stage. Stage fright is a fear of the sensations you will feel when you go on the stage. Huge stars don't not have stage fright, they just have an enormous capacity to experience their sensations because they have a great desire to be on the stage. It could be said that they're like the dogs who break through the invisible fence because their desire to get to the outside is so great that they're willing to experience the sensations that go with that freedom.

So, by not being willing to experience certain sensations, we have cut off huge parts of the infinite world of possibility from our experience. When we become willing to be with whatever sensations we are experiencing, the simple (but not always easy) act of doing that reopens endless possibilities. We now have access to unlimited thoughts, and those possibilities MUST appear, since what appears in the world is nothing more than an exact reflection of our thoughts.

So perhaps the most important step in the process is that once you identify the thought you want to take on and actually take it on, you must pause and ask yourself, "What physical sensations am I experiencing?" If you want to be with the thought so that you can see it manifest, you MUST be with the sensations that that thought brings up.

If you see something in the world that is not the manifestation of the thought you wish to hold, it doesn't mean that your thought didn't work. It simply means that you have exchanged the thought away, and the mirror of the world is showing you that. And the reason you have exchanged the thought away is undoubtedly that you don't want to experience the sensation that the thought generates. DO NOT FIGHT WITH THE MIRROR. Immediately go back to the thought you wish to hold, and EXPERIENCE THE SENSATIONS that go with it.

This is your key to unlimited possibility and unlimited manifestation.

CHAPTER 13
THE PROTECTIVE THOUGHT

Once we understand how experiencing sensations opens the door to the entire invisible world of the Great Un-Manifested, we can begin, sensation by sensation, to heal our childhood wounds and reopen the world of infinite possibility for ourselves.

Every time we have a thought, it generates a sensation. At this point, we have two choices. We can either experience the sensation and stay with the thought we took on, or jump away from the sensation in the only way possible, by exchanging the thought we're holding for a different thought. Some call this different thought a sabotaging thought, but that's not really what's going on here. In Thought Exchange, we call this different thought a protective thought, because it is taken on to protect you from the sensation you are afraid to experience.

As we discussed earlier in the book, making the choice to stay with the sensation allows the thought to be transformed into a belief, which results in the thought reflecting in the mirror of the manifested world. To put it more simply, staying with the sensation allows us to see the thought manifest.

Making the choice to jump away from the sensation by exchanging our thought for a protective thought will definitely replace our sensation with one that feels more tolerable and safe, so this new thought will do its job of relieving us from the sensation we're afraid of.

But here's the problem.

PROTECTIVE THOUGHTS NEVER ULTIMATELY WORK

The new protective thought will get us away from the sensation we're afraid of, but in the process, it will also produce a result which is not what we've been going for. In fact, since protective thoughts are invariably of the "I can't, I won't, It will never happen" variety (to get us away from the thoughts that are causing the uncomfortable sensation, which are invariably thoughts like "I can, I will, It's gonna happen") the results they produce are usually the exact opposite of what we want.

So, although we will feel temporary relief from the sensation, in short order we will notice that we don't have what we wanted and we will go back to having the thought of what we want.

ALL ROADS LEAD YOU BACK TO THE SENSATION YOU'RE AFRAID OF

And guess what happens when we exchange the protective thought for the thought of what we want? You got it! The sensation we were afraid of appears again, and 'round and 'round we go through the same pattern.

In short, YOU CAN RUN BUT YOU CAN'T HIDE! If you try to avoid the sensation created by the thought of what you want, the mirror will give you infinite opportunities to "take another crack at it."

SENSATIONS – STAY OR RUN – YOUR CHOICE (BUT NOT FOR LONG)

We've already discussed that the original point of choice is in the thought you choose, but as soon as you choose a thought, you immediately come to a second, and perhaps more crucial point of choice. Whether to stay with the sensation the thought has produced and see the thought pass through and become a belief and manifest, or to jump to a protective thought, see that thought manifest, realize it's not what you want, become aware of the thought you do want, take on that thought and find yourself right back at the sensation you were trying to avoid by taking on the protective thought.

Here's a chart of what all the options look like:

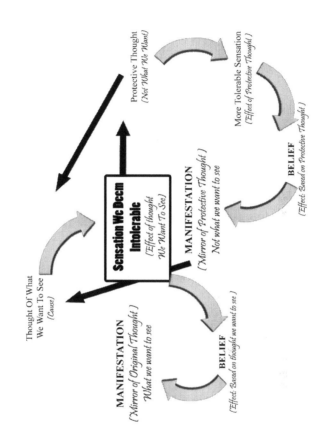

Protective Thought
(Not What We Want)

More Tolerable Sensation
(Effect of Protective Thought)

BELIEF
(Effect: Based on Protective Thought)

Sensation We Deem Intolerable
(Effect of thought We Want To See)

MANIFESTATION
(Mirror of Protective Thought)
Not what we want to see

Thought Of What
We Want To See
(Cause)

MANIFESTATION
(Mirror of Original Thought)
What we want to see

BELIEF
(Effect: Based on thought we want to see)

So, looking at the chart, we see that all roads lead us back to the sensation we need to feel in order to stay with the thought of what we want and see it manifest. Holding the thought immediately produces that sensation. If we jump away from the sensation, we will go to a protective thought. If we notice we're having a protective thought, we can do a thought exchange and go back to the thought we want to hold, and we'll be right back at that sensation. If we are unaware that we've taken on a protective thought, the thought will produce a manifestation that we will experience as an upset, and we'll immediately remember our original thought, go back to it, and before we know it, we're right back to the sensation we've been trying to avoid.

So the universe is "rigged" to always send us back to the sensation that is attached to the thought of what we want, so that we can experience it and move through to manifestation. Looked at in this light, the universe completely shifts from being something that is constantly attacking and frustrating us to a benevolent place where, no matter what, we're being guided toward experiencing the sensations that will allow us to see what we want appear.

THE MISSING PIECE

This was truly the missing piece in the original Thought Exchange, the answer to why we were exchanging thoughts and not sticking with our new thoughts. In areas in which we're having "problems" or "lack" in our lives, it is always nothing more than a reflection of a protective thought. So often, we think these incidents are "proof" that we can't have things, but they are, in fact, just the opposite. They are pointing us back toward the thought of what we want, but the problem has always been that we expected to feel good when we held that thought. In fact, it is that very thought, the thought of what we want, that always brings us right back to the sensations we've been afraid of. If we can learn to expect those sensation, and know that they are harmless and are truly the path to manifestation, we can choose to stay with them and see the thought finally manifest.

So avoidance of sensation has been at the heart of all those issues that we have grappled with throughout our lives and which have continued to frustrate us. The things that we go for over and over and never seem to get. The only reason we don't get to see what we want manifest is that we think we can't stay with the sensations that the thought of having what we want produces, so we exchange the thought of what we want for a protective thought and immediately see a different result. A result we don't want.

If we understand that what we see in the manifested world is simply a reflection of the thought we're holding, and we understand that each thought generates a sensation, then it's simple (not necessarily easy) to realize that all we have to do to see a thought manifest is be able to stay with the sensations that the thought produces.

As you will recall, that chart (the original Thought Exchange Chart) looks like this:

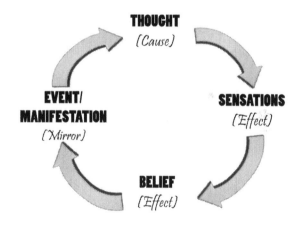

Simple. But!!!!! That chart may FEEL like this.

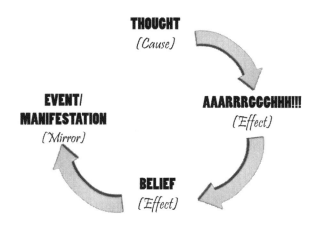

Not easy.

So all you have to do to be able to see the manifestation of the thought you wish to hold, is be able to be with that AAARRRGGGHHH!!!! that the thought produces.

In simple terms, this is called maturity. It's called growing up.

Let me explain what I mean.

GROWING UP – ADULTS CAN HANDLE SENSATIONS THAT CHILDREN CAN'T

When we're 2 years old and we want candy, if we have to wait in a line for it, we may not be able to tolerate waiting in that line, so we will burst into tears and run off the line and not get the candy. (Or an adult will have to wait in line and get the candy for us.)

As an adult, we also don't like waiting in line, but because we know we want the candy, we tolerate the sensation of waiting in line and the result is that we have the candy.

So it could be said that all the things we want and can't get, because we can't stay with the sensations that the thought produces, are simply a matter of our being stuck in childhood, and shying away from or thinking we can't tolerate a sensation that, although we couldn't tolerate it in childhood, we're perfectly capable of tolerating in adulthood. When we grow up, we realize we can tolerate these sensations, and thus we can stay with the thought of what we want.

This can be very challenging, because the sensations are still viewed as extremely painful because they're associated with events in which they did signal danger. But our healing depends on our being with them anyway, without giving them thoughts, without running, just being with them.

Once we understand this, we begin to heal, sensation by sensation, and reclaim our world. We take on the thought of something we've always wanted, experience the sensation that goes along with it, and make the choice to experience the sensation just as it is. And suddenly, all sorts of thoughts and actions are available to us, and all sorts of things happen that bring about the result we desire.

Now at this point, many people ask, "Does this mean that I will have to experience this sensation (the one I hate) forever? The seemingly bad news is, "Very possibly yes." But the good news is that once you don't have danger associated with the sensation, once you are able to experience it whenever it arises, you almost always find that the sensation is simply a run-of-the-mill tightness or itching or heat or cold that you're perfectly capable of experiencing. It wasn't really the sensation that was dangerous or intolerable, just the thoughts about it that you had taken on as a child. So the sensation becomes totally tolerable and after a while you don't even notice it.

But a strong warning here. If you go into this process with the goal of getting rid of the sensation, that implies that you're holding the thought that the sensation has to be gotten rid of in order for you to be OK. This thought becomes just another tactic (another protective thought) to try and circumvent the sensation. If this is what you're thinking, you're still stuck in a pattern of avoidance, because the sensation will reappear every time you take on the thought of what you want, and you'll jump away to a protective thought that will bring about a result you don't want.

The only way to have mastery is to know that no matter how, when or where the sensation arises, you're perfectly capable of being with it and staying with your thought.

You might have a situation in your life where every day you have to stand on a long line to get something you want. The sensation that you experience standing on that line may never go away, but you are always capable of having what you want by simply standing on that line, day after day after day. After a while, you'll hardly even notice the line. It will simply become a fact of life on the way to what you want.

Every time we are able to be with the sensations that are associated with a thought we are having about a particular issue, a piece of the Un-Manifested re-opens to us. This is a process that goes on for the rest of our lives. In fact, it is the way life works. We have a thought, we have a sensation, we stay with the sensation, and the thought manifests. And what happens next? You got it. We have another thought which brings on another sensation, and if we can stay with that sensation, that thought manifests. The object of life is not to get to the point where we don't have sensations. The real object is simply to know that we have everything available to us at all times, and all we have to do is see something in our mind, stay with the sensations that come with that thought, and we will get to experience whatever we want.

CHAPTER 14
BRING IT ON!
INVITING OUR CHALLENGES IN

So let's review what we've observed so far.

We get to choose whatever thought we want to think.

When we think a thought, it generates a sensation. When we stay with that sensation, the thought turns into a belief, which is a thought we think is true (even though no thought can actually be TRUE – it's just a thought.) And when we hold a thought as a belief, it appears in the Manifested world, which is nothing more than a mirror of our thoughts.

When we hit the point of sensation, we have two choices. If the sensation is one we think we can tolerate, we simply experience it, and the thought continues on through to become a belief and to manifest. If the sensation is one that we think we can't tolerate, we will exchange the thought we're holding (the thought that produced the sensation) for one which will produce a different sensation. In this case, we will not feel the sensation we've been afraid of, because the new "protective" thought will produce a different sensation that we perceive as more tolerable. But the new thought will also produce a result that is not the result we desired.

When we get this result, and see that it isn't what we want, we will immediately remember what we DO want, and that thought will bring us right back to the sensation we've been afraid of. If we want to see that thought (the thought of what we want) manifest, we will have to, at some point, choose to be with the sensation that goes with that thought, no matter how uncomfortable it feels. Otherwise, we will keep going around and around the frustrating circle of wanting and not getting, forever.

So, in order to allow a thought to manifest, we must be able to stay with the sensation it produces. We originally began shying away from that particular sensation to protect ourselves when we experienced it in a childhood situation where we were helpless to take action or where we got no support for feeling the sensation. We then continued to shy away from it every time we hit a situation where it would come up. By doing this, we limited ourselves, being unable to stay with the sensation and thus being unable to stay with the thoughts that would bring us what we wanted in that area of life.

With this understanding, we can see that the only way to reopen this area of possibility would be to be able to experience the sensation. And since sensations are caused by thoughts, the only way to experience this sensation is to have a thought that will bring on the sensation.

And if we're not having that thought (because we're holding a protective thought) the way to know that we're not having that thought is to see a circumstance that reflects back to us that we're holding the protective thought and not the thought we want to hold.

So, in an effort to heal, and as a mirror of the thought we're holding (the thought of what we actually desire) we keep bringing up situation after situation where we have the chance to experience the sensation and make the choice to stay with it, so that our thought of what we desire can appear in the manifested world.

With this understanding, it becomes clear that we actually seek out these situations that we call upsetting. We bring on incident after incident where this sensation comes up. And then, we erroneously think that "this is happening to us" and we run from it. And what do we do next? We bring on another situation to give us another opportunity to experience the sensation.

It would be like if you fell off a horse, horses kept coming by to give you another opportunity to conquer your fear of falling off so you could ride, you kept getting on each new horse, experiencing the sensations you felt when you fell off, screaming "I can't take this" and jumping off the horse. I'm sure you can see that the only way you would ever get to ride a horse again would be to get on the horse, experience the sensations that go with it, and STAY ON THE HORSE!

So suddenly, within this paradigm, all those repetitive incidents become re-contextualized. Rather than being examples of how you can't have anything, or of how your original childhood incident is "true," they become opportunities that you have brought on in order to heal, in order to give yourself the chance to understand that incidents that were unmanageable to a child are not unmanageable to an adult, and sensations that could not be tolerated by a child can be tolerated by an adult.

In this context, rather than fighting or trying to change these incidents, we can truly be grateful to them as opportunities to experience, in our adult selves, the sensations that frightened us as children. And the payoff for doing this is that we will be able to hold thoughts of prosperity and success and happiness that we were unable to hold before (because we couldn't stay with the sensations they produced) and actually see them come to fruition.

RE-EXPERIENCING SENSATIONS
FROM AN EARLIER TIME

Since our lives have been stopped off by our avoidance of sensations that came with incidents that appeared earlier in our lives, we need to find a way to re-experience those sensations as adults so that we can re-generate the sensations and stay with them.

In an effort to do this, many therapies try to dig up the original incident and get you to feel what it felt like to experience it. The problem with this is that, as an adult, you won't experience the incident the same way you did as a child, because things that are impossible to handle for a child are not impossible to handle for an adult.

So you don't even have to know what the original incident was, because that incident, in most cases, would not have the same effect on you and would not generate the same sensations or outcome today. For example, if your original incident was that your mother hit you, if she tried to do that to you today, with you being an adult, you would simply stop her. If one of your parents were treating you badly today, you could leave the house. The incident wouldn't have the same effect on you, because you didn't have an empathetic adult with you then. But you do now. YOU.

You are present with the child inside who is experiencing the sensations, and you can hold the child and allow the child to experience them. Had you been there, as an adult, during the original incident, you could have interceded and changed the events and the child's experience of them. But you weren't, so the child did the only thing the child could do. Took on thoughts that would keep him or her away from anything that might bring on the same sensation.

So now, in creating incidents that give you the opportunity to experience that sensation, the childhood incidents won't do. They won't affect an adult in the same way. So you have to bring on incidents that are parallel but will have the same effect on you as the incidents had on the child. Those incidents tend to be HUGE. They have to be, in order to have the same effect. So you may have a spouse leave you, lose all your money, or develop a serious illness.

These things seem so real that we often forget that they are simply a mirror of our thought that we can't have things. If we can remember this, we can look at these events and ask the basic Thought Exchange question. "If this is a mirror of what I'm thinking, what must I be thinking?" And we will find the thought "inside" that is producing the reflection we're seeing "out there." The protective thought that is being reflected as the disease; as the loss of money; as the marital problem. The thought we took on to get away from the sensation that would be produced by the thought of what we desire.

It may seem crazy that we would call thoughts that produce disease, poverty and dissatisfaction "protective." But if you want to see how protective they are, try exchanging them for thoughts of health, wealth and happiness.

The moment we exchange these protective thoughts for thoughts of what we want, BOOM, the full force of the sensations we've been running from our whole life comes up. The tight throat, the hotness, the breathlessness, whatever. These are not dangerous, they are just invisible sensations, but because we have associated them with danger, we think they're dangerous.

Here's the amazing thing. All we have to do is stay with them. Period. When we do this, it immediately becomes clear to us that we can choose any thought, and when we choose the thought of what we want, the problem disappears and is replaced by what we want.

Now when I say this, people often reply, "I tried that, I experienced the sensation and took on the thought and the problem didn't go away."

Remember, the mirror is an EXACT reflection of what you're thinking. It has no power to do anything on it's own, and you have no power to think anything without it immediately and exactly being reflected in the mirror. So if you take on the thought and you still see the problem in the mirror, all you know is that you have exchanged the thought back for one that is still reflecting as the problem. How do you know? BECAUSE YOU SEE THE PROBLEM IN THE MIRROR! If I change my shirt in front of the mirror and come back to the mirror in a few minutes and see my old shirt in the mirror, THERE CAN ONLY BE ONE EXPLANATION. I changed my shirt back. If I look in the mirror and see I've lost 5 pounds, and a few weeks later I look again and I see that the 5 pounds are back, THERE CAN ONLY BE ONE EXPLANATION. I gained 5 pounds.

When we understand this, our whole life changes. Rather than being upset, we begin to welcome each challenge because we know that it is here not to hurt us but to heal us. Each thing that happens is another chance to experience the sensation we've been running from so we can stay with it, stay with the thought of what we want, and thus see what we want appear in the manifested world. At last!!!!

One thing I wanted to remind you of at the end of this chapter so you'll be sure to remember it is this. If you look at this process, you will see that IT IS THE THOUGHT OF WHAT WE WANT THAT BRINGS ON THE SENSATION THAT WE THINK WE CAN'T TOLERATE. I reiterate, IT'S AN ERRONIOUS NOTION THAT WHEN WE GET WHAT WE WANT WE WILL FEEL GOOD.

When we get what we want, we will feel the sensations we've been running from our whole lives, sensations we've been avoiding by making sure we NEVER GOT what we want. As I always say, "The bad news is that we may have these sensations forever. The good news is that these are just sensations, and once we cease to assign them the meaning we've been assigning them in order to stay away from them, we become perfectly able to experience them and tolerate them, and our experience of them totally changes.

PART 4 LIBERATION

CHAPTER 15
WHERE YOU ACTUALLY LIVE
YOU ARE INVISIBLE

With the understanding that everything we see in the manifested world is just a mirror, and that the only purpose of this mirror is to direct our attention back to sensations we've been avoiding so that we can hold the thoughts we've always wanted to hold, and thus experience what we've always wanted to experience, our lives become completely turned around.

Knowing that the "visible" world is actually the mirror in which the "invisible" world of experience is being reflected, we can now begin to explore the REAL world. All this time, we've been calling the physical world the "real" world, and the invisible world of consciousness, thought and sensation the "imaginary" world. Now, as it turns out, it's just the opposite. The REAL world is the invisible world of the Great Un-Manifested. And the real "you" exists ONLY in that world. You can't possibly exist anywhere else.

As it turns out, who you really are is not your body, not the things you possess, not the things you have achieved or will achieve, not the things that "happen to you." All these things are simply reflections of your thoughts. Who you are is invisible! You cannot be seen, you cannot be measured, you cannot be located, you cannot be reached or hurt or destroyed by anything in the physical world, any more than you could be destroyed by your reflection in the mirror.

As you may recall from the first chapter of this book, I spent the entire first few decades of my life thinking that the purpose of life was to acquire money, success and love in order to be "happy." Now suddenly none of those things matter because none of those things are located where I actually live. This can be a real mindbender. Here we are, having spent our whole lives calling the physical world the "real" world, and the invisible world of thought and imagination "unreal," and now we find out it's just the opposite.

You wouldn't call what's in the mirror the "real" world. But you would call what's in front of it the real world. By the same token, if the physical world is a mirror of our thoughts, then the physical world is just a reflection of our thoughts, so our thoughts are part of the real world, and the physical things and situations we see in front of us, aren't.

Now it's one thing to say this, but it's another thing entirely to actually experience it for yourself. A good way to begin is to do the following meditation.

A Meditation on Where We Actually Live

(After you read this you might want to memorize it or record it so that you can actually do the meditation with your eyes closed. If you record it, be sure to leave a 20 or 30 second space every time it says, "Take a few moments.")

(Close your eyes.)

With your eyes closed, notice how you know that you are here. Notice how you know that you exist. That you are present. There's a sense of consciousness, a sense of I Am. This sense of consciousness doesn't have your name on it, it's not located in any particular place. In fact, it's invisible. It can't be seen. I can't look over at you and see your consciousness. You can't see your consciousness. But it's definitely here, as an experience. An invisible, non-physical, non-locatable experience.

So it could be said, that who you are is an invisible consciousness.

Now, notice that you have sensations. Itching, tightness, shortness of breath, hotness, coldness, pain, throbbing, relaxation, calmness, pounding, rushing. With your eyes open, you might think of these as "physical" sensations. But with your eyes closed, you can't even be sure you have a body. All you know is that within your consciousness you are experiencing sensations. And the experience of these sensations, like your consciousness, is invisible. I cannot see your experience of hotness or coldness or tension. You cannot see it. You may see the results of it, but you cannot see the experience itself.

128

You may attribute it to some physical world location or "cause," like a leg cramp, heart palpitations, or a stiff neck, but what it "feels" like to be experiencing those things lies completely in the invisible world of experience. Everyone experiences them differently. What may seem intolerable to one person may seem like nothing to another.

Take a few moments to be with and notice the sensations you're experiencing. Notice whether they stay the same or keep changing. Just be with them.

So it could be said that who you are is an invisible consciousness experiencing invisible sensations.

Now notice your thoughts. Notice that you can think of ANYTHING. Locate a baboon in your thoughts. Say "Got it" when you've got it. It shouldn't take you more than the time it takes to think of it for you to get it. And the time it takes to think of anything is infinitesimal. Now see yourself doing the twist on the rings of Saturn. Say "Got it" when you've got it. If you're having trouble seeing this, or are finding yourself saying, "Well that's impossible. Saturn's rings are not solid and you can't breathe on Saturn," remember, I didn't ask you to take this into the physical universe or figure out how you're going to accomplish it. I just asked you to see it in the invisible world.

Notice that all the things you "see" in this realm are invisible, not solid or physical.

You have infinite choice of what you can see here, unlike in the physical world, where it seems much harder to see things. And this infinite world is inside you and always available to you.

So it could be said that who you are is an invisible consciousness experiencing invisible sensations and containing unlimited, invisible thoughts.

In fact, what I have just described is YOUR ENTIRE WORLD OF EXPERIENCE, and is the ONLY PLACE IN WHICH YOU LIVE.

Think about it. How do you experience anything? How do you KNOW something is out there? All you've got is a consciousness which experiences physical sensations and has thoughts. If I were to stab you, you would only experience that stab by having a physical sensation about which you would notice a thought you're having. Physical sensation. OUCH! Thought. "I'm going to die." (Or, possibly, the thought "I'll be fine," or any other thought for that matter.)

That's it. You live only in the invisible world and you cannot ever get into the physical world. Things appear before you, but how do you "know" they're there? Only by your experience of them. You might say, "Well everybody agrees that there is a table there." But you only "know" that because you are seeing an "everybody" inside of you. Is "everybody" really there? No way of knowing. Except you have an experience of an "everybody." An experience that takes place inside you and ONLY inside you.

So you can't ever get into the manifested world, just as you could never get into a mirror. You see the reflection in the mirror clear as day, but if you tried to walk into the mirror, you'd HIT THE GLASS. And anyway, the reason you can't walk into a mirror is that THERE'S NOTHING IN THE MIRROR! It may look like there's a "you" standing 5 feet in back of the glass (if you're standing 5 feet in front of it) but there isn't.

With this understanding, that you live only in the invisible world and everything else is a reflection of that world, go inside to the unlimited, invisible world of your thoughts, or as we call it, "The Great Un-Manifested" and notice, as we did when we first began to explain Thought Exchange, that everything is in there. Every illness and every cure for every illness, unlimited amounts of money, every job, every relationship of every kind, every home, every success and every failure. All you have to do is think of something and it's there.

Now find something in there that you've been regarding as a problem. Something you've thought you were missing, that was lacking, that "needs changing." Got it? Now, with your eyes still closed (they should have been closed through this entire meditation) pull that "problem" out and place it in front of you, outside you, in the mirror, as it were.

You are now "looking" at your problem in the "outside" world. You are seeing your thought of lack of money or lack of a relationship or poor health, whatever. But what you are seeing is not the problem, but merely the reflection of the thought of a problem that you are focusing on inside. Furthermore, you can see that this "problem" did not happen to you, but that in fact, YOU PUT IT THERE! It's not real in and of itself. It doesn't mean anything. It's just the tiny piece of the infinite thoughts in the Great Un-Manifested that you've been focusing on.

Knowing this, take the problem or circumstance you picked, and suck it back into the Great Un-Manifested, into the "soup" of infinite, unlimited possible thoughts that always must exist inside you. Stir it up until it dissolves. You now have a "solution" in which that particular problem is mixed up in all the other unlimited possibilities. You can't really see the problem as distinct. It's as important or unimportant as anything else in there.

Now, reach into the "soup" of The Great Un-Manifested, and pull out the problem solved. You don't have to know how this happened, just that it's solved. So if you needed money, see yourself having all the money you want, without knowing how it came to you. (That's not your job. That's the mirror's job to reflect your thought of how much money you think you can have.) If it's a relationship you want, see yourself in a relationship. You don't have to know with whom or how it happened. Just see it. If you have been holding the thought that you are ill, simply see yourself well, without knowing how that happened, and without checking in the physical world to see if that's so. (That would be holding the thought that you're not well, and since a mirror MUST reflect what's in front of it, the physical world will reflect illness.

So, knowing that your entire experience is invisible, that you are an invisible consciousness experiencing invisible sensations and the unlimited possibility of invisible thoughts, and that whatever "problems" you see are merely an exact projection of the ones that you're thinking about, slowly open your eyes and know that you are there, inside, invisible, safe and sound, and you are looking at a mirror.

Usually, in a Thought Exchange workshop, whatever it is that we chose to project into the manifested as our "problem" is what we work on. We notice the protective thought we've been holding that has been projecting as the "problem," exchange it for the thought of what we want, and then notice the sensations that arise with that thought and do our best to stay with them, rather than running from them (as we may have been our whole lives) by using a protective thought.

For a recorded version of this meditation, go to David's Thought Exchange Meditation CD, at WWW.THETHOUGHTEXCHANGE.COM

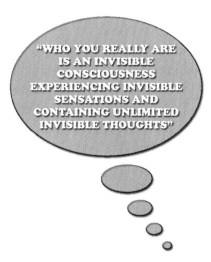

CHAPTER 16
WHO YOU REALLY ARE

Imagine if nothing that happened, and nothing you felt or thought, could affect or diminish you in any way. No matter what, you always knew that you had infinite supply, infinite possibility and infinite safety.

This, in fact, is who you really are.

To have a first-hand experience of this, read or record the meditation I describe in the next six paragraphs and then close your eyes and try it. This is something you can do any time you feel stuck or overwhelmed with sensations, thoughts or circumstances.

A *MEDITATION* ON WHO YOU REALLY ARE

Close your eyes, and notice any sensations you're having. Just notice them. A tightness in your chest, an itch, a feeling of fullness, shallowness or deepness of breath, just notice them. They don't have to be big or small, important or unimportant, scary or comfortable. They just are whatever they are.

Now notice your thoughts. You may be thinking about the sensations you're having, interpreting them, cringing from them, enjoying them, whatever. You may be thinking about what you're going to have for dinner tomorrow night, or the stock market, or that you're going to run out of money in 12 years, or that you'll never meet the love of your life. Just notice your thoughts, whatever they are. If you begin to interpret them, simply notice that you're interpreting them.

Now go back to noticing your sensations for a few moments.

Now go back to noticing your thoughts.

Now notice who's noticing all this.

I think you can see that the one who is noticing is neither the thoughts nor the sensations. The Noticer has no opinion, cannot be hurt by these thoughts and sensations, has no need to change them, and loses nothing by observing them. Any thoughts you're having about your sensations or thoughts are not the Noticer. They are what's being noticed by the Noticer.

The Noticer is who you actually are. It is located nowhere, has no name, and not only can what's going on in the world not affect it (it just observes) but what's going on in your body can also not affect it because it is also outside the Noticer, being observed.

Now open your eyes, knowing that you are the Noticer.

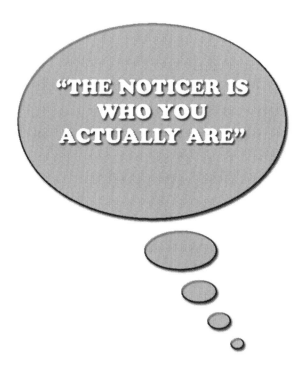

CHAPTER 17
LIVING IN THIS NEW WORLD
TORN BETWEEN TWO WORLDS

If you are like many people, you may be thoroughly freaked out at this moment.

When I ask people, as I always do after this meditation, 'What was your experience?" people often say things like, "I don't believe it. That was interesting to imagine, but what good does it do me in the 'real' world? Do you mean to say that my husband doesn't exist? Do you mean to say that this table doesn't exist? This is all well and good but how do I pay the rent? Isn't it selfish and narcissistic to think that you're the only one who's here and there's nobody else? What happens when someone else does something to you?" (There is no "someone else, only you. Another potentially upsetting concept.)

Knowing that you live in this invisible world and not in the visible world does upset the apple cart, because, like much of the information in this book, it goes directly against everything we've spent our lives learning. We suddenly think we're alone, we have nobody to relate to, nobody to work with or fight against or blame, nothing to work on.

So, if it's true that we only live in the invisible world (and I'm not asking you to believe it. Like everything else in this book, I'm only asking you to suspend disbelief long enough to examine the hypothesis and decide for yourself) what is the purpose of life? What are we here for? What are we supposed to be doing? Where are we supposed to be getting? Why get up in the morning?

First, let's explore how things work in this new paradigm, the rules of the road if you will.

WHO YOU REALLY ARE
IS DOUBLY PROTECTED

We've talked about the invisible barrier between the invisible interior world of sensations and the physical world. You can never actually get into the physical world, you can only observe it and experience it inside you, in the invisible world, via your experiences of sensations and thoughts. No matter what you do, you can not get out of your invisible self and into the physical world, because even the body you live in is once removed from the invisible, interior you. So there seem to be two separate worlds, one on the "outside" and one, protected by an invisible shield, on the inside.

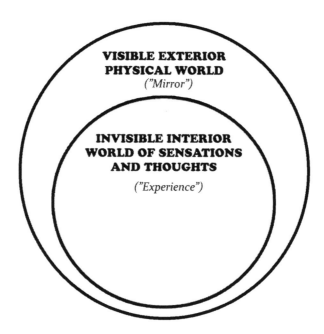

VISIBLE EXTERIOR
PHYSICAL WORLD
("Mirror")

INVISIBLE INTERIOR
WORLD OF SENSATIONS
AND THOUGHTS

("Experience")

When you understand this, you understand that nothing that happens in the physical world can pass through the barrier into the invisible world. You see something, and you generate your sensations, but all the changes in the invisible world are created on the inside, not on the outside.

136

This inside, invisible world of sensations and thoughts is closer to the real You, because you can have a direct experience of it, but even it is not the real You. There's something behind that that is you, and that something is the Observer or Noticer.

With the discovery of the Observer, we have created an even deeper, safer place, because the Observer is not only shielded from the "outside" world, but is also shielded from the invisible world of your sensations and thoughts. No thought or sensation can have any effect on the Observer, because the Observer is just watching. So the Observer is the most protected of all. It cannot be punctured or injured or in any way lose the infinite possibilities it always has, no matter what happens on the "outside" and no matter what sensations and thoughts are generated on the inside. It just IS. No opinion, no fear, no need to run, no attachment, no preferences. Just watching and seeing everything. Sort of like the way lots of religions describe God. Infinite Love, because it has no judgment or preference; Infinite Possibilities, because it cannot be limited; Infinite Patience, because it doesn't require anything to happen; Infinite Faith, because it knows that it is always safe and always has everything it could ever need (which is both nothing and infinite possibility;) Infinite Peace, because if peace is the ability to be with what is, it has infinite ability to do that because it just watches.

And THIS INVISIBLE, INFINITE, UNASSAILABLE OBSERVER IS YOU!

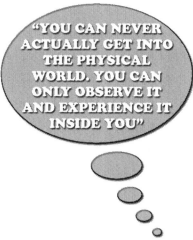

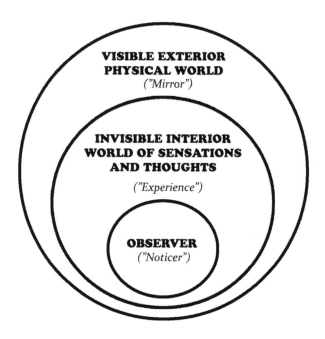

Take a moment and see if you can identify with the Observer. If you're worried or have an opinion or a preference, that's not the Observer. If those things are happening, just notice them. When you can experience yourself as the observer, you are in a position to allow yourself to experience any sensation you're experiencing and to notice any thought you're thinking. When you can do this, you have completely mastered the key to all the riches of the universe. You can think anything because you're not afraid of the sensation the thought will produce, and your life immediately begins to reflect those thoughts so you can see them in the world.

You're home free!

CHAPTER 18
YOU ARE NOT CAUSING
THINGS TO HAPPEN
IT'S JUST A MIRROR

A big question that often comes up, especially around the area of illness, is, "Are you saying I caused this? Are you saying I brought on the cancer myself?

This is a valid question, and when we can truly understand and come to terms with the answer, our consciousness shifts in a way that turns our life upside down, changes our whole perspective on where we actually live and on the way the world works, and puts us in a position to never again be at the mercy of ANYTHING that happens.

As we know, one of the basic principles of Thought Exchange is that the manifest world is an exact mirror of our thoughts. Think about seeing your image in the mirror. Would you say you "caused" it? In order to have caused it, there has to be something there. If you see a red shirt in the mirror, is there actually a red shirt in the mirror? Of course not. There's a reflection of a red shirt, there's light on a flat piece of glass, not a real shirt. The only use the image has is that it allows you to see what you're wearing.

When we understand this, we can clearly see that THE ONLY USE ANYTHING WE SEE IN THE MANIFESTED WORLD HAS, IS TO ALLOW US TO SEE WHAT WE'RE THINKING.

Think about a dog who sees itself in the mirror and doesn't recognize that it's looking in the mirror. It sees an attacker. Or it sees a possible friend or playmate. But the minute it tries to treat it as such, all the reflection does is do exactly what the dog does. And the dog can't seem to get to the reflection because it keeps running into the glass. Once we can recognize that everything we're seeing is a reflection, then if we don't like the reflection, we understand that the only place to change it is within ourselves.

Think about what it might be like if you had been blind your whole life and could suddenly see. You would look around and see a lot of people. When you looked in a mirror, you would also see a person. That person would, of course, look exactly like you, but since nobody can ever see their own face, you wouldn't even know that. You would actually think you were looking at another person. You might then, after a while, notice that that other person had the irritating habit of doing exactly what you're doing at every moment. "What an irritating person! No independence. Doesn't think for himself. Just does what I do!"

At some point, you might figure out that there's no person in there, that you can't have a conversation with him or her, that he has no independence from you, and that in fact he can't do anything to you.

You would now be "enlightened" to the truth of who that person is and begin using him for what he's really there for. To see yourself.

You don't put on an outfit so that it can look good in the mirror. You put it on so that it can look good on you. When you look in the mirror and see something you don't like, you make the adjustment on the outfit, not in the mirror, and when you're satisfied with the way YOU look, that's the exact image that appears in the mirror. And then YOU go out of the house. The mirror doesn't.

Another important point is that the mirror doesn't reflect who you ARE. It simply reflects the part of the infinite possibilities of the Un-Manifested that you are thinking about. So if you see something you don't like in the mirror, it doesn't mean you're bad, or doomed, or stuck. It just means that you need to go into your infinite source of possibilities and find one that you'd like to see reflected in the mirror.

If you think of thoughts in terms of outfits, when you see an outfit on yourself that you don't like, you wouldn't say, "Oh well. I'm stuck with this outfit. I'll always have a black dress on." You have a closet full of outfits. And if you don't happen to have the outfit you want in your closet, you have thousands of stores you can go to. And if you don't find what you want in the stores, there are fabrics and designers and you can have one made. It's the same thing with thoughts. When you see a thought you don't like reflected in the mirror, you must know that you have an infinite choice of thoughts. And just like an outfit, when you exchange a thought, you must instantly see it reflected exactly in the mirror. If you don't see it, the only thing you know is that you haven't exchanged it. And fortunately for you, very fortunately for you (and this concept can be one of the most difficult to grasp) YOU ALWAYS HAVE A MIRROR IN FRONT OF YOU TO SHOW YOU WHAT YOU'RE THINKING. And that mirror is the Manifest World.

So when we begin to use the mirror for what it's there for, to show us what we're thinking, we stop focusing on the cancer, the financial difficulty, the lack of a job or a partner, and allow those appearances to direct our attention to the place where we actually have unlimited possibilities, unlimited choice, and where, in fact, we have, have always had, and always will have, everything we could ever want. The Great Un-Manifested. The invisible world.

CIRCUMSTANCES DON'T MATTER

Remember, in the first chapter of this book, when I described what I, and so many of us, have been taught is the meaning and the goal of life? To have stuff? To achieve things? To make sure certain things happen and certain things don't?

When you are aware that you live in the invisible world, none of these things matter, because none of these things mean anything.

It's not that we don't want to live comfortably. Of course we do. But when we have made the transition to knowing that the invisible world is where we live, we understand that the source of all the "things" we want, the source of our comfort, is inside, in the invisible world, not outside. When we understand this, since the "outside" world is nothing but an exact mirror of the inside world, we will see those comforts appear as soon as we know we have them on the inside. But we will recognize those comforts as merely a reflection of the comfort we already experience on the inside, and not as an end in themselves. And as we get more adept at being with this truth, we will recognize that those comforts are merely a reflection of the comfort that we ALWAYS have available to us on the inside, no matter what the circumstances.

Comforts or possessions mean nothing in and of themselves. It is only our experience that means anything, because our invisible experience is the only way we know that anything happens, and our experience happens in the only place we live, on the inside.

How many people do you know or know of who have millions of dollars but who do not experience happiness or safety or comfort? And how many people do you know who do not have that kind of money who do experience happiness and safety and comfort? So obviously, having money, or a gorgeous body, or fame, or a relationship, is not the source of our happiness or abundance. In order to have a true sense of happiness and safety, we have to know where the source of that is. And THE SOURCE OF EVERYTHING, THE PLACE WHERE IT EXISTS AT EVERY MOMENT, AND THE <u>ONLY</u> PLACE WHERE IT <u>EVER</u> EXISTS, IS IN THE INVISIBLE WORLD. INSIDE.

MANIFESTATION IS JUST A WAY TO SEE OUR THOUGHTS. NOTHING IN THE PHYSICAL WORLD HAS ANY INTRINSIC MEANING

Now that we know that we are not "causing" things to happen (because there are no things to cause to happen, the world of things is simply a reflection of the world of thoughts) we have an opportunity to understand more deeply what it means to be "seeing our thoughts reflected in what we see before us."

Nothing in the Physical World has any intrinsic meaning. The only thing we can see in it is what we're thinking, the meaning we assign to it. So when you see something in the "mirror" of the physical world, notice what it is you are thinking at that moment. It will seem like what you're seeing "made you think" that, but since what you're seeing is only a reflection, whatever it is you notice you're thinking when you see the physical object is the thought you have that is "causing" the object to appear the way it does to you.

For example, let's say that you're 10 pounds overweight but don't know it. You will go along being 10 pounds overweight and not even be aware of it. One day, you look in the mirror and you see 10 extra pounds. You suddenly have a sensation, and a thought "Ugh, I'm overweight." Did the mirror "cause" you to be overweight? Did you "cause" the mirror to be overweight? Did the mirror cause you to think "Ugh" as opposed to "I look wonderful?" Of course not. You just saw something that is on you and can be nowhere else but on you, reflected in the mirror.

Just as the only purpose of a mirror is for the person in front of it to see what they look like, so the only purpose of the physical world is to reflect back to us what we're thinking.

It doesn't matter what form that reflection takes. There are many things that will reflect back the same thought to us. In fact, when we hold a thought, EVERYTHING reflects it back to us. It doesn't matter what mirror you go to, you will see that thought in it. Because there is no objective reality in the physical world, only the meaning you assign to it.

Let me give you an example.

Take an anorexic. Somebody who is anorexic thinks of themselves as fat. They can look in the mirror and see someone who weighs 70 pounds and say, "I look too fat." Most people would say, "That's not true. You're emaciated." But that has no effect on the anorexic, because the anorexic is holding the thought "I am fat," and so that's all the anorexic sees in the mirror.

You can force feed an anorexic all you want, or the anorexic could get down to 30 pounds, and it still will not change their thought. Because the thought is on the inside and the thought is causative of their experience. Only when the anorexic can exchange that thought for a thought that would reflect as a "normal" weight (a thought that is extremely challenging for someone in that position to take on because of the sensations that thought will produce – the anorexic has created this condition to protect themselves from sensations) will normal weight appear. So treating anorexia is totally about treating the thought.

When the thought shifts, the reflection of that thought appears as a more "normal" weight. (I keep putting normal in parentheses because normal is only what we agree is normal. There's actually no such thing as normal.)

This reminds me of that wonderful episode of The Twilight Zone where surgeons are doing plastic surgery to try to alter the face of someone who is deemed terribly ugly. You only see the surgeons' hands and the bandaged face of the patient. At the end of the episode, they unwrap the patient to reveal a gorgeous blonde. They all gasp in horror, calling the operation a failure, and as the camera pans back, you see that all the surgeons are green-faced, pig-nosed aliens. By the standard of beauty they made up (as are all standards of beauty) what we would call a blonde bombshell is ugly, and pig-nosed green faces are gorgeous.

So it is not the particular incident that our thoughts are causing, and it is not the particular incident we're trying to change. By looking at any incident, we can notice what we think when we look at it, and that is the reflection that our thought has generated so we can see our thought. Once we see this, the object is not to try to change the reflection, but rather to notice that the reflection is revealing a particular thought, among all possible thoughts, that we are having. This thought is generating sensations and beliefs and experience. We then have the opportunity to exchange this thought for the unlimited thoughts that are available to us, be with the sensations the exchange generates, and have a new experience. When this experience appears in the mirror as something that we are satisfied with, we will have what we want:

AN INTERNAL EXPERIENCE THAT IS REFLECTED ON THE OUTSIDE AS SOMETHING WE WISH TO SEE THERE.

But let us not be confused and think that it's the thing on the outside that we want. That's not the point. It's the thing on the inside that we want (and that we always already have, we're just not aware of it.) When we become aware that we have that on the inside, we will see whatever is on the outside as what we want.

This can be difficult to grasp when we are living in the illusion that objects are real and are the point. People often resist this point of view because they don't want to give up their objects. But we're not giving them up. We're simply seeing them for what they are; reflections of a joy or sadness, thought of possibility or impossibility that lives within us, and is ours to choose.

As we come to understand this, our reaction to not seeing what we want in the "outside" world shifts. Instead of going after things in the outside world (which would be like going after them in the mirror) we automatically go to the place where everything is and where everything is instantly accessible. The Un-Manifested. In this place, it takes no time to get anywhere, there is no work involved in finding anything, we already have EVERYTHING. And when we know this, we almost cease to care what appears in the mirror. Our focus is on knowing that we already have everything, and lo and behold, it MUST appear in the mirror.

But make no mistake about it. It is the knowing we have everything, right now, in the invisible, that gives us all our real security, all our real happiness, and all our true prosperity. Knowing this, puts an end to striving and an end to worry. It doesn't put an end to sensations or to doing things. But our life becomes a process of looking in the mirror, seeing what we're thinking, going inside and finding whatever we wish to be thinking, and seeing it in the mirror. And when we do this, we have sensations, and if we can stay with these sensations, we can stay with these thoughts and know that we have everything all the time.

The manifestation in the physical world now becomes just a way to enjoy the thought we're having, just as you might enjoy a beautiful dress by looking at it in the mirror so you can see it. But the dress, like the thought, is actually on you, not in the mirror.

IF WE THINK WE LIVE IN THE PHYSICAL WORLD, NOTHING IN SPIRITUALITY MAKES SENSE

When we become aware that we live in the invisible world, spiritual principles that used to seem weird or airy-fairy suddenly make sense. When I would hear someone who was sick say, "I am totally well and whole," my first response would be, "No you're not, you have the flu." And if you think the physical world is real, that's true. But when you know that the physical world is just a mirror, you immediately realize that all we see when we see the flu is the person's thought that they are not well and whole. And by using that reflection and going inside to the place where they do have the thought, "I am well and whole" they are well and whole RIGHT NOW. And when they're truly holding that thought, well and whole will appear in the physical world. Perhaps as the flu disappearing. Perhaps as being perfectly OK with having the flu, or even seeing the advantages that having the flu might bring them, like giving them the chance to rest or contemplate. Or even perhaps as the person dying. The circumstance doesn't matter. This can be the most challenging thing to get, but once we get it, not only do we have the capacity to find happiness, comfort and abundance at any moment in any circumstances, but in fact, circumstances, as a reflection of this happiness and comfort, have a way of clearing up and being re-placed by circumstances that we regard as happy and comfortable.

EVERYTHING WE SEE IS HELPING US

Gradually, as we learn to accept that we live in the realm of the Un-Manifested, we begin to see EVERYTHING that happens to us as good. The reason for this is that all that is happening is that we are see-ing a reflection that is directing us to go to the place where we already have everything. Our thoughts. So every incident, every occurrence, frightening or comfortable, inconvenient or convenient, wanted or not wanted, loses its old meaning and simply becomes a way of returning ourselves to the knowledge that we have everything, all the time.

With this knowledge, the whole object of life changes. The object is simply to know that we have everything. (In religious circles, people might say "the object is simply to know God." In Thought Exchange, we think of God as The Great Un-Manifested, the way things work, the infinite, ever-available possibilities that always exist inside us.)

Once we know this, the purpose of life becomes simply to live it. To experience it. It would be like living in a luxurious house where you have a swimming pool and a great kitchen and a piano and TV sets and a stereo. You don't use them all at once, but you always know they're all there, so depending on your mood, you experience each of them whenever you wish. And you don't worry about the other things not being there when you're not experiencing them, because you can always go back to them.

WE ARE ALWAYS SAFE
(NOTHING CAN BE TAKEN AWAY)

When we understand that we live in the Invisible world, and in the Invisible world only, we become aware that we are ALWAYS safe, no matter what is happening.

When you know that you are an invisible consciousness with invisible sensations and unlimited invisible thoughts, there is no way "the outside world" can harm you. To think that something from the outside world can harm you would be like thinking that something could come out of the mirror and harm you. As if something could step through the glass and hurt you or take something away from you.

The reason nothing can step from behind the glass is because THERE IS NOTHING BEHIND THE GLASS. The mirror is an illusion, a reflection of what's in front of it. Just as you cannot step into the mirror, so the mirror cannot step out toward you.

What this means is that nothing can ever be taken away from you. No matter what you see in the mirror, the unlimited possibilities of thought in the invisible world always exist. If you see yourself lose all your money, does that mean that any of the possibility of having unlimited money is taken away from you? Of course not. If your husband or wife leaves you, does that mean that any of the possibility of having love in your life has been taken away? Of course not. If you've taken 50 wrong turns on the way to getting somewhere, does that mean that you can't get there? Of course not.

So you are safe, no matter what you see in the mirror, because you live in a bubble where you have everything at all times. Nothing can be taken away. Nothing can hurt you where you live. Yes, you will experience sensations, but SENSATIONS CAN'T HURT YOU! The whole reason for upset when we experience a sensation we don't like is because we take our thoughts back out to the manifested world, and think the sensation means something is going to happen. It doesn't mean anything. It's just an opportunity to heal, if you are just willing to be with the sensation. It's an opportunity to expand your world, to reopen opportunities that you have closed off, and to remember that you already have everything.

This is what we mean when we say, "Nothing is lost in spirit." It can't be, because it is not physical, it is always pure potential, and this cannot be touched or damaged or taken away. Period.

THE SPECIFIC MANIFESTATION DOESN'T MATTER

In the world in which we actually live, can you see that what we specifically manifest doesn't matter? Since the manifestation is only a signal to us to reflect us back what we're thinking, manifestation is no longer the goal. Manifestation is no longer an end in itself, but rather a means to remembering that we have everything.

So often, we think that we have to have a specific achievement, a specific situation or a specific person in our lives for us to be happy. But why do we want that achievement, situation or person? So that we can see the reflection of a thought we're having. And when we don't see that achievement, situation or person before us, all we know is that we have taken on a thought that something is missing, a thought of lack, or a thought that we can't have something we want.

This can be hard to grasp, but is most important to remember when something "big" happens. When someone dies or we have a financial crisis or we don't get a job we wanted, it often seems like these things are real and like we have lost something. After all, you can't get the person who died back. You may be in danger of losing your home. That specific job is not yours.

These things seem big because they generate large sensations, and we have associations with these sensations that pull us back into the physical world, where we think there are such things as loss or danger.

But in the invisible world of our experience, what does someone's death mean? It means that we have a powerful sensation, which feels uncomfortable, and we have thoughts that we are missing something, that we can't go on, that we will never be happy. Is this true? If someone you love dies, is it impossible that you will ever feel happy again? Is it impossible that you will ever find someone to love? Of course not. So what you really want is still available to you. You may not get the dead person back (although according to the story of Lazarus in the bible, even that is possible) but the things you think you lost by that person dying are not lost, because they always have been and always will be inside of you.

This may seem like a very cold way of looking at life. Are you saying it doesn't matter if my husband dies? Of course it matters, because we experience powerful, painful sensations. But in fact, where you live, it doesn't matter, because not only is all the love and happiness still available (if you can be with the sensations that arise, and experience the death) but also, the only part of your husband to which you can truly relate is still as here as it ever was. The invisible part.

WE ARE NOT ALONE

Often, when we talk about nobody and nothing being "out there," nobody else causing anything, no antagonist, no problem, just a mirror, people get upset. "You mean I'm all alone in here, inside the bubble of invisibility, and everyone and everything I see isn't real? I have no friends? I have no spouse? I have no job? It's all an illusion?"

Yes, it's all an illusion, but the interesting thing is that when we truly understand that it's all an illusion and that we really live inside, in the invisible world, with everything, when we truly get this on an experiential level, we suddenly realize that everybody "else" is also here in the same invisible consciousness and we are not only connected to them, they are the same thing as us.

Remember, in the meditation, when you took note of your consciousness, of your "I Am-ness" and noticed that it didn't have your name on it? It's just consciousness, and everybody and everything is in it. So we are all in the invisible together, as one consciousness.

Even though we say it all the time, it can be very difficult to grasp the concept that we are all One. The reason for this is that in the illusion of the physical world that we see in the mirror, we definitely are NOT One. We are separate people, doing things to each other, having and losing things, wanting things that appear to be outside of us or "other" than us. In this world it is impossible to merge with or connect with anyone, we are definitely separate, and thus there is distance and time and hard work and striving and loss.

When you know that you live in the invisible world of infinite possibility (and remember that knowing this comes with sensations) there's no need to strive for anything. There's no need to push anything away. Struggle ceases. Wars cease, because you don't have to throw off your sensations by attacking the mirror. Nothing can hurt you. Nothing can be taken away. This changes everything.

To use an example that everyone is familiar with, when the World Trade Center incident happened, many people immediately said, "Who is responsible for this? We've got to track them down and punish them." The reason they said this was that they were having tremendous sensations that they thought they had to get rid of by "attacking" whatever it was in the "outside'" world that they perceived as causing them.

My first thought was, "What am I thinking that 'caused' this to happen? (I put 'caused' in quotes because I know I didn't cause it, but merely that I'm seeing a reflection of my thoughts.) The incident can only be going on inside of myself. I must be seeing a reflection of a thought of danger, and of actions on my part that have been manifested as these occurrences. I'm not to blame for this, but neither is anyone else."

Can you see that if everyone in the world had thought this way, none of this would have happened? And by most people in the world not thinking this way, thinking that the incident is real, all we got were two more wars and more throwing back and forth of sensations in a grand illusion that can have no resolution as long as people don't realize that they're looking in a mirror."

When we go inside to our experience of invisible consciousness, as opposed to outside to the mirror, we find that we're in here with everyone and everything. We find that we're deeply connected to everyone and everything on the only level on which we can ever connect to anyone or anything. Suddenly we're aware that everyone and every thing in the universe is right here, within us and available to us right now.

This is why when you hold a thought, things seem to happen that are outside you. People call from far away, circumstances reverse themselves in surprising ways, things break through that have seemed to be stuck. Because in the invisible world, you and everybody and everything are not separated by time and space. In fact you're not separate at all. YOU ARE THE SAME THING.

So rather than the invisible world being a lonely place, where nobody "else" exists, it is a place where you are connected to and part of everyone and everything all the time. In the context of the physical world, this makes no sense, but when you've made the shift to knowing where you actually live, it not only makes sense, but fulfillment and peace and safety become a way of life. The only way of life. No matter what you're seeing before you in the mirror of the manifested world.

THE PURPOSE OF LIFE
(REVISED)

When people first become aware that they live in the invisible world, they often get upset because they think, "What am I going to do now? I've lived my whole life thinking that the point is to manifest things, and now I find out that that doesn't matter." Have no fear. Manifesting still matters, but for a different reason. Just as we need a mirror in order to see ourselves, we have the tool of manifestation to allow us to see our own thoughts so we can remember that we have everything. So just as we use a mirror to enjoy looking at the beautiful outfit we have on or the great makeup job we've done, we use manifesting to experience that we have everything.

So even when we know that we live in the invisible world and that the physical world is just a mirror of our thoughts, we use manifestation to experience and see the abundance in which we live. So we keep striving for the things we want, we keep shopping, we keep decorating the house, and dating and getting married. But we do all these things knowing that they don't intrinsically matter, knowing that we're just doing them to see ourselves, knowing that we're doing them so we can experience the sensations that go with them so that we can heal.

And we stop fighting things that we know are unreal. We stop fighting wars, or blaming other people for things. We may actually be tempted continue to do this from time to time, but we quickly know that this is an illusion. Life may look the same, but there's a joy, a safety, and a sense of play, fulfillment and connection underneath everything we do, underneath everything we experience.

Make no mistake about it, this transformation will not stop things from happening. People who have "awakened" or are "enlightened" still experience pain, still experience illness and disappointments and challenging relationships. But they now experience them as a part of life's learning and as a way of constantly being reminded that they have everything.

So what happened to money, success and love? They're still here. They're still appearing (or not appearing) in the mirror of the world. But I now know that I already I have them. Inside. The only place where they really count. And the only place where they have been all along.

"SEEK YE FIRST THE KINGDOM AND ALL ELSE WILL BE GIVEN"

So it all boils down to this. The Kingdom (The Kingdom of God if you will) is invisible, is infinite and is inside you. When you go to this Kingdom, you immediately know you have everything. And knowing you have everything can only reflect in the world as seeing everything.

Sometimes this can seem difficult to do, because the sensations that arise when we "dare" to think thoughts of abundance and success, thoughts that were dangerous for us to think as children, can be powerful and can be experienced as disturbing. But when we understand that the sensations themselves cannot hurt us, and that the incidents that are arising that produce them are here simply to help us experience them in a different way, we begin to welcome both the incidents and the sensations that that they produce as signs of healing.

When you know this, all of the work, all of the exchanging of thoughts, all of the analysis, all of the incidents, can be distilled into one simple act. Experiencing your sensations.

If You Remember Only One Section of This Book, Remember This:

THE KEY TO A SENSATIONAL LIFE

WHENEVER YOU FIND YOURSELF IN AN UNCOMFORTABLE CIRCUMSTANCE, CONFUSED, UPSET, OVERWHELMED, THINKING THERE'S SOMETHING YOU NEED OR THAT SOME-THING'S MISSING, THERE'S ONLY ONE THING TO DO.

GO TO YOUR SENSATIONS!!!

DO NOT THINK, DO NOT ANALYZE, DO NOT STRUGGLE. SIMPLY EXPERIENCE THE TIGHTNESS, POUNDING HEART, HOTNESS, COLDNESS, WHATEVER PHYSICAL SENSATION YOU'RE EXPERIENCE AS A SENSATION, WITHOUT GIVING IT MEANING AND WITHOUT TRYING TO GET AWAY FROM IT OR HAVE IT GO AWAY.

WHEN YOU DO THIS, THE ENTIRE WORLD OF UNLIMITED POSSIBILITY AUTOMATICALLY OPENS TO YOU, YOU KNOW WHAT TO DO, YOU KNOW WHAT TO THINK, AND THE RIGHT ACTIONS HAPPEN BY THEMSELVES.

WHEN YOU'RE NOT AVOIDING SENSATIONS, THERE IS NO REASON NOT TO TAKE ON THE THOUGHTS OF WHAT YOU WANT AND SEE THEM MANIFEST.

Use It to Open the Door

You now have the Sensational key to instantly and automatically knowing that at every moment you already have everything you could ever want.

EXPERIENCE YOUR SENSATIONS

It's that simple. And when you do it enough, it actually becomes easy.

You're free. You have everything. You cannot lose anything.

Try it.

And enjoy your *Sensational* life!

PART 5 STAYING WITH SENSATIONS

CHAPTER 19
AFFECT TOLERANCE
BEING WILLING TO JUST FEEL WHATEVER YOU FEEL

As I've said, when you take on a thought, sensations are caused, beliefs are formed, and the thought appears in the mirror of the world as manifestation. Often, the sensations, beliefs and occurrences that happen as a result of that thought (which are absolutely necessary to bring about the fulfillment of that thought in manifestation) are sensations, beliefs and occurrences that we are afraid of. In fact, one of the main reasons we don't take on the thought we want, even though we are clear that that thought will be reflected as the desired result, is that we think we cannot "tolerate" the sensations we will have to experience as the thought gets fulfilled in the physical world. Since this fear is often unconscious (we're not aware of it) in order to prevent those sensations from coming up, we simply keep ourselves away from the thought (by taking on a protective thought) or else have the thought for a little while and then exchange it for the protective thought as soon as we begin to experience the undesired sensation. This may seem complicated, but it's actually very simple.

If you had a fear of spiders and I told you that you would definitely completely get over that fear by simply walking through thousands of spiders for two blocks, you might not choose to do that. Even if you truly believed that that would get you over your fear, the act of walking through spiders might be too terrifying for you to allow yourself to do it. You would either be in touch with your fear and not walk through the spiders because of it, or perhaps you might find another line of resistance (protective thought) like deciding that it wouldn't work anyway, saying you don't really care about your fear and it's fine if you have it, etc. In any case, any of these forms of resistance would be for the sole purpose of keeping you away from having to feel what you would feel were you to do the thing you fear, which in this case, would be walking through spiders. So, if you subscribe to the premise that walking through the spiders would get you over your fear, and you want to get over your fear, the only thing you have to be willing to do is feel and tolerate the sensations you experience while walking through the spiders. Can you see that this ability in itself, the ability to feel and tolerate what you're feeling, would already be tantamount to being over your fear?

As I write this, I'm sitting on a ship headed for the Caribbean with my partner, Shawn. At the first stop there's a snorkeling trip that sounds wonderful. A serene and scenic boat ride, beautiful fish, gorgeous coral reefs, and cool water in the hot island sun. Shawn loves beauty and loves comfort, but he professes to be uninterested in the trip. Why? Because Shawn, like many people, cannot put his face in the water without holding his nose and closing his eyes, and thus cannot wear a snorkel. I've tried many times to teach him to do this in swimming pools but he can't allow himself to do it. Is it because he is just one of those people who can't put his face in the water? Of course not. It's because he gets a sensation when he's about to do it that reminds him in some way of some childhood trauma, and he's afraid to experience that sensation. The protective thoughts he's taken on to avoid getting anywhere near these sensations began with, "I can't do it" and now have escalated to, "I don't even want to do it."

I'm sure you can see that because of the avoidance of a sensation, which is probably something like a tightness in the throat or chest, Shawn does not get to do something that he would surely enjoy. In the case of a snorkeling trip it's not really a big deal. We'll go on a hike or go to the beach. But if we look in our own lives, we can all see things that we really would like to do, successes we would like to experience, that we take away from ourselves because of the avoidance of a harmless, totally tolerable sensation. Simply because of fear.

FEAR, SHAME AND GUILT

At this point, I think it's important to define what fear is. Fear is not, as many people believe, a sensation. Fear is a thought about a sensation. When you say, I'm afraid, what you're really saying is, "I'm feeling a sensation that I don't want to feel, so I'm making up the thought that there is something dangerous about this sensation." So it could be said that all that fear is a tactic to get away from experiencing a sensation. The same is true about shame and guilt. "I'm so ashamed that this happened. I feel so guilty." Both of these are not sensations, but rather thoughts we take on to give us a reason to try to stop doing the thing we're doing that is bringing on the sensations we're having. And like all protective thoughts, they usually do the job of getting us away from the sensations, but the result is, of course, that we don't see what we want appearing in the Manifested World.

DON'T BOTHER WITH THE FEAR – GO STRAIGHT TO THE SENSATION

Think of something you do on a regular basis that involves some measure of fear that you have learned to tolerate. Something that some other people might be too afraid of to do. Driving. Swimming. Going on stage, if you're a performer. Skiing. Speaking in public. If you regularly do any of these things, and stop to think about them, you will realize that there is a certain measure of fear involved. If you look more closely, you will realize that it's not necessarily that you don't have this fear, but that you're accustomed to it, you don't "give it a thought" as it were, but keep your thought on what it is you see yourself accomplishing....driving, skiing, performing, etc. Because you're willing to be more focused on the thought of what you want than on the sensations the thought produces, you're able to have the sensations and do what you want to do anyway.

And if you notice that you have the thought of fear, you are willing to immediately exchange it for the thought that you can do whatever it is you want to do. So fear becomes merely a signal that you are jumping away from a sensation. All you have to do is go back to the sensation, be with it, and you will be able to hold on to your original thought and see the result you desire appear.

When you decide you are going to simply hold a thought and thus have the reflection of that thought appear in the mirror of your life, you must be willing and able to tolerate whatever sensations come up, without wavering from the thought, without running to fear, guilt or shame. If you had been attacked as a child when you spoke out, then if the thought you are holding is going to stimulate speaking out, you need to be able to tolerate the sensations you feel, generated by your memory of what happened (or might have happened) when you spoke out as a child. The facts are not the same now, you know that you are no longer a child and that nobody is going to do to you what they did then (and even if they did, you would be able to stop them or tolerate it) but you still might feel those sensations when you let your guard down. So when you allow yourself to have the thought, the risk you are taking is not that you will be attacked, but rather that you will feel the sensations you felt when you were actually in danger of being attacked. Can you see the distinction? We will often say that we don't want to speak out because we're afraid of being attacked, but a moment's logical thought will show us that that's not true. What we're actually afraid of is the sensations that will come up because of our history. Again, there's that paradox, that THE SENSATIONS WE FEAR COME UP WHEN WE TAKE ON THE THOUGHT OF WHAT WE ACTUALLY WANT.

So this is what we have to do in order to allow ourselves to hold the thought we want to hold. First, notice that we are thinking that we are afraid. Second, say to ourselves, "If I'm grabbing for the thought 'I'm afraid,' it can only be because I'm having a sensation that I don't want to feel. Third, go to the sensation that our original thought has caused, and simply be with it. The thought will always bring about the desired result, but in order to allow ourselves to stay with the thought, we have to be able to feel and tolerate the harmless sensations that come up. This is simple, though of course not easy. It takes a willingness to tolerate things that feel very painful, even though they won't actually hurt you.

One thing that many people have found helpful is to substitute the word "withstand" for the word "tolerate." In saying, "I can withstand my sensations," what you are saying is that you are able to <u>stand</u> with your sensations, stand in the same place as your sensations, experience them, and continue to hold your thought. Thus, sensations are viewed as part of the process, not something that is attacking you or coming at you.

So, when you take on a thought, simply notice whatever sensation you are feeling — be it comfort, tightness, tingling, shortness of breath, whatever —and sit with it. Be with it. Just feel it. Do your best not to act on it, react to it, push it away or direct it at someone. Just have it. If you're in a situation that's been perennially difficult for you, you might even try encouraging those sensations to appear by saying to them, "Come on, 1 want to experience you, appear so I can see and experience what you are."

An important adjunct to this is that you must not expect to feel good, or motivated, or excited when you take on the thought of what you want. One of our biggest defenses against sensation is often to say, "Oh, this will never happen. Why am I even trying? I don't care," etc. Just go to the sensation and hold the thought, and the actions and results will happen spontaneously. No matter what harmless, meaningless sensation you're experiencing.

As you develop your ability to simply be with your sensations, you not only become more able to allow yourself to hold the thoughts you want to hold, but the old wounds that those sensations contain begin to heal.

It is not your sensations that are causing the problems, the stuck-ness, the inability to hold the thought you want and allow it to manifest. It is the FEAR of those sensations and the RESISTANCE to those sensations that knocks us off the path time and time again. Hold the thought, allow whatever sensations that are there to be there, and you have mastered the art of Manifestation. The rest does itself.

THE "NEGATIVE" THOUGHT –
OUR "DRUG" OF CHOICE

So often, I've heard people in new thought circles say things like, "You're just addicted to negative thoughts" or, "Thinking negatively is just a habit." I've always found those statements extremely dismissive and irritating, as though that meant you could simply change and "stop doing that!" Even if those statements are true, they are about as useful as saying to an alcoholic, "You're addicted! Stop drinking!"

I've always known that it is naïve to think that a drug addict or alcoholic's problems end when he or she stops drinking or taking drugs. In fact, although it is necessary to stop doing those things in order to recover, it's been my experience that the addict's problems really begin, or shall we say, surface, when he or she stops using the drug.

So I looked at the statement "You're addicted to negative thoughts," and thought to myself, "Why do we get addicted to things? Why do we drink? Why do we take drugs?" And I realized, there's only one reason why we turn to our addiction, to our substance of choice, ☐and that is to escape from pain.

So I asked the question, "When we turn to a "negative" thought, how does it help us to escape from pain?"

Now, the common wisdom is that negative thoughts cause pain and that if you can just exchange the "negative" thought for a "positive" thought you will feel better and be rid of pain. But if that is the case, why do so many smart, spiritually aware, powerful, willing-to-do-their-work people continue to choose the "negative" thought? Why do so many people continue to be "addicted" to thinking thoughts that prevent them from realizing their dreams and doing what they want to do? It MUST be because those thoughts protect them from something. Otherwise they wouldn't pick up the "drug."

So if you are noticing that you're thinking a thought that is not producing the result you desire, ask yourself, "What painful or difficult sensation is that thought protecting me from?" And just as, at a certain point, in order to face the sensations and heal, the alcoholic puts down the bottle, or the drug addict decides to kick the habit, you can decide, "I'm going to stay with the thought that will produce the result I desire, and not take the drug to alleviate the sensations." And just like what happens when one gets off drugs or alcohol, you might feel anxiety or go through "withdrawal" or experience some level of pain that you didn't experience when it was being dulled by the "drug." But getting off this "drug" eventually leads you to be able to experience and tolerate the sensations, which allows you to stay with the thought that will produce the reflection in the world that you desire.

It's Not The Sensations That Cause the Problem, but Our Resistance to Them

Years ago, I worked with a body worker who made Rolfing seem like child's play. She would start the session by putting her elbow in my solar plexus and leaning her whole body weight on it. That was the light stuff. From there, she would dig in more and more in an effort to release my body's deepest holdings.

Sometimes, she'd press on something and I'd say, "You're killing me. I can't take this." She'd keep pressing, and a few minutes later I'd say, "Did you stop pressing? This is suddenly not painful." And she would say, "No, I'm pressing harder, but you stopped resisting."

It is not the sensations themselves that are hard to take. We all have the same spectrum of sensations, tightness, tingling, hotness, coldness, itching, "pain." We have these sensations when something upsets us. We also have them when something wonderful happens, like falling in love, or winning, or getting a lot of money. These sensations only become hard to take when we are holding a thought about them and letting our minds run to all sorts of "what if's" in order to resist the sensations. Once we can just be with the sensations, we realize that they are just run-of-the-mill sensations that we can easily tolerate.

A funny example of this comes to mind. Years ago, for reasons we can't explain, both my partner, Shawn, and I were experiencing a strange buzzing sensation that went from the solar plexus to the groin. The sensations went on for about four months.

During that time, Shawn interpreted them as a sign that his chakras were opening to new spiritual awareness. I, with my history of hypochondria, chose to interpret them as a sign that I was having an aortic aneurism. So for months, he would go, "Ah, I'm growing" and I would go, "Oy, I'm dying" every time the symptoms appeared. After four months, the symptoms spontaneously went away. Shawn had just been through four months of joy, and I had been through four months of terror.

Can you see that it wasn't the symptom itself, but the meaning we each gave it that determined our state of mind and happiness?

THE 20-POUND WEIGHT

When people first begin to feel their powerful, upsetting or difficult sensations, and are told that what they need to do is tolerate them whenever they come up, one of the first comments we often hear is, "Do you mean I'm going to have to feel this way for the rest of my life? I'd rather die."

The truth is that, in fact, it is possible that those sensations might be here for the rest of one's life, or at least that they may come up from time to time when we hit stressful moments that resemble earlier stressful moments. But this doesn't mean that they will be intolerable. The sensation doesn't have to change, just our ability to tolerate it.

I like to use the example of the 20-pound weight. If you hadn't worked out for years, and began to go to the gym, lifting a 20-pound weight might be difficult to do. When you lifted it, you would feel strain, you would get tired easily, and you probably couldn't hold it for very long.

If you worked out for a year, gradually increasing the amount of weight you could lift, you might reasonably get to the point where you could lift a 100-pound weight without too much difficulty.

At this point, after a year of practicing with weights and building up your ability to lift them, were you to go back to lifting a 20-pound weight, it would seem incredibly light and easy to lift. The fact is though; it's still a twenty-pound weight. It hasn't gotten lighter. It hasn't gone away. It hasn't changed at all. The only thing that's changed is your ability to lift weight.

In the same way, a sensation that seems intolerable now might come to be at first familiar and then almost unnoticeable. It's still there, it doesn't have to go away or even diminish, but it ceases to be perceived as problem, and often it ceases to be perceived at all, because you have increased your capacity to be with sensations.

TAKING ON THOUGHTS THAT HELP YOU STAY WITH SENSATIONS

If you find that you're getting stuck in the sensations, or that you continue to experience them as intolerable no matter how many times you try to exchange an old thought for a new thought, stop for a moment, and see if there is a new thought that might help you to reframe and stay with the sensations more effectively.

Ellen (not her real name) came into the group noticing that she was not allowing herself to express herself to her full potential. When she looked at her thoughts, she realized that she was thinking, "If I express myself, I will be ridiculed and stopped." She exchanged that thought for, "I Gotta Crow!," the quote from Peter Pan, which seemed to embody, for her, the sense that it was important, in fact necessary, that she express herself no matter what obstacles might be presented to her.

She came in the next week saying that all sorts of wonderful things were manifesting as a result of that thought, but that her anxiety was increasing and she noticed she was starting to take on the thought, "I shouldn't be doing this, it's dangerous for me." No matter how many times she exchanged that thought for, "I Gotta Crow!" the anxiety continued to increase.

We discussed the notion that the object was not to get rid of the anxiety, but rather to be able to just have it. She understood that it was most likely anxiety from a situation in her childhood when she had dared to have the thought, "I Gotta Crow!" and was cut down for it. At that time, understandably, she had been unable to allow herself to tolerate the sensations, so she took on the thought, "I shouldn't be doing this, it's dangerous for me," to make sure she never put herself in line to experience that sensation again. She understood that her childhood situation did not exist now, but even so, she was having a hard time with the sensations. So it became apparent that we had to find a new thought to exchange for, "I shouldn't be doing this, it's dangerous."

As we talked, it became clear that Ellen needed a thought that would allow her to re-contextualize what her sensations meant. The problem was not that she felt that sensation every time she took on the thought, "I Gotta Crow!," but that she was giving that sensation the thought, "I shouldn't be doing this."

The thought she came up with was, "Sensations are just sensations." Now every time she took on "I Gotta Crow!" felt that "anxious" sensation, and took on the thought, "I shouldn't be doing this," she could immediately exchange that thought for, "Sensations are just sensations."

This thought helped her to re-contextualize and tolerate the anxiety, stay with "I Gotta Crow!" and see how that thought reflected in her life.

Gradually she could return to "I Gotta Crow" and the thought, "Sensations are just sensations" would have absorbed into that, or would at least always be consciously available to her whenever anxiety might arise.

In another example from my own life, when I found my dream home in Connecticut after 20 years of searching, and was thinking there was no way I could afford to buy it, I exchanged the thought "I can't have what I want" for "I am allowed to have what I want." Out of that thought, the money for the house appeared, in the form of my selling an apartment I already owned for an enormous profit, and I was able to find a dream rental apartment in New York City as well. I was very excited and happy about all that had happened, but I noticed that I was getting progressively more anxious, wondering if I would be able to enjoy the house, or if some illness or disaster would befall me. This anxiety culminated in my falling down in the street, banging my head on a pole while standing up in subway car, and bumping my nose while looking in a store window, all in the same evening. I was not seriously injured in any of these mishaps, but I took the falling, banging and bumping as a wakeup call. I realized that out of the anxiety I was feeling, I was taking on the thought "I can have what I want but I will be retaliated against." I suddenly remembered that when I was a child, I had had an incident where I had fought hard for something I wanted, only to be told in the end that I could have it, but that if I chose to have it, something else extremely important to me would be taken away.

That made me see that the thought I had been holding did not quite cover all the aspects of the situation, so I exchanged it for two thoughts that extended its range. One was "I am allowed to have what I want without retaliation," and the other was "I am allowed to have what I want and enjoy it." Inside of these thoughts, I stopped falling, banging and bumping, and I began to enjoy my new home and all the preparations and plans that went along with it.

EDWENE GAINES' 21 DAYS OF NOT COMPLAINING

Last year, Edwene Gaines came to give a workshop at Unity of New York. Edwene is the most inspiring, expert prosperity teacher I know, and she always transforms the lives of everyone who comes in contact with her, and increases the abundance and prosperity of any church or community she visits.

In the course of her workshop, Edwene asked that we all go on a non-complaining diet. The instruction was to refrain from complaining for 21 days straight. If we slipped, and accidentally complained, no problem. We shouldn't beat ourselves up, just simply start the 21 days over.

A week after Edwene left, I held a meeting of The Thought Exchange, and people were going wild with the 21 days. They were frustrated because they said they could not stop being angry and upset — in fact, their angry and upset feelings had escalated. I pointed out that Edwene had not asked them not to be angry and upset, all she had asked them to do was not complain. She hadn't asked them not to feel or believe anything, she just asked them to not complain.

In fact, when you stop complaining, you usually feel worse, because you become conscious of your thoughts and sensations. That's the point. So it's literally impossible to stop complaining if you insist on not feeling anything. The only way you have the power to stop complaining is to be willing to experience and accept your thoughts and sensations.

169

A friend of mine once came to me and said, "I don't know why I drink so much." I asked him if he wanted to find out, and he answered, "Yes, I do." To which I replied, "Stop drinking, and you'll find out immediately why you drink." Since we usually drink to obliterate certain sensations that we perceive on some level to be intolerable, the moment we stop, those sensations will appear. Then, the challenge is to be able to take on a new thought that will reflect as not drinking, and to be able to tolerate the sensations that come up as the effect of the thought that reflects in the "mirror of life" as sobriety.

As I see it, this is the basic principle behind organizations like Alcoholic Anonymous. People come to these places wanting to change their behavior, and they accomplish this by taking on new thoughts and receiving the support they need to tolerate the sensations that those thoughts bring up.

GETTING MORE HELP WITH SENSATIONS (THE BENEFITS AND PITFALLS OF THERAPY)

As you do Thought Exchange and begin to encounter and deal with strong sensations that feel difficult to stay with, there are numerous other ways to get help (that can be done in conjunction with Thought Exchange) that can assist and support you through the challenges of going through this process.

Therapy can, of course, be the most useful, in that your feelings (your thoughts about your sensations) will be mirrored and understood and worked through. In Thought Exchange work, it's important to not get mired in the reasons or in the particulars of what happened, since we're approaching things from the standpoint of exchanging a thought and letting the natural healing process occur spontaneously. But if you're finding that it's extremely difficult for you to tolerate the sensations you're experiencing and the thoughts you're reaching for in order to attempt to get away from those sensations (thoughts which will cause you to not see the manifestations you desire) you might want to work with a therapist.

Numerous experiential modalities of therapy, from Gestalt to Somatic Experiencing to TMS Therapy, Inner Child Work, Codependency Work and many others in between, directly address the question of developing affect tolerance, or the ability to simply stay with your sensations as sensations. These will also help you to not jump out of the sensations into creating new thoughts based on them, and will ultimately allow you to stay in the thought you want to stay in and produce the result you wish to see. Another advantage of therapy is, of course, that you're working with someone who can help you to hold and frame your sensations, just as a good parent would.

A word of caution. If a therapist or practitioner promises to "get rid of the sensations" or to "release them," you might want to be a little suspect. When we are experiencing sensations that are challenging to us, we will often reach for any straw that promises to allow us to circumvent them. That's the reason we go to the protective thought. If these sensations are associated with the thought of what you want, there is no way to circumvent them and still see the thought manifest. The only way is through them. It's an erroneous notion that these sensations must be released. What they must be is experienced and incorporated into the experience. When we do that, we either cease to notice them, or cease to be disturbed by them.

Another pitfall of therapy can be that often people think they have to remember and return to the original incident that generated the sensation in order to heal. Although it can be helpful to know what the incident was, in that it can give you some "rationale" and "justification" for why you're feeling as you do, there are two fallacies to the notion that it's necessary to remember and relive the original incident.

The first is that the original incident happened to a child, and does not have the same impact on an adult.

For example, when I was a child, I didn't want to go to summer camp. I complained, cajoled and argued for months, to no avail. On the day I was to leave, I threw a major tantrum. My mother got so frustrated that she finally said, "OK, you can stay home from camp but nobody in the family will talk to you all summer." I was 12 years old. I had to go to camp.

I couldn't tolerate the thought that nobody would talk to me all summer.

If that happened to me now, as an adult, I'd say, "Fine, don't talk to me all summer." First of all, I could tolerate that, and second of all, I know that my parents would be able to keep that up for about ten minutes before they'd relent and be speaking to me again.

So knowing that this was what happened years ago would not have the same effect on me now as it had then.

In order to direct ourselves back to the sensations we've avoided and need to be able to tolerate, what we do is create things in the present that actually will generate them. That's why we lose all our money, have terrible breakups, get sick, etc.

If we use these incidents to allow us to experience the sensations and be with them, rather than trying to go back to the original incident, two things happen. One, we heal, and in the process of healing, often the original incident, which we may have repressed, immediately comes to mind. The reason this happens is that the only reason we have suppressed this incident is because we've been afraid of our sensations. Once we can experience our sensations, there's no need to repress the incident and it pops up. Then the whole thing heals. Once we can tolerate the sensations, we have no need to rehash the incidents that caused them, and our lives begin to really change.

The second problem with insisting that we remember the original incident is that we are often using that to avoid sensations in the present. I can't tell you how many people I meet in Thought Exchange who spend years talking about something that happened in their childhood, saying it's the reason they can't have what they want now. That's not true. The reason they can't have what they want now is because instead of experiencing the sensations they're having now, around the incidents they've created in the present, they're busy experiencing the sensations around a past incident (which to an adult are actually easier to tolerate) in order to avoid the present sensations.

SENSATIONS ARE NOT INTOLERABLE
(WE ONLY SOMETIMES THINK THEY ARE)

As I've said many times in this book, most sensations are not intrinsically intolerable. It's only our particular associations to them that make them seem intolerable to us.

"This sensation is intolerable" is a thought, not a fact. You feel something, it feels as it feels, it hurts, it stings, it contains pain, but it is your thought that says "This is tolerable; This is intolerable; This is healing me," or "This is destroying me." It's important to remind ourselves of this distinction, in order to help ourselves to be able to stay with the sensations we need to stay with.

In the group, when someone is thinking that they're overwhelmed or that their sensations are too big or unusual, I usually stop for a moment and ask the group, "Who else feels or has felt like this?" Invariably everyone in the group raises their hands. This gives assurance to the person going through the sensations that they are not alone, not strange, and that this is just a part of everyone's process.

We must remember that sensations are a very important part of the healing process, perhaps the most import part. They are not to be gotten rid of, but are actually signposts, showing us what we are thinking, and ultimately, how to heal. When we realize that we need to stay with them, experience them as just sensations and not "give them a thought," we are guided back to knowing what thought is behind them. If this is a thought we wish to hold, we can choose to simply be with the sensations, and the thought will continue on to become a belief and to manifest in the mirror of the physical world.

Again, I want to stress, that having that new thought doesn't mean you will definitely have a sensation to "match it." But as you become more able to stay with the sensation that arises, no matter what it is, you will gradually notice that your thoughts, sensations, beliefs and manifestations make more and more sense to you and become more aligned.

173

It's not that the sensation will necessarily change, but you will see it as part of the thought you're holding, and not only will you not fear it, but in time may cease to even notice it.

As one person in one of our groups said: "When I'm feeling, I'm healing."

Or to put it another way, "To feel better, you've got to "feel" better.

PART 6

APPLYING THOUGHT EXCHANGE
TO OTHER AREAS OF LIFE

CHAPTER 20
LOVE, RELATIONSHIP, HEALTH, MONEY AND DIETING

In this section, I discuss how the Thought Exchange specifically relates to various issues and endeavors that we come across in life. Although we've touched on some of these in other places, I felt it would be useful to have a variety of situations and applications discussed, in greater depth, in one place.

FINDING LOVE

I was in a very long relationship that I was committed to staying in for the rest of my life. There were numerous things that were not working about it, so I prayed, every day, that my partner would love me in the way I wanted to be loved. After about 14 years, I unconsciously changed my prayer to, "I am willing to be loved in the way I want to be loved." And the voice within me, call it God, call it spirit, call it the universe, said, "Are you really willing to be loved in the way you want to be loved?" And I said, "Yes."

Now, I was unwilling to leave him, but since the mirror of the world MUST reflect our thoughts, and it was obviously not possible for me to be loved in the way I wanted to be loved by him, the next thing that happened was that out of the blue, my partner had an affair and left me.

How could this be the reflection of my thought, "I am willing to be loved in the way I want to be loved?" I was totally bereft for three years. His leaving me was the one thing that I had never wanted to have happen.

During those three years, I had the thought, based on his leaving me (since at that time I thought that my thoughts, sensations and feelings, were caused by the things that "happened to me" and didn't know that it was I who was choosing those thoughts) that I was worthless, that

177

nobody could love me or be interested in me, and that I would never find anybody. And during those three years, surprise, surprise, that's exactly what appeared before me. I could hardly get a date, and if I did get one, it was totally disastrous.

Three years after our breakup, I was invited to participate in a retreat, the subject of which was "Healing Your Heart." I entered that retreat thinking that although, in my head, I wanted to move on with my life, my heart was broken and I couldn't. After doing the work of the retreat for 5 days, which involved going into my heart and taking on new thoughts, I was sitting by myself in a small chapel when I suddenly realized, "It's not my heart that's broken. My heart cannot be broken. It's filled with unlimited possibilities, unlimited thoughts, unlimited potential feelings. It's my head that's broken. It's my thought."

And I suddenly had the thought, "Patti LuPone must have auditioned for Cats on Broadway, but she didn't get it because Betty Buckley got it. Patti didn't make the assumption from that audition that she couldn't do a Broadway show. She went on to do lots of them. Why am I assuming, because one guy dumped me, that I'm no good? I'm a great guy. I have lots of wonderful attributes. I could make someone a fantastic boyfriend." My thought had shifted, and at that moment, the very moment I had that new thought, the door opened, and in walked Shawn, someone I had known peripherally for years, who was running sound and leading the meditations on this retreat. Shawn sat down and began chatting with me, and after about 10 minutes I looked at him and thought, "This guy is hitting on me. I haven't seen that in 3 years."

Shawn and I ended up being partners, and are to this day.

As an interesting aside, Shawn later told me that he'd been in love with me for the past five years! But because I'd been holding the thought, "Nobody could love me," I could not possibly have seen him, since someone loving me could not reflect in a mirror that had "Nobody could love me" standing in front of it.

So, for years, I had been afraid to have the thought, "I am willing to be loved in the way I want to be loved," because the next thing that had to happen to fulfill that thought was that my current partner had to leave. That seemed like a disaster at the time, but it was the universe's way of reflecting my thought perfectly, since it would not have been possible for me to be loved in the way I wanted to be loved with that person. He was a reflection of my thought (that I wasn't even aware I was having) that I am not worthy of the kind of love and respect I want. He did his job extremely well. He's not to blame. For 15 years he stood in the mirror and reflected me. When I exchanged my thought, he disappeared. (There's a wonderful book called Radical Forgiveness by Colin Tipping that explores this concept in greater detail.)

RELATIONSHIP

Whether in romance, friendship or business relationships, Thought Exchange is a useful way to work with any difficulties that might arise. Often, in relationships, we think that the reason we feel a certain way is because the other person is acting a certain way, or the other person is crazy, or the other person needs to change. We make the mistake of trying to change the other person, or we walk away from the other person, only to find that the same set of circumstances appears elsewhere. Doing this is like looking in a mirror, not liking what you're wearing, and walking to another mirror hoping to see something different reflected there. It sounds ridiculous, but that's exactly what we do in relationships when we fail to acknowledge that they are a reflection of our own thoughts.

So when you have a problem in a relationship, the first thing to do is ask yourself the question, "If I'm seeing this in the mirror before me, what must I be thinking?" You may then uncover thoughts such as, "I'm not worthy; I never get what I want; I can't be loved; I'm not a member of the club; People don't like me;" any number of those "negative" thoughts that we hate to admit we have. If you're sitting there saying, "No, I'm totally positive and know that I deserve the best, etc." and you're not seeing that in front of you, then you're not telling yourself the truth about what you're thinking.

Once you've identified the particular thoughts that are most likely being reflected by what you see happening in the relationship, you can

179

can then work on exchanging those thoughts instead of working on the reflection of them by trying to change the relationship. You will begin to notice that when you exchange the thoughts, what's appearing in front of you begins to change.

The interesting challenge in this work is that you don't get to decide HOW it changes, you just see that it changes. So let's say you're in a relationship with someone who seems to be not holding the space for you, and not allowing you to have your feelings and go through your process without criticism or objection. Your first thoughts might be "I want him or her to hold the space for me, they should do this, they should do that, they should be different." When you come around to knowing that your thought must be being reflected in their not holding the space, you will uncover thoughts within yourself like, "I don't deserve to be taken care of; It's not possible for someone to see my needs and meet them; etc." If you then exchange these thoughts for something like, "I know that in the Great Un-Manifested of Infinite Possibilities it is possible for me to be in a relationship where the space is held for me," you will see that appear. The only catch is, you don't control HOW that appears, so it might appear as your current partner changing and beginning to hold space for you, but it also might appear as your current partner disappearing, and someone else coming in to hold the space. Can you see that it is not your concern HOW it appears, just THAT it appears? Often, people get stuck because they want this particular person to be the one who offers what they want, and this particular person is not the one who's going to offer it. Can you see how that makes it impossible to move?

If you were in a troubled relationship and I gave you two choices: one, to stay in that relationship forever no matter how bad it was, or two, to leave the relationship and both of you would find true happiness, which would you choose? It's amazing how many people would choose the former.

When you begin to understand that it is always your thought reflecting as the satisfaction or dissatisfaction that's in your life, you begin to work on the thoughts, and not concern yourself with the specifics. Having said this, I would like to add that it's amazing to me how, when we exchange our thought, our partner often actually seems to become a different person, giving us things we never dreamed we could get, and acting in ways we never would have imagined him or her to be capable of.

This has certainly been the case, time after time, in my relationship with Shawn. In fact, I attribute the success of this relationship to that fact that for the first time in my life, I'm viewing my partner not as someone who's here to make me happy and do what I want, but as someone who is here as a reflection of what I think relationship is and can be, so that I can see my own thoughts and work on them inside of me. As a result, I've been able to expand my awareness of what's possible in relationship, and the relationship has expanded accordingly.

Years ago, right after the breakup of my very long-term relationship, I did the old exercise of writing down everything I wanted in my next relationship, everything I wanted my next partner to be. I put it away and forgot about it, but years later when I was already well into my present relationship, I found it. To my great surprise, my current partner, Shawn, was every single thing that I had written down on that list. I very excitedly and lovingly showed him the list. Although, of course, he was very gratified, his first response was, "You idiot! Why didn't you write down multi-millionaire?" He was, of course, kidding, but the point was well made.

The Buddhists actually say that relationship is one of the most challenging soul-growth opportunities because you are ALWAYS standing in front of a mirror. So as you look at your relationships, try looking at them from the point of view of The Thought Exchange and notice how a change in your thought creates an immediate change in what you see before you in your relationship.

Thoughts that might be being mirrored as problems in relationship	Thoughts you might exchange them for that would allow for successful relationship
I can't have the love I want.	THE LOVE I WANT HAS ALREADY BEEN CREATED AND IS ALREADY HERE FOR ME (perhaps still in the Un-Manifested)
Nobody would want to date me. I am not attractive. I am not smart. I'm too old. It's too late for me.	THERE ARE ALREADY PEOPLE IN EXISTENCE WHO WOULD BE DRAWN TO EX-ACTLY WHO I AM.
I'm not a member of the club.	THERE IS NO CLUB. I CAN HAVE IT HOWEVER I THINK IT.
Thoughts I'm currently having about my relationship	**Thoughts I'm exchanging them for**

At the beginning of this chapter, I told you about how my willingness to be loved in the way I wanted to be loved resulted in my current partner leaving, followed by three very challenging years which I had to go through in order to meet my next partner.

Now, Shawn was very different from my previous partner in every way. And yet, as time went on, I began to notice that he actually began to develop certain traits that my ex had exhibited. Now how could that be? Was it just my "bad luck" that every partner I chose seemed to be perfect and then turned out to have the same problems?

Fortunately, I was wise enough to realize that the only common denominator in the two relationships was the presence of ME. Somehow, this had to be a reflection of my own thoughts.

But still, I was becoming increasingly more unhappy.

Shawn and I were in Paris on a vacation, when things came to a head. We were having dinner one night, and I was railing about how he wasn't treating me the way I wanted to be treated, wasn't supporting me, wasn't being kind to me, etc. At one point, Shawn stopped, looked me in the eye, and said, "When you're ready to have these things, you'll have them." To which I replied, "I know, but it may not be with you." His answer was, "That's right. But we'll cross that bridge when we come to it. You just become willing to have these things, and let's see what happens."

From that point on, I let go of caring about whether I was with Shawn or without Shawn, and just concentrated on my thoughts about knowing that it was possible for me to have the things I wanted in a relationship. When I would see Shawn behaving in ways I didn't like, I would simply regard it as a reflection of my thought about what I was allowed to have, and exchange the thought.

And lo and behold, Shawn began to radically change, and today, almost all of those issues are no longer issues any more. Unlike with my former partner, who had to leave in order for me to have what I wanted, Shawn ended up being the demonstration of what I wanted.

It just goes to show, you never know how something will appear, but if you're thinking it, it MUST appear.

ILLNESS

Thought Exchange can be extremely useful in dealing with physical illness and medical conditions, but before we get into the topic, I want to make a few very important points.

Many metaphysical teachings deal with how our minds, thoughts or beliefs "create" illness. Although I'm quite sure that this is true, one of the pitfalls of dealing with illness in this way is that people begin to feel guilty, to take on blame, to think their illness is their "fault." Overzealous practitioners often say things like, "Why are you doing this to yourself? Why are you making yourself sick? You're not really sick, you're just causing yourself to feel this way. Illness is an illusion. Stop it!"

I want to be very clear that we are not talking about blame or guilt or shame or fault when we discuss employing the Thought Exchange in dealing with illness. What we are saying is that illness may be a reflection of a thought we're having, an attempt to avoid sensations that are perceived as painful or dangerous, or a way of dealing with fears, sadness, frustration, psychological pain or other difficulties we might be having. Illness may, in fact, be the body's way of trying to hold and handle those difficulties.

From the point of view of the Thought Exchange, we're looking at how we can get in touch with what we're seeing about our own thoughts when we see an illness, to see if we can take the physical illness back into the realm of thought, where we can transform and exchange it.

It's important to remember that we're not causing the illness, any more than we could say that we "cause" our reflection in the mirror. We stand in front of the mirror and our reflection is there. But it's not real, It's just a reflection. In the same way, it could be said that an illness is not real. It's not solid. It's just a reflection of our thought. So we're not causing it, because there's nothing to cause. It's actually just a signpost, as is a mirror, reflecting us back to what is generating it, which is our thought. The only thing that will change what we see in the mirror is a change in what's in front of it, which in this case, must be our thought.

So there's no cancer, just your thoughts being reflected as a "picture" of things that "look" like cancer, so you can see your thoughts. There's nothing out there, so there's nothing for you to have caused.

Of all the concepts we've discussed so far, this can be the most difficult to wrap your mind around. "Are you saying the world isn't real? Are you saying this table isn't here? Are you saying that my cancer isn't real?"

No. I'm not saying that. But I'm saying that just as you recognize your reflection in the mirror as a reflection, these things must be recognized for what they really are. A reflection of your thoughts.

So, if cancer is here to reflect a thought of yours to yourself, then when you can go in and find that thought and exchange it, the reflection will no longer appear as cancer. (Or the cancer will mean something very different to you and be experienced in a different way.) But the change has to be within you. You cannot change the image in the mirror by working on the mirror. You have to change it within yourself.

So when we begin to use the mirror for what it's there for, to show us what we're thinking, we stop focusing on the illness, whatever it is, and allow its appearance to direct our attention to the place where we actually have unlimited possibilities, unlimited choice, and where, in fact, we have, have always had, and always will have, everything we could ever want. The Great Un-Manifested. The invisible world.

With this in mind, let's explore some thoughts for which we can exchange the thoughts we might currently be holding about illness.

The first, and to me, most important thought regarding illness is: "EVERY ILLNESS HAS A CURE." Now I can see people, especially doctors, bristling, saying, "That's not true. We have many illnesses for which there are no cures!" Actually, that statement is not correct. What is correct is that we have many illnesses for which we have not yet revealed a cure. If the illness has been generated, there MUST be a way to un-generate it.

Think of the illnesses that were "incurable" 100 years ago that are now run of the mill. Tuberculosis, polio, smallpox, leprosy, bubonic plague, were all diseases for which no cause was known and no cure or prevention available. Now those diseases hardly exist. Did we "create" a cure for those diseases? No, the cures were already created. They already existed. We just discovered them. Revealed them. And how did we reveal them? People began to have the thought that a cure must exist, and the actions they took inside that thought appeared in the mirror of the world as a reflection of that thought, and revealed a cure.

If you have a disease for which the statistic is that 1/10 of 1 percent recover, that means that a way to recover from that disease already exists. It's already been created. There already exist physical, chemical or mental processes that make the disease disappear. Medications or herbs or other treatments already exist. There is something you could take, or something you could think or do, that would make it go away. It may not have been revealed yet, but it does exist.

So the first thought, EVERY ILLNESS HAS A CURE, is one that we can take on with complete confidence that that is a fact. Within that thought, the possibility of complete healing exists.

You then look at the illness, the symptoms, and see what thoughts you're choosing "about" them. As I've said time and again, it usually seems like we're having thoughts because of something that happens, but in Thought Exchange, we're looking and seeing what result we get if we turn that around and work on the assumption that we're seeing things happen as a reflection of our thoughts.

Following this premise, we can return to our original Thought Exchange Circle (Thought causes Sensation causes Belief causes Event or Manifestation) and enter it at the point of Event. In this case, the event, or manifestation we're seeing is the illness. We can then notice what thoughts we seem to be choosing "about" the illness. Given that we know that thoughts are Cause, and manifestation is Effect, and not the other way around, we have now arrived at the causative thought. This is the thought that is appearing in the mirror of the world as the illness. And whereas an illness (manifestation) cannot be exchanged, a thought can. So we are now positioned to work on the illness in the only place in which anything in the manifested world can be worked on. In thought.

For example: I do shows, and often, a week or so before I have to go onstage, I will get physical symptoms. Anxiety, or a headache, or a back spasm. I stop, and notice what, in the back of my mind, I am thinking about those symptoms. I most often find that what I am thinking is, "Oh no! If I have that symptom I won't be able to perform." Now, I know that what I'm anxious about is having to perform. I acknowledge that the thought I'm having is that performing is dangerous, and that I have actually chosen that protective thought as a way to possibly get out of having to perform. Even though my adult self doesn't want to get out of performing, my child self, the part that remembers some earlier incident in which the sensation I'm now having was perceived as dangerous, is creating the symptom in order to give me the opportunity to avoid a situation that it regards as dangerous. (For more on this, see the chapter on Inner Child.)

Knowing this, I can then take on a new thought about performing, be with the sensations that that new thought generates (which may be uncomfortable, but I know they're just sensations) and I will see the outcome I desire appear before me.

Years ago, I was hired to take over the job of conducting the show Song and Dance on Broadway. It was a very difficult show to conduct in that it consisted of no dialogue, just wall-to-wall music, so there was a lot to learn in a very short time. I was very nervous about being able to be ready in time. During the rehearsal period, I developed a stuffed ear. It wasn't terribly painful, but it was annoying. So I went to an ear doctor in New York who was well known for prescribing a lot of drugs. He gave me a prescription for prednisone as well as another steroid and several other drugs. I took the drugs, and the stuffed ear opened up. But I experienced the "side effects" of the drugs, which were dry mouth, sleeplessness, restlessness and anxiety. I suddenly had the realization that what I was experiencing was not the "side effects" of a drug, but was in fact, my fear of not being up to the task of doing the show. I was more afraid than I wanted to be while learning a Broadway show, so I developed the symptom of a stuffed ear to hold that fear for me, and then when I forcibly blasted the symptom away, I was left with what I had taken on the symptom to cover in the first place.

So I said to myself, "Get off the drugs, you won't be anxious, you'll just have a stuffed ear, and right after opening night it will go away." And that's exactly what happened. In fact, it happened sooner than that, because once I was able to know and tolerate the idea that, of course, I was nervous about the show, but that I could certainly do the show whether I was nervous or not, I didn't need the symptom or the anxiety.

The thing to know about illness, is that our body, which is always trying to help us deal with things and right itself, sometimes resorts to illness to hold something for us that seems unthinkable, undoable or impossible to deal with. So, if you are experiencing an illness, ask yourself, "What thoughts am I having about this illness? What would it prevent me from doing? How am I feeling about it?" and see if you come across a thought that might be reflecting as the illness. Such a thought might be: "If I'm ill I can't do my performance next week. — If I'm ill, I won't be able to go here, or there. — I'm so angry. — I'm so hurt. — I'm so weak. — I'm such an idiot."

The thoughts you're likely to come across may be thoughts that you don't want to have. Be both gentle and unsparing with yourself. Allow yourself to know and accept thoughts that you really might wish you weren't thinking, or that scare you or upset you. They're just thoughts. Remember, it's only by getting to the truth of what you're actually thinking that you put yourself in the power position where you can exchange your thoughts that are reflecting as illness for ones that reflect as health and well-being.

So one of the first thoughts you come across might be: "I can't deal with this." That thought might be replaced with "It is possible to deal with this." This is something that's true. There are forces and powers and ideas in the universe, already created, already here in the Great Un-Manifested, that would allow you to deal with this. It's just a matter of revealing them through thought.

Illness can be dealt with, in thought, on several levels:

The first thoughts one must choose are thoughts that it's possible to heal this. That a cure already exists.

The second group of thoughts are about looking at the symptom, seeing what thoughts it brings to mind, exploring the possibility that those are the thoughts that are actually being reflected as the illness, and then exchanging them for thoughts that might be reflected as health.

It's an ongoing process. Keep digging for the thoughts you might be having that are reflecting as illness, and keep exchanging them for thoughts that might reflect as health.

Thoughts that might be being mirrored as a health challenge	Thoughts you might exchange them for that would allow for healing and perfect health
There is no cure for this illness.	A CURE FOR THIS ILLNESS ALREADY EXISTS. EITHER SOMEBODY ALREADY KNOWS ABOUT IT AND IT'S POSSIBLE TO FIND THAT PERSON, OR WE MAY NOT HAVE REVEALED IT YET BUT IT IS DEFINITELY ALREADY HERE.
I can't handle the thoughts and sensations that come up for me when this I think about illness.	IT IS POSSIBLE FOR ME TO HANDLE THE FEARS, SENSATIONS, THOUGHTS AND ISSUES THAT COME TO ME WHEN I THINK ABOUT THIS ILLNESS.
My body cannot get better from this.	MY BODY IS CAPABLE OF HEALING, AND ALREADY KNOWS HOW TO DO IT.
I am sick.	UNDER ANY ILLNESS, WELLNESS ALREADY EXISTS IN THE UN -MANIFESTED.
Thoughts I'm currently having about my illness	**Thoughts I'm exchanging them for**

An important point, that can't be overstressed, is that when you take on the thought you want, you may very well feel sensations. Often illness is what I call a "second line of defense." Something happens, you have a sensation, you don't want to experience that sensation because it reminds you of the event that you thought you couldn't tolerate, so an illness forms to distract you from the sensation. You then focus on the illness, thinking that if you could just get rid of it, you would be fine. But when you get rid of it, you'll be right back to the sensation you were afraid of in the first place. If you still think you can't tolerate the sensation, you may take on the illness again to get away from it. Can you see that at the center of this is the ability to be with the harmless sensation that comes with the thought of what you want? When you don't have to dodge those sensations, but can simply experience them, you get to take on the thought of health and success you wish to hold.

Early in my career, I used to get 103° temperature every time I had to conduct an opening night on Broadway. What this illness did was distract me from the fear I had about opening night, because all I could think about during the show was living through the evening and getting home to bed. I now see that I had unconsciously developed this distraction because I thought I couldn't tolerate the issues and pressures that came with an opening night on Broadway. That thought led me to believe that experiencing these issues and pressures would make me unable to do the show, so I developed a symptom to make sure I wouldn't experience opening night.

I was about to take over the show Grease on Broadway, and I noticed that once again I was beginning to develop a fever. I suddenly stopped and thought to myself, "I'm developing this fever because I'm afraid, and I'm afraid to be afraid. Grease is an easy show to conduct. Why don't I just be afraid and see what happens?" So I did that, experienced the sensations that came with being afraid, and on opening night, not only did I not have a fever, but I wasn't afraid either.

So by being willing to know what I was thinking, and being willing to exchange that thought, and experience whatever I experienced, I was able to deal directly with the issue at hand, and didn't need the disease to distract me from it.

In short, don't let yourself be distracted by disease. Go to the thoughts and sensations that underlie it, and all your actions will be directed toward making it disappear.

I want to be very clear that I'm not saying not to treat the disease, but when you know that it is just a reflection of thought, an exchange in thought will cause you to take actions that result in healing, whether those actions be medical, mental, or a combination of both.

MONEY

The first thing to know about money is that there is an unlimited supply, and it's available for everyone. Money is not a THING. Think about it. Add up all the billionaires, all the millionaires, all the corporations and businesses, giant and small and in between, and all the rest of the people in the world, and get an idea of what the total amount of net worth is in the world. Do you really think there are that many bills around? Obviously not. Money is an idea, an energy, a concept. Money is the reflection of a thought.

We are swimming in money. The majority of it is invisible, yet all around us, and the question is, how do we manifest it? We never own it. It appears, we use it, it goes back into the Un-Manifested.

I like to think of myself as wading through invisible piles of money, so much so that it's almost hard to walk. It's right there, and in our hypothesis, what brings it out is not work, not special knowledge, not luck or privilege (although these things may be things that occur or appear on the way to money appearing) but THOUGHT.

So when you look at your particular money condition, as always, look at what thoughts you might be having that could be reflecting as the condition you see before you. Thoughts like, "There isn't enough; I don't get to have what I want; I'm lacking something that others have; I can't make money in the stock market; You have to have special knowledge or skills to be rich." Even thoughts like, "Rich people are always unhappy; It's selfish to be rich." The list is endless.

Money is one of the chief ways in which our thoughts get held up before us by the mirror of the universe so that we can see them. Instead of fighting with your reflection in the mirror, trying to figure out how to get more money, look at your thoughts. Look at your abundance consciousness. Look at your thoughts about your ability to have freedom and plenty. When you've determined what those thoughts actually are, take a trip to The Thought Exchange and trade them in for thoughts that would be more likely to reflect as the money you would like to see in the mirror of your life, and watch ideas, jobs, surprise checks, inheritances and sources you never even dreamed of appear.

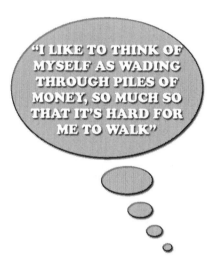

Thoughts that might be being mirrored as money problems	Thoughts you might exchange them for that would allow for financial abundance and success
I can't have money.	UNLIMITED MONEY IS ALREADY THERE AND EQUALLY AVAILABLE TO EVERYONE.
It's not possible for me to make money in the stock market, or business.	THE POSSIBLITY OF ANY-ONE MAKING MONEY IN EVERY ONE OF THESE AR-EAS ALREADY EXISTS.
I don't have the skills or knowl-edge or talent to be rich.	BEING RICH IS NOT AT ALL RELATED TO SKILL OR KNOWLEDGE OR TALENT.
It is evil to be rich . People who are rich lead miser-able lives.	BEING RICH, IS NOT CON-NECTED TO BEING EVIL OR MISERABLE, NOR IS IT CON-NECTED TO ANY OF THESE OTHER THINGS, EXCEPT AS WE THINK IT IS.
Thoughts I'm currently having about money	**Thoughts I'm exchanging them for**

Once you have taken on your new thought about money (or about anything for that matter) you must remember that it is the sensational component that will allow you to stay with that new thought and see its reflection manifest in the physical world.

When you take on your new thought about money, the thought you wish to hold, you will experience physical sensations. Money has often been such a hot topic in early life, that we feel endangered when we <u>dare</u> to think that we can have money. Because of this, often when we take on our new thought, we will notice that we immediately "get scared" and go back to thoughts of lack. We must be able to look under that fear and find the sensation we're experiencing that we're trying to jump away from by returning to old thoughts. Once we can be with that tightness or shaking or "empty" sensation, we can continue to hold our new thought. If we interpret that sensation as meaning that we can't have money or that there is some danger in having money, we won't be able to stay with our new thought. If we simply experience the sensation as sensation, without interpretation, we will be able to stay with the thought that money is unlimited and available to us, no matter what we're seeing before us, and this new thought will reflect in the world.

Perhaps the reason so few people seem to get to experience great wealth is that so few people are able to stay with the sensations that go with it. Many of us hold up the idea of great wealth as a way to get away from or to get around experiencing sensations we're uncomfortable with. If this is what we're thinking, then when those sensations begin to increase as we move toward great wealth, we will take on the thought, "This is dangerous" and find ways to make sure we never really have money. Only by being willing to experience the sensations that go with great wealth, no matter how uncomfortable or surprising they might be, can we allow ourselves to actually see the manifestation of that wealth.

A few years ago, I experienced a financial "disaster." I was heavily invested in a stock that completely took a nose dive, and I suddenly found myself without enough money to pay my bills. Since I had three mortgages, two car payments and an expensive office at the time, this was a real problem. Naturally, at first, I panicked. I had thoughts like,

"Why does this always happen to me? I'm going down the drain. I'm going to have to sell everything. I'll be living in the street. I'll be humiliated." You name it, I had it.

I helplessly watched it get worse and worse, until one day, I suddenly stopped and said, "Wait a minute, Mr. Thought Exchange! Put your money where your mouth is and apply the principles you're so busy teaching everybody else!"

I immediately took a look at the situation I was seeing and asked myself the basic Thought Exchange question. "If you're seeing this in the mirror, what must you be thinking?" The thoughts I came up with were, "I'm not allowed to have money; I will always lose; Everything gets taken away from me at the last minute."

I suddenly realized that this loss of money was not real. It was nothing more than a reflection of my deep thoughts of lack. The mirror was simply showing me that I was thinking that I couldn't have money.

With this new perspective, I went inside, to the Great Un-Manifested and located the infinite amount of money that is there and is always available to me.

Based on the knowledge of this truth, I exchanged the thoughts I was having for, "Infinite money is here for me right now and always available to me."

I next looked for my sensation, which wasn't difficult to find, since a huge heaviness appeared in my chest. I just sat there with it and experienced it.

At the time that this was happening, I was involved in rehearsing a show, which I was truly enjoying. I continued to rehearse the show while simply holding the thought that there was unlimited money available to me and allowing myself to experience the heaviness in my chest. I walked around all day having a great time while experiencing this heaviness in my chest. I decided not to watch the stock market, since there was nothing I could do about it.

Three weeks later, I opened my stock account, and all the money and more had come back.

The following year, I was teaching a class at the same theater, and I told this story. Everyone was shocked that I had been having a financial problem when I had been there the previous year. They told me that through the whole rehearsal period I had seemed so happy and relaxed, and had given no indication that I was in crisis.

This was because I had been able to hold the thought, which is the truth, that in the Un-Manifested, unlimited money is available to me at all times, and experience the sensations that the thought brought on, without jumping away from them. Because I was able to do this, I had the freedom to choose any thoughts I desired, and I chose to enjoy myself. (Enjoy literally means, "to put joy into myself.")

So there's one thought to hold around money, and that thought is, "It's unlimited." If you can experience the sensations that go with that thought, you will always be living in unlimited financial abundance.

Try it and see.

DIETING

If we approach our weight from the premise that our thought is somehow reflecting in both our eating habits and in the size and shape of our body, we have a handle on how to break into the difficulties we might be having while dieting.

Look at your weight and your diet, notice what's there, and then notice what thought you might be having that would be reflecting as the "problem" you're seeing before you. Typical overriding thoughts are: "I can't lose weight; It's difficult to lose weight; I'll have to starve myself to lose weight." The way that you know you've come upon the right causative thought is when the result before you falls within or appears to match that thought. So, if you've been dieting for several months and have gained weight, that might be a reflection of the thought "I can't lose weight." Generally, we think that the reason we have the thought

"I can't lose weight" is because we've dieted for a month and haven't lost any. But in the premise we're exploring, we're hypothesizing that the lack of weight loss is a reflection of the thought rather than the cause of it.

When you've identified the thought, look for what thought might be one within which the desired result would appear in the mirror of your life. For instance, if you identify "It's NOT possible for me to lose weight," notice that there is also a thought, "It IS possible for me to lose weight."

Remember, we're not visualizing or affirming here. Although visualizing and affirming are wonderful tools, we're looking only for what is TRUE RIGHT NOW. When you say, "I am a slim, toned person at the perfect weight" is that true right now? NO. So what is it you are actually affirming? What can we KNOW is true?

What we can KNOW is true is that in the realm of the Great Un-Manifested, one of the infinite possibilities that already exists is your being at your perfect weight. That has already been created. There's a way to get there. Even if you don't know what it is right now, there are things you can think, things you can do, processes that can happen, that will lead to that result. So what you want to do is affirm that that possibility already exists. That it is something that is DEFINITELY true. The possibility exists, it's already here. Now the only task is to bring it forth. And in our experiment, we are testing to see if Thought, in fact, does bring it forth.

So take on a thought that might reflect in the mirror as the possibility you might want. Like, "It is possible for me to lose weight." Or, "The diet that will accomplish this already exists."

This is a very subtle process. Although a thought like "It's easy for me to lose weight" sounds good, if it's not true for you at this moment, don't take it on. That's more of an affirmation. One thing we want to do is make sure we're not plastering a "positive" affirmation over a "negative" thought that lies beneath it. We want to get to the bottom of the thought, so that we can notice and know what we're truly thinking, not what we wish we were thinking. Once you know what you're truly thinking, you have the power to exchange that thought for another. If you don't acknowledge what you're actually thinking, or you don't know what you're actually thinking, you lose the power to exchange that thought. The best way to know what you're actually thinking is to look at the result you're getting. What's actually happening in your life is the sure mirror to what your thought is, just as your reflection in the mirror is a sure way to know what you're wearing.

So, look at the result you're getting, find the thought that would be reflecting as that result, and then take on a thought within which your perfect weight might be likely to appear. Then just notice what happens, what ideas come to you, what information comes to you, what you're inclined to do, what diet facts and tips are revealed to you. Do not worry about how you feel, whether it's hard or easy to diet, or whether you believe the thought you've taken on. As I've said before, in this process, it doesn't matter how you feel or what you believe, just what the thought is. If the thought causes the result to appear, you will be led through whatever path the universe takes to manifest that result. It might be a difficult path, it might contain things you were afraid to do because they were difficult or made you uncomfortable, but no matter what is on the path, if you hold the thought, the result MUST appear in the mirror of your life. So don't decide how the process will work or how you're going to feel, just take on the thought and see what happens. Whenever you feel uncomfortable, don't focus on the discomfort, simply hold the thought.

Here are some examples of how you might specifically use The Thought Exchange in support of your diet:

Thoughts that might be being mirrored as an unsuccessful diet	Thoughts you might exchange them for that would allow for successful dieting
It's impossible for me to lose weight. I'm just built to be overweight. It's a glandular problem.	THE POSSIBLITY OF MY BEING AT THE PERFECT WEIGHT, OR THE WEIGHT I DESIRE TO BE, ALREADY EXISTS IN THE GREAT UN-MANIFESTED. IT HAS AL-READY BEEN CREATED.
I don't know how to diet. Diets don't work for me.	THE DIET THAT LEADS ME TO MY PERFECT WEIGHT ALREADY EXISTS.
I can never reach my perfect weight.	IT IS POSSIBLE FOR ME TO BE THE WEIGHT I WANT TO BE.
I can't do it.	I CAN DO IT.

Thoughts I'm currently having about my body or my diet	Thoughts I'm exchanging them for

Of all the issues we're discussing in this chapter, successful dieting may be the one that most depends on our ability to experience and stay with our sensations.

When we take on the thought that we can be the weight we wish to be, the natural outgrowth of that thought will usually be some sort of diet. Since, 99 times out of 100, we have overeaten and gained weight in order to suppress a sensation that we have found uncomfortable, the moment we begin to diet we will experience that sensation. If we can't allow ourselves to be with it (which can be challenging since the sensation is usually associated with something from the past that we were afraid of, even though it's harmless now) we will come up with a million reasons why we have to eat.

My favorite one of my own is that whenever I diet, if I begin to lose weight quickly, I notice that I suddenly think, "Oh no, I'm losing weight so quickly, I must be sick. I'd better 'test' that by eating a lot to see if I have the ability to gain weight."

Ridiculous, I know, but it's just one of the many tactics we use to get away from the sensations that arise when we stop doing the thing that we were doing in order to suppress them. (Overeating)

When all is said and done, the only thing you need, to be able to stay on a diet, is the ability to allow yourself to experience what it feels like to be hungry. That's all. The only thing that breaks diets is that people can't tolerate the experience of wanting to eat and not eating, so they eat to stop the sensations.

As I've said time and again in this book, when you get what you want, you will not necessarily feel good! But if you can stay with those sensations, they become nothing more than neutral, meaningless, harmless sensations, and only by staying with them can you see what you want appear.

CHAPTER 21
FOR PEOPLE IN THE CREATIVE ARTS

Since I originally came to Thought Exchange through my work as a musician, I have had the opportunity to apply many of its insights to my own work. This section is about music, because that's the area in which I have personal experience, but it could just as easily be applied to dance, painting or any other creative art.

SINGING THROUGH FEAR

One of the best ways to demonstrate how what we're thinking appears as manifestation, is through singing. As part of my work as a composer, conductor and music director, I have been coaching and teaching singers for many years. When I lecture around the country, I often do the following demonstration to bring home how powerfully our thoughts appear as what we see in the manifested world, and how quickly what we see can change with a simple exchange of thought.

After a brief explanation of the principles of Thought Exchange, I ask for a volunteer, someone who is terrified to sing and thinks they can't sing. Generally someone comes up who is absolutely shaking. I ask them what they think of their singing, and they usually say things like, "I can't sing; My voice is ugly; I can't sing on key, People will humiliate me" — something along those lines. Often, they will tell a story about some teacher in school who told them they couldn't sing or said they should keep quiet during choir practice, or a parent or sibling who made fun of them when they sang. In one case, someone was actually told, "You have retarded pitch." If they do have a memory of someone telling them some such thing, they usually think that that memory is the reason they can't sing, not realizing that although someone may have told them that long ago, it's the taking on of that thought, over and over again in the present (in order to avoid the sensation that they had when they were told whatever they were told in the past) that is the only thing keeping the condition alive.

Once we have heard what their thoughts are about their singing, I ask them to sing a few lines of a familiar song that everybody knows. After some trembling and hemming and hawing they usually do so, off pitch, unable to open their eyes and look at the audience, forgetting the words — you name it. Then I ask the audience, "Having just heard the person sing, would you say that their singing accurately demonstrated their thoughts about their singing?" The answer is always, "Yes. They were off pitch. They were shaky. Their voice did sound ugly."

I then ask the singer, "What do you think a famous singer, who knows they have a fantastic voice thinks about their singing?

We come up with thoughts like, "I'm here to share my gift. Everyone is excited to hear me sing. I have a beautiful voice. I sing on pitch. The audience is transformed by my singing to them. I'm here to bring the people an important message that they need to hear."

Our singers always struggle with taking on these thoughts, not only because they think the thoughts are not true, but also because it means they will have to look at people, feel frightened, be seen, whatever their fear is. I point out that I'm not asking them to think it's true or to believe it, but just to acknowledge that of all the unlimited possibilities that exist in The Great Un-Manifested, these thoughts are among them. Furthermore, I'm not saying they have to feel good, or feel any particular way when they do it. I'm only asking that they exchange the thought they're having for the new thought, experience the sensations that go with that thought, and see what happens.

When they finally allow themselves to just take on the new thought, the same thing happens every time. Their sensations escalate, they're shaking and they're panicked, but their voice immediately transforms to being on pitch, they look the audience right in the eye, the world reflects exactly what they are thinking, and their singing becomes meaningful and filled with feeling. Regardless of how they are feeling, their singing takes a great leap forward as an exact reflection of the new thought about singing that they took on. Invariably, they get a standing ovation. Give them a chance to do this over and over, and they will become used to the sensations that come with the thought that they can sing, and they will be able to confidently sing in front of audiences.

BEING EXPERIENCED AND SUCCESSFUL DOESN'T MEAN YOU DON'T HAVE FEAR

I was standing on the podium, about to do my first performance ever on Broadway as a conductor, when Charlie Blackwell, a stage manager who had been on Broadway for over 30 years, came up to me and said, "Well David, this is your first Broadway show and this is my fiftieth. The difference between us is; You feel like you're going to die, and you think you really will. And I feel like I'm going to die, and I know I won't."

What Charlie was saying was that it didn't matter how nervous he or I felt. Performers frequently feel sensations that might be called terrifying, and often those sensations never go away. But it's the thought they have about those sensations that determines whether they'll go on stage and fulfill what they want to do, or not. I've carried Charlie's statement with me throughout my entire career. I now realize that I have changed, through years of experience, into someone who knows he won't die during the performance, even if I still feel like I will.

MORE ABOUT SINGING

How we sing is one of the most misunderstood and mis-taught aspects of music. People are constantly talking about technique, but what is technique really? Do we really know exactly how our vocal cords or lungs move on each note, or how our mouth forms?

The way singing actually functions is that we hear something and our body knows how to produce it. There are basically two things we must work on in singing. The first is to know what we want to hear, and the second is to be able to get out of the way of our body (our instrument) so it has the freedom to produce exactly what we want to hear in the way that it knows how to do. (And, in the way the we DON'T know how to do.)

For example: Say "hello." Now say "hello" in whatever your impression of a British accent is. It doesn't have to be good, just whatever your impression is. How did you do that? Did you purposely choose to form your mouth differently? Of course not. You simply heard a different sound in your head, and based on what you heard, all different groups of muscles did something different, your breath was used differently and your body produced a totally different sound. With no conscious movement on your part.

Notice that whenever you speak, you're not consciously moving your mouth. You're simply thinking words, and as a reflection of that thinking, all sorts of mouth movement, throat movement and diaphragmatic movement is spontaneously happening as your body reflects in the physical world (with words) the words you are thinking in the invisible world of your mind.

So singing technique is really learning how to clearly think exactly what sound, tone, pitch, word you want, and how to get out of the way of the body so the body can produce it. After you have done this on a particular note over and over, you come to expect and know what the body is going to do to get that note, to the point where it seems like you are intentionally doing it. That's what we call technique. But in fact, it is doing itself.

Another exercise I like to do that demonstrates the way singing works, is to ask someone to stand about two feet from the piano, and reach out and touch their index finger to a particular spot on the piano. They, of course, do this easily and effortlessly. I then ask them to do it again, but this time, the moment they start to move, I grab their arm and try to move it toward that spot on the piano. Invariably what happens is their arm starts to swing wildly and they have trouble touching the piano. When I ask them what they think I was trying to do, they always say, "You were trying to interfere with my touching the piano." They're always shocked to find out that I was in fact trying to make them touch the piano. Usually, to convince them, I have to allow them to do it to me. The point of this is that our arm knows how to touch the piano. As soon as we try to "help," our arm has to struggle with the interference we provide (since we don't know how our arm moves, only our arm does) and this invariably throws our arm off.

In the same way, when we hear a note, our voice knows exactly how to create it. When we try to "help" (by adding physical input or adjustment) the voice is immediately thrown off. Furthermore, our thought that there is a need to add input could only come out of the thought that our voice is somehow deficient. That thought shows up immediately as deficiency in the voice, since the voice can do nothing but mirror our thoughts exactly.

Every detail of our thoughts about our voice shows up (is mirrored) in our singing. For instance, if you think you can't sing on pitch, you will hear the notes off pitch in your head, and your voice will be off pitch. If you think your voice is ugly, you will hear notes as ugly in your head, and your voice will precisely reflect what you hear and will sound ugly.

Sometimes, when people are obviously trying to "fix" their voice through physical means, and I ask them why they're doing that, they will say, "I didn't like the way it sounded so I tried to fix it." They think that what they're doing is listening to their voice and hearing something they don't like, but that's impossible. In fact, since the voice can only do what we're thinking, they must actually be hearing the note the way they don't want it in their head (based on the thought they're having that their voice can't sing it.) All the voice is doing is mirroring this. So if you hear something in your voice you don't like, don't go to the voice. Go to your head, and when you hear what you like in your head, it will come out of your voice in exactly that way.

If you refer back to the meditation at the beginning of Part 4, you will remember that the sum total of who we are is an invisible consciousness experiencing invisible sensations and having invisible thoughts which contain infinite possibilities.

The physical world is not part of who we are. We can never be in or act in the physical world. We can only see our thoughts reflected in it.

If we contemplate what this truly means, we see that we actually can never DO anything. We can only think things, and our body, or the physical world, does them.

In terms of singing, this means that any attempt to "fix" a note or "adjust" our position physically, is not actually us doing something, but can only be a reflection of our thought that our voice doesn't know how to sing the note or that there's something wrong with it.

And as we've seen over and over again, if that's our thought, that's what we're going to hear in the note. So it's futile to do anything other than hear the note and get out of its way. If you see yourself trying to do anything else, or do not like what you're hearing, simply go back to how you hear the note, leave it alone and watch your body create it, often in a way that will surprise you.

This obviously applies to anything you would do in life, and is another example of how our thoughts instantly manifest in the mirror of the physical universe.

Thoughts that might be being mirrored as difficulty in singing	Thoughts you might exchange them for that would allow for successful, comfortable, better singing
I can't sing.	I CAN SING.
I can't match pitch.	I CAN MATCH PITCH.
My voice can't sing that note.	MY VOICE KNOWS HOW TO SING ANYTHING I CAN HEAR.
I have to know how my voice works.	I ONLY HAVE TO HEAR WHAT IT IS I WANT IN MY HEAD, AND GET OF THE WAY.
Thoughts I'm currently having about my singing	**Thoughts I'm exchanging them for**

Conducting an Orchestra

When I think about it, the first place that I consciously experienced the ideas and theories that led to The Thought Exchange was when I was conducting on Broadway.

It had always been a dream of mine to conduct on Broadway, and when I was in my 20s, through a series of synchronistic events, I suddenly found myself conducting a major show on Broadway. Even though I hadn't had any experience doing that, I used my talent and my intuition and figured it out. I became quite a successful conductor and began going from show to show on Broadway. There was only one problem. I really didn't know how to conduct. I could wave my arms and hope for the best, but in my heart of hearts, I knew that I wasn't controlling the orchestra but that, in fact, they were controlling me. It was a very uncomfortable feeling, sort of like living a life in which you're completely at the mercy of events and never have any idea what might happen next.

I had just finished a two-year run of a show, and I decided I'd had enough of being scared and insecure, so I found a great conducting teacher, Rob Kapilow, took three years off, and took six hours of lessons a week in an effort to really learn how to conduct.

When I finished my course of study, I signed on to conduct the show *Song* and *Dance* on Broadway, just to see how everything worked.

When I was conducting the overture in my first few performances of Song and Dance, I noticed that the orchestra was always a little bit behind me, playing slightly slower than I wanted them to. The overture was a fast piece with a steady rhythm. It stayed in one tempo, and thus should have been very easy to conduct. Yet each night, though I tried to be clearer and clearer, laying down the beats, accenting the beats, trying harder and harder to demonstrate exactly where I wanted the beats to be, the orchestra was still playing late.

I wondered why this was happening, and my mind started to wander to all the usual places it would go when people around me weren't giving me what I wanted. Did the orchestra not like me? Were they opposing me on purpose? Were they not as talented as I thought they were? Were they not watching me? Was I conducting unclearly? Was the world just against me in general? Whatever the reason, my perception was that I was asking people outside of me for something and they just weren't giving it to me. And that didn't feel good.

Fortunately, instead of continuing to spin off into those fantasies, I decided to investigate and see if I could find out the truth.

There were several players in that orchestra whom I really trusted, and I asked them if I was being clear. To my surprise, each of them assured me that I was being perfectly clear, and that they were absolutely able to follow what I was showing them with no difficulty.

This was not good news to me. In fact, it threw me into deep despair. Until I'd asked that question, I'd been living in the illusion that there was something outside of me that was functioning incorrectly, and if it would just change, stop opposing me, pay attention, everything would be fine. I had been thinking that the orchestra was somehow at fault and responsible for the problem, which was upsetting, but which held the possibility that if they would only change, I would get what I wanted. I now discovered that here I had an orchestra that was totally cooperative, watching me, had the talent, the willingness, and in fact, the desire to play anything I showed them, and that it was I who couldn't show them what I wanted. In fact, I was clearly and distinctly showing them something I didn't want. How did I know that? Because that's what they were playing, and when I asked them, they were telling me that I was being perfectly clear and that it was easy for them to play exactly what I was showing them. The proof of this was that all of them were playing the thing I "didn't want" in perfect unison, so obviously everyone was seeing the same thing.

So I had to face the disturbing news that it was me, not them. I had to face the fact that the orchestra was playing what I was showing them, and that the problem lay not in the orchestra's inattentiveness or inability to play what I wanted them to play, but in my inability to show them what I wanted. Far from opposing me, the orchestra was in fact doing my exact bidding — carefully, perfectly and supportively mirroring what I was showing them. The only trouble was, I was showing them something I didn't actually want, and I couldn't seem to do anything else

Why could I not show them what I wanted? What was I actually show-ing them? Why was I showing them that?

I called my teacher, told him the problem, and asked if he would sit in the orchestra pit and watch me conduct to see if he could figure out what I was doing wrong. He came down to the show, and right before I went on, he said, "I have one instruction for you, and that is; at no time are you to think about what the orchestra is playing or where your hands are, only about how the music goes. Just think, in your head, of how it sounds, allow your hands to move to that however they do, and let the orchestra play whatever it plays."

So, with trepidation, because this meant I was giving up "control" of the orchestra and leaving what they played to "chance," I took the po-dium, closed my eyes, went inside, and began to conduct the overture. Immediately I noticed that I seemed to be conducting about a half beat ahead of the orchestra, and with a completely different beat pattern. Rather than hitting the beat hard and with emphasis, I was through the beat and half way back up toward the next beat by the time the orches-tra played. It felt so out of control that I actually began to physically shake — remember I was doing this live in front of an audience of over a thousand people — but I did notice, to my great surprise, that the orchestra was playing exactly what I was hearing inside. Exactly what I wanted them to play.

It was only after the show that I was able to sit down and analyze why this had worked. I realized that when I had been conducting before, I had been conducting over the subtle, almost unconscious thoughts that I couldn't be clearly seen, that this was difficult, and that the orchestra did not want to follow me and thus would play slower than I want-ed them to. In order to "compensate" for these thoughts (i.e. get the orchestra to not do the thing I was afraid they were going to do) I was trying to lay down the beat extremely clearly and forcefully. In doing that, I was actually slowing down slightly before each beat. The players could see this, and were unconsciously waiting for me to hit the beat before playing it. Thus, in my belief that they would play too slowly, I was hearing them play too slowly in my head; my hand was demonstrating the slower tempo that I was hearing; they were seeing my hand; and lo and behold, they _were_ playing too slowly.

When I simply focused on how I heard the music in my head (and not on how the orchestra was going to get it) my hands demonstrated the music exactly as I heard it, moving through the beats at the exact moment I heard them, and the orchestra played exactly what I wanted with no difficulty at all.

What's important to understand is that the orchestra saw no difference between the two ways I was conducting. Both times they were simply, cooperatively, unconsciously playing what I was showing them. I envisioned slow, they played slow. I envisioned faster, they played faster. They made no value judgment, they had no opinion, they just played what they saw. In one case, I was looking out at the orchestra, paying attention to what I believed they would play. In the other, I was looking inward, paying attention only to the music. The difference was astounding, and at that moment, conducting became a joy.

As an addendum to this story, years later I was playing piano at the first rehearsal of a piece which I had written, with a large orchestra and chorus and a well-known conductor at the podium. We ran the piece down for the first time, and at the end of the piece, I said to the conductor, "It needs to be faster." The conductor replied, "I was trying to get you to go faster but you wouldn't go." This was surprising to me, since I had been watching him carefully, and I knew I was playing at exactly the tempo he was showing me. Hearing his words, "I was trying to get you to go faster but you wouldn't go," I realized that what must be happening was that he was thinking that he couldn't get me to go faster, and his hands were demonstrating that thought. I couldn't very well say this to this distinguished conductor, so instead I said, "I'm sorry, let's do it again and I'll try to follow you better."

During the second run-thru, he conducted at the same slower tempo, but I simply played faster than he conducted. At the end, he said, "Now that was the right tempo!" And from then on, he conducted the piece correctly, in the right tempo. What had happened was, because I gave him the experience of having me play in the tempo he wanted (rather than the tempo he was showing me) he unconsciously lost the thought that I <u>wouldn't</u> play fast enough and replaced it with the thought that I <u>would,</u> which resulted in his easily and comfortably conducting in the correct tempo.

Thoughts that might be being mirrored as poor conducting	Thoughts you might exchange them for that would allow for clear, excellent conducting
The orchestra won't follow me.	THE ORCHESTRA IS ALWAYS PLAYING WHAT I'M SHOWING THEM.
I have to know what my interpretation of the music is.	THE INTERPRETATION OF THE MUSIC IS REVEALED TO ME IF I LISTEN TO THE MUSIC INSIDE ME.
I don't understand why the orchestra is able to follow me.	I DON'T HAVE TO UNDERSTAND WHY THE ORCHESTRA IS ABLE TO FOLLOW ME. I JUST HAVE TO KNOW THAT THEY CAN.
I have to know exactly what my hands are doing to show what I want the orchestra to play.	I SIMPLY HAVE TO THINK WHAT I WANT, ALLOW MY HANDS TO MOVE, AND THE MIRROR OF THE ORCHESTRA WILL REFLECT WHAT I'M THINKING.
Thoughts I'm currently having about conducting	**Thoughts I'm exchanging them for**

As is always the case, we must remember that when we allow ourselves to simply think the thought of what we want and let the universe simply and exactly reflect that thought, we will experience sensations. Because of childhood experiences and earlier associations that we might have with these sensations, we may notice that we have thoughts like, "I'm throwing myself to the wolves; I'm out of control; This will never work."

When we realize that these thoughts are simply our efforts to get away from these sensations, and can experience the sensations as harmless and meaningless, we can allow ourselves to stay in the position of simply thinking, and allowing what we're thinking to appear before us.

One of my favorite things is when someone says to me, "I've finally decided to give up control." My answer to that is always, "You <u>had</u> it?!?!?

We do not have direct control of anything, but we can harness the way the universe works by knowing that whatever thought we're having is appearing before us. We can only do this if we are willing to experience the sensations that arise when we simply hold a thought and allow it to reflect in the universe without our interference.

So hold the sound of what you want to hear in your mind, allow whatever sensations you experience to simply be there, and what's in your mind will appear before you.

Or to put it more simply; Think, shake, and watch what you're thinking appear.

Chapter 22
APPLYING THOUGHT EXCHANGE PRINCIPLES TO CORPORATE COACHING

Through a series of surprising and synchronistic events (aren't they all?) I found myself doing Thought Exchange work with a major corporate coaching firm, going into Fortune 500 companies and coaching their highest level executives.

At first I thought, "What could I possibly have in common with corporate folk?" But as I got involved with them, I realized that they're just people, with the same basic desires and subjected to the same basic laws of the universe as everyone else. One of the interesting things about them is that their goals, aspirations and achievements are the same as the average person's, but often on a much larger scale. I found it fascinating to explore not only what made them capable of such high levels of achievement, but what was holding them back.

Corporate Culture

In corporate culture, the very thing that makes it so productive is the thing that can often be its downfall.

Corporate culture is, naturally, focused on productivity, on achievement, on money, on results and on the "bottom line." As I'm sure you can see, all these things are in the physical world. And as you know, from reading other parts of this book, the physical world is nothing more than a reflection of the invisible world of thought, and as such, is not real, any more than a reflection in a mirror is real. It's there, but it's not the thing it looks like. It's just a reflection of that thing.

Since corporate culture is so committed to these physical-world "things," it can be very challenging to make the point that all this is not real. But only by understanding this, can we understand the powerful idea that, because they're not real, these things cannot be manipulated by trying to do things in the physical world, any more than the reflection in a mirror can be manipulated by trying to manipulate the mirror. The only way we will see a real shift in these things is by going to their actual source, to the only place that IS real. And that place is Thought. In order to solve the problem, we must find the thought that underlies it, exchange that thought, and then find ways for our clients to hold that thought and not exchange it back.

Most often, when corporate coaches are called in, they are called in to "correct" some behavior in order to "produce" results. We commonly hear that someone is not being "executive" enough, is not being "communicative," is "going underground" or "hiding out," being "manipulative" or not a "team player."

The coaches often analyze these behaviors, interview everyone around the person to get a handle on how the person is being perceived, and give the coachees tactics, assignments and techniques for changing these behaviors.

When all this doesn't work, I get called in.

Now before I go on, I want to say that the work that many of these corporate coaching firms do, particularly the one I work with, is excellent and important. But where it runs into problems is that unless it is done within the context of exchanged thought and the ability to experience the sensations that go with that exchanged thought, it will not hold.

THE SOURCE OF THE "PROBLEM"

In order to effectively deal with a problem or issue, we have to go to its source. Behaviors, productivity and results are all effects, not cause, and any attempt to change them without going to the cause must be futile, because we will just see the cause reflected in other ways.

Thus, when I'm sent in to fix a problem, I never directly address that problem. The first question I ask is, "What is the person thinking that is appearing as that problem?" When we can find the answer to this question, the person can exchange their thought, and the world will immediately, often miraculously, appear differently. When we begin to look at EVERYTHING as just a reflection of thought, problems that seemed firmly entrenched immediately begin to shift. And when our clients backslide, we know where to go to get them on track. Not to the problems themselves, but to the thoughts that underlie them.

In corporate coaching jargon, this is called "Changing your story." One of the first things that many corporate coaches do is ask, "What is your story about this?" and then ask, "How could you change that story and take on another one?" This is actually right on track, but the challenge we see over and over again is that people seem to change their story and then, in very short order, change it back.

More than anything, it's at this juncture of "stuckness" that I get called in.

So the question to ask is, "What is it that keeps people from changing their stories? And once they have changed them, what keeps them from staying with their new story so that they can see a new result?

The Secret To Successfully Changing a Story
(And Staying With the New Story)

As I've said throughout this book, whenever you take on a thought, that thought generates physical sensations. We're not talking about feelings, like anger, sadness or love, but about actual physical sensations like pain, hotness, coldness, emptiness, shaking, tingling, tightness, numbness, etc.

If the new thought you take on is one that you have been steering clear of, the reason you've been steering clear of it is usually that it comes with a sensation that you have associated, from your childhood, as dangerous.

For instance, if as a child, you were slapped for taking independent action, whenever you make a decision without consulting your "superiors" you will have a sensation that signals you that you're in danger. This sensation is often a run-of-the-mill, innocuous tightness or tingling, but to you (or more specifically, to the child inside of you that remembers the old incident even if you don't) it signals danger. To get away from that sensation, you will exchange your thought, probably for one like, "I'd better not make any decisions without asking someone's permission."

This thought, that you cannot act without permission, will then appear in the physical world as "non-executive" behavior. Even if you have been told in no uncertain terms that your boss wants you to take the initiative and think independently, if you can't be with the sensation that comes with doing that, you will quickly revert back to the other behavior and potentially be thought of as uncooperative, incapable or resistant, by the executives and coaches who are trying to get you to change.

When you see that behavior, which is merely a reflection of your thought, not of you, you will think, "See, I AM incapable of taking the initiative," and reinforce that thought. The reinforcement of that thought will then produce more, "I can't function independently" results, and the cycle will continue to escalate.

If we understand that the purpose of that mirror is simply to reflect back the thought that we are thinking, in this case, "I can't make a decision without permission," we can teach our clients to use the mirror to direct themselves back to their own thoughts, which is the only place the change can be made. Once we identify the thought the client is holding (by looking in the mirror of the world and seeing it there) we can ask the client to choose another one.

But the moment this new thought is chosen, the client will experience the old sensation, the one that he or she has been afraid of since childhood. At this point, we must get the client to simply sit with the sensation and experience it. Not interpret it, not decide what's going to happen because of it, just to experience it and describe it as sensation.

Only when the client can do this can the client stay with the new thought.

When the client understands that the new thought may always come with this sensation, but that this sensation is intrinsically harmless, the client can then hold the new thought and see new results.

It's important to know that what we're afraid of is not success, not the consequences of the present circumstance, not "getting slapped." What we're afraid of is simply the sensation we get when we take on the new thought. There is no reason to fear these sensation in the present, as adults, even though in our childhoods they meant something. As adults, we can tolerate and be with them, and this is the key to getting the results that a new thought will bring.

I often find it amazing to learn what simple sensations are causing executives to make BIG decisions that work against the results they desire. One president of a huge corporation wanted to quit his job every time the CEO yelled at him. When we explored why, we found that he had a tingling sensation in his chest every time this happened. It turned out that this tingling in his chest was the same tingling he felt as a boy when his father yelled at him. When he was able to experience the tingling simply as tingling, he was immediately able to exchange his thought about the CEO to, "He's just a gnat buzzing around the room." His desire to quit left him as he was able to tolerate the "tingling."

It is one of the big misconceptions of the modern new thought movement that you will feel good when you get what you want. On the contrary, when you get what you want, when you achieve success, you will feel whatever sensations have been connected with the thought that has allowed you to manifest the achievement. Only by being with these sensations, however comfortable or uncomfortable they might feel, can you hold the thought you want to hold and see the result you want to see reflected in the mirror of the world before you.

THOUGHT EXCHANGE CORPORATE COACHING – STEP BY STEP

With the above principles in mind, knowing that the world is just a mirror of our thoughts, I have laid out this step-by-step guide to successfully coaching corporate clients using Thought Exchange.

SEE THE "PROBLEM" SOLVED IN YOUR OWN MIND

Thought Exchange coaching begins with the coach identifying his own thoughts about a situation. Remember, if everything we see before us is a reflection of our own thoughts, then the whole problem can be nothing more than a reflection of those thoughts that we ourselves are holding. It cannot be someone else's problem. It is our problem.

When we first see or are told about a situation, we usually see it as a problem, as though there's "something wrong." The first step is for the coach to search the world of unlimited possibilities that exist in his or her own thoughts, and see the situation solved. The coach doesn't have to know what the solution is, but must know that the solution to the situation already exists, right now, in the world of unlimited possibility. So if someone is not working up to par, the coach must see that it is possible that the person could work up to par, even if the coach can't see how that could possibly be. Just as when we have a serious disease we know that even if only 1% of people have been cured that it is possible to cure it, we must focus totally on the FACT that a solution exists.

IDENTIFYING THE ISSUE WITH THE COACHEE

Knowing that the solution exists, we present the issue to the person being coached. There are two basic possible scenarios here. In one, the coachee knows and acknowledges that the issue exists. In the other, the coachee argues with or resists the assessment.

In either case, you ask the coachee to present what he or she sees is happening from his or her point of view. There should be room made for the coachee to express this exactly as he or she sees it, i.e. "This person is trying to stab me in the back; I'm being blamed for things I didn't do; I don't seem to be able to do the job; People don't like me," whatever. Or, "I'm being wrongly accused; There's nothing going on; Everyone else is at fault." We want to see what the coachee is seeing in the mirror of the world, so we must be very careful not to correct or guide him or her at this point. We just listen, because in order to determine what the coachee is thinking, we must get an accurate picture of the reflection that the coachee is seeing.

IDENTIFYING WHAT THE COACHEE MUST BE THINKING

Whatever the coachee sees, ask him or her, "If what you're seeing were an exact reflection of your thought, what would you have to be thinking in order to be seeing it in the mirror of the world?" It can often be challenging to hone in on the answer to this question, and it must be done with no blame, no shame, no judgment. We are simply saying "You're seeing a black dress in the mirror. What must you be wearing?"

After some searching (this can be the longest part of the coaching, and the coach must keep going until this is found) the coachee will usually land on thoughts like, "Nobody likes me; I'm no good at what I do; I can't get the support I need at work; Everyone is against me," etc. These thoughts do not have to be rational, in fact, usually people don't know they're having them. This is the value of seeing the world as a mirror. We have a constant way of knowing what we're thinking, by what we're seeing before us.

WHAT WOULD YOU LIKE TO SEE?

When you have identified the thought the coachee is holding that is reflecting in the world as "the problem," you ask, "What would you like the world to look like?" The answers will pertain to seeing the problem solved. "I'd like to see myself completing my work in a way that's satisfying to me and to the company; I'd like to be respected by my peers; I'd like to get the support I desire at work."

EXCHANGING THE THOUGHT

Once you have the desired outcome in mind, you ask the coachee, "What thought might you exchange the one you're holding for, that might appear in the world as what you want to see there?" And you search around until you find one. It's not an affirmation. It's not a thought about what will be. It's a thought that, reflected in the world, would appear the way we want to see the world. Thoughts might be: "I can get the support I need at work; I can get the work done; I can get along with my coworkers." Thoughts that acknowledge that possibility exists. We find these thoughts in the unlimited invisible world of all possible thoughts, and we don't worry about how we're going to achieve them. Just as we don't worry about whether the outfit we have on will be reflected in the mirror, we simply "put the thought on" and let the mirror do the rest. How, is not our concern.

NOTICE THE PHYSICAL SENSATIONS YOU'RE HAVING

This is perhaps the most important and most overlooked part of the process. There are many methods, both in the corporate and spiritual world, which talk about taking on a new thought, but the question of why we don't hold our new thought is one that I have sought to answer. And what I have come to is that we resist certain thoughts because they come with sensations that we think we can't tolerate, because we couldn't tolerate them in our childhoods. For example, if as a child, you said, "I can do that" and someone slapped you across the face when you said it, every time you take on the thought "I can do that" as an adult, you're going to feel a sensation similar to the one you had when you were about to be slapped. Instinctively you will flinch from that sensation, think of yourself as in danger, and take on a protective thought to get away from that sensation. And that thought will obviously be, "I can't do that." So now you will be safe from the sensation, but of course, you can't do the thing you wanted to do.

IN ORDER TO BE ABLE TO STAY WITH A NEW THOUGHT OR NEW STORY, YOU MUST BE ABLE TO EXPERIENCE THE SENSATIONS THAT GO WITH THAT NEW THOUGHT OR STORY.

And those sensations, contrary to popular belief, are often uncomfortable.

So once the coachee has identified the new thought, ask, "What sensations do you experience when you think the new thought?" Sensations are not feelings. Feelings, things like anger, sadness, fear, are merely our interpretations of sensations. Some people feel a tingling in their chest and say "I'm angry." Some feel it and say, "I'm in love." Same sensation, different interpretation. So we're looking for the sensations. Tingling, tightness, shortness of breath, hotness, coldness, emptiness, pain, constriction, comfort, ease. Whatever.

When the coachee identifies the sensation, ask him or her to simply be with it, without interpretation, while holding the new thought.

We take on thoughts like 'I can't; I won't; It's impossible," to PROTECT ourselves from these sensations. Only by being with the sensations can we stay with the new thoughts.

STAYING WITH THE NEW THOUGHT

Ask the coachee to simply stay with the new thought and the sensations that come with it as they go through their week. If they see a result that is not what they want, it's not that the new thought didn't work; it's that they exchanged away the new thought to get away from the sensation. Simply tell them to go back to the thought and experience the sensation whenever this happens.

If you see the coachee slip back, ask yourself what YOUR thought is, where YOU have exchanged your thought for "It's not possible."

Remember, this is all going on inside of you.

A WORD ABOUT RATINGS, 360'S AND TESTING

In the world of Thought Exchange, ratings, 360's and testing do not show us facts. This is not to say they are not useful. In fact, they're extremely useful in showing us what the coachee thinks of him or her self. So if a 360 reveals that someone is not, say, "Executive Material," all that means is that the person doesn't think of themselves as executive material.

When going over these tests and reports with people, using the Thought Exchange model, the question to ask is, "What are you thinking about yourself that has caused this result to appear in the mirror of the world before you?"

When the coachee can look at these things from this perspective, there's no blame, nobody is attacking them, they've just been done the favor, not of seeing how other people see them, but of seeing how they see themselves. By working inside themselves, they can change what they see in the world.

"THE FIRST QUESTION I ASK IS, 'WHAT IF THE PERSON THINKING THAT IS APPEARING AS THE PROBLEM?'"

CHAPTER 23
FORGIVENESS – THOUGHT EXCHANGE STYLE

Forgiveness can be such a hot topic that I thought it deserved its own chapter.

WHO ARE YOU FORGIVING AND WHY?

In New Thought, as well as in religious and psychotherapeutic circles, we are told that one of the most important elements in healing and recovery is Forgiveness. We are told that forgiving doesn't mean condoning; that you can love a person and not love his or her behavior; that you have to "let go" of the past; that "holding a grudge is like taking poison and hoping the other person dies" (one of my favorites.)

I have listened to all these statements and tried to forgive others in many ways, but I always found that there was something missing, something fundamentally "off" when I tried to forgive someone else for something they had done or not done to me.

When I began to work with Thought Exchange, I realized that if the "other" is merely a reflection of my own thought, then there is no "other" to forgive. All the work has to be done inside myself. When that work is done, the world will reflect that work and the "other" will appear differently.

I had just spent a weekend at a Prosperity Seminar with Edwene Gaines, and she had said that all financial debt was a product of non-forgiveness. Since, at the time, I was experiencing some financial debt, I decided to give forgiveness a try.

The first thing Edwene recommended was to write, "I, David, forgive myself" 35 times in the morning and 35 times in the evening, for a week.

The premise was to forgive 7 times 70, as Jesus had done. I began to do this, writing, "I forgive myself, I forgive myself" over and over. Suddenly, I asked myself, "For what? I forgive myself for what? What am I forgiving myself for?"

I realized that whenever something upsetting had happened or someone had "done something" to me, it wasn't the actual act that was the problem, but rather the thoughts I had taken on about it in order to get away from the sensations I experienced when I had tried to go for what I wanted and had been thwarted or hurt.

So when I had been hit as a child, it wasn't the hitting that lingered. It was thoughts like, "I'm in danger, I deserve to be punished, I can't have what I want," that I had taken on and made a part of my life, in order to try to make sure I would never again feel the sensations associated with the original incident. It was those thoughts that were still manifesting in the present. Rehashing the incident or blaming someone else did nothing to diminish them. Trying to be nice to someone else, or saying it was OK, or forgiving them in some way, also did nothing to diminish the sensations that arose every time I took on the thought of what I wanted. The only way to "get over it" would be to take on the new thought of what I wanted and be able to be with the sensations that came with it.

Rather than forgiving somebody else, I realized that I would have to forgive myself for having taken on these thoughts and having taken actions based on these thoughts that had only served to cause them to repeat and repeat and to be reflected in my current life. Once I realized that it was I who had taken on these thoughts, I could exchange them, feel the sensations that went with the new thoughts (sensations that I had been avoiding for years because of my inability to be with them at an earlier time in my life) and stay with the new thoughts that would appear as new things in my life.

The "sensational" part cannot be emphasized enough. Many of us go through the process of choosing a new thought, only to find that before we know it we are back with the old thought. We must be prepared for the fact that if we are choosing a thought that we have stayed away from for years (to protect ourselves from experiencing a harmless, meaningless sensation that had become associated with pain or danger) that new thought will come with sensations that we might find uncomfortable or think of as endangering. It is only when we can stay with the sensation the new thought brings up that we can stay with the new thought.

With this understanding, I went through my whole life and forgave myself for everything about which I had taken on thoughts that had limited me. I forgave myself for the thoughts I had taken on about failing. I forgave myself for the thoughts I had taken on about leaving jobs. I forgave myself for the thoughts I had taken on about falling and hitting my head. I forgave myself for the thoughts I had taken on about bad investments I had made. I forgave myself for the thoughts I had taken on about my mother dying.

When I shared this with my Thought Exchange classes, some people said, "Why should you have to forgive yourself for those things? Many of them weren't even your fault." That's just the point. I'm not forgiving myself because things were my fault. I'm forgiving myself because I took on thoughts about those things that are limiting my life today.

With this knowledge, I expanded my forgiveness of myself to include things that many would consider good things. I forgave myself for having written hit songs. Why? Because based on those hits I took on thoughts like, "I can never do that again" or "I have to write another song as good as that one," and these thoughts were affecting my ability to be open and relaxed in my writing in the present. I forgave myself for conducting successful Disney movies, because whenever I would enter a period where I was working less, or working at something I was interested in but that paid less, I would beat myself up for not having the kind of success in the present moment that I had had before. This prevented me from enjoying and working with the natural ebb and flow that is so important to any artistic career.

The forgiveness list went on and on, and every day I read it over and added to it. Doing this has helped me to heal, to remain open to life, to live in the present and, incidentally, to manifest a great deal more cash and get out of debt.

Try making your own list. The only one you have to forgive is yourself for the thoughts you took on based on the reflections you saw in the mirror of the world. When you do this, the world appears to change, because like a mirror, it can do nothing but reflect your thoughts.

CHAPTER 24
PANIC "ATTACKS"
DON'T BE FOOLED BY YOUR SENSATIONS

As I mentioned in section 1 of this book, at the age of twenty I suffered from a debilitating case of panic "disorder." Because of this, and especially because of my work with Thought Exchange, I have become sort of an expert on the subject, and am often called upon to work with people who are going through what I went through. I'm happy to say that my work in this area has been extremely successful, so if you're suffering from panic, you've come to the right place. Although panic "disorder" can be terrifying and confusing, getting over it is actually a very simple process. The process can, of course, be challenging, but it definitely can be done in less time than you would imagine.

In case you're wondering why I put the words "Attack" and "Disorder" in parentheses, it's because once you go through this process, you will come to understand that Panic is neither an attack nor a disorder, but simply an understandable misinterpretation of sensations and what they mean. So for the purposes of this chapter, we'll just call it panic.

My panic began in my senior year in college. I was standing on stage singing in a chorus concert with the New England Conservatory Chorus, when suddenly, for no apparent reason, I felt like I was going to faint, and thought "I have to get out of here." I somehow made it through the song, and hurriedly left the stage. The moment I left the stage, I felt better, but over the course of the next few weeks, this sensation would recur from time to time, and I would panic and "run from it" each time. (Of course there was nowhere to run because it was happening in my own body, but that didn't stop me from trying.) I was petrified. I didn't know what was happening to me. I first assumed that there must be something terribly wrong with me physically, but doctors couldn't find anything. Soon I was having the panic, or living in fear of the panic, almost constantly. I couldn't go out of the house without my head spinning, my heart pounding, and the street seeming to be heaving in front of me.

I couldn't go on the subway, couldn't sit in a theater, couldn't perform, and was afraid to get into a car or onto a plane. I had all sorts of psychosomatic symptoms, and went to a lot more doctors, still to no avail. I was placed on various tranquilizing medications, but none of them seemed to do anything other than make me feel sleepy and out of it. Nor did psychotherapy seem to have any effect on stopping the panic. Delving into my past, into my anger, into my relationship with my parents, may have caused me to grow emotionally, but it didn't stop the panic symptoms. Efforts to get me to relax and breathe deeply didn't help either. No matter what, even if I went through brief periods where I felt better, there was always the chance that the panic would return. And since I thought I couldn't take that chance, I became extremely limited in what I could do and where I could go.

After a short while, my life essentially stopped, and I ended up in a mental hospital. I stayed there for two months, on heavy medication, participating in group therapy and psychotherapy, and occasionally taking forays out into the world to see if I could "do it," but the panic didn't change. I finally checked myself out of the mental hospital, only because it wasn't helping, but still the symptoms continued. I thought my life was over, that I'd never be happy again, and that I would have to give up on achieving any of my goals and dreams.

If you are having this kind of panic experience, I'm sure you are recognizing many, if not all of these symptoms. Because you are dealing with something that's going on inside you, something that you can't seem to control that comes and goes unpredictably and for no apparent reason, after a while it seems hopeless. Even if you've felt OK for a while, there's always the chance that the panic will return.

As you can see, I was in the same place as you, so I understand perfectly what you're going through. But fortunately for me (and fortunately for you since you're now reading this) through a series of events, some of them seeming to occur by chance, and others that were brought about by careful and painstaking practice and research, I have come to a deep understanding of how panic works and what it takes to completely disarm it.

As I said at the beginning of this section, because of my extensive, first-hand experience with the subject and the discoveries I've made, I now work with many people who are experiencing panic. I go on the subway with them, I take walks with them, I see them in private sessions, and in every case, in short order, they are able to bring their lives back to normal with this simple, albeit sometimes challenging process.

MY FIRST BREAKTHROUGH (STOP TRYING TO GET IT TO GO AWAY)

My first breakthrough was when I accidentally came across a book called "Hope and Help For Your Nerves" by Dr. Claire Weekes. If you're suffering from panic disorder, I recommend that you get this book and read it immediately.

In this book, Dr. Weekes talks about panic symptoms being nothing more than adrenaline firing because your system has become sensitized. Her suggestion is that you notice the sensations you're experiencing and "float" through them. Your panic about the sensations is causing the adrenaline to fire even more, so the condition just continues and escalates. The fact is that adrenaline can only do so much, so there's a limit to how much the sensations will escalate, even though it doesn't feel that way. Knowing this, the first step is to accept that the sensations are there and not fight them.

This "technical" explanation of panic gave me great relief. As a person who is very psychotherapy-minded, I was constantly trying to analyze the problem, in hopes of finding an emotional cause for it which, once found, would make it go away. This wasn't working because, as I was to learn, the object is not to make it go away, but to be able to have it.

With this technique, I began to learn that I could actually be with these sensations and still do things. I was still experiencing the sensations, but was becoming able to function with them. Perhaps the biggest turning point in my recovery was the day I finally said, "OK, fine. I'm going to have these sensations for the rest of my life. What do I do now?" At first I thought, "I might as well kill myself. There's no way I can go through life having these 'terrible' sensations."

Although, at first glance, it might seem like accepting that I might have these sensations for the rest of my life would mean that I was giving up hope, in fact, that acceptance was the beginning of my healing. Remember, one of the basic principles of metaphysics is "What you resist, persists." In terms of panic, this does not necessarily translate into the sensations disappearing, but when you don't resist them, you can begin to incorporate them into your experience. And the more you do that, the more you become able to do more things, even while having the sensations.

So, based on the premise that it was possible that I might have these symptoms for the rest of my life, I began to do things, expecting to have the sensations. I found that I could walk through Macy's on Christmas eve, experience the sensations, and walk through anyway. I found I could get on the subway, albeit trembling and shaking, but I could get on the subway. Within a few years, I was in New York, conducting on Broadway.

Now imagine the terror, for someone who had experienced the kind of panic I had experienced, of being confined to a small orchestra pit from which you can't escape, standing in front of over a thousand people, doing something that you are not allowed to stop doing for 2 hours. A panic-person's worst nightmare!

I put a sign on my music stand that said, "So Die!" What I meant by this was, "Drop dead and someone will carry you off, but don't leave the podium, no matter what you feel." The sensations continued for years, but gradually I got used to them, came to expect them, and could navigate them. After a while, they became part of my life, and my experience of them was that they were an annoyance but didn't stop me from doing anything. In truth, they probably did still stop me in subtle ways, because they were always a factor in deciding whether I would take risks. Things that were well within my capabilities, that people without my history of panic would not think twice about, were still big decisions for me because of the panic factor.

I didn't really come to a full understanding of how panic could not only be dealt with, but actually be something that was healing, until I was several years into the development of my Thought Exchange work.

DISARMING PANIC ONCE AND FOR ALL

Looked at in Thought Exchange terms, what I came to understand about panic is that it is nothing more than sensations, often fairly innocuous sensations, that have been associated with something traumatic that happened earlier in life. The first panic may arise because something in a present situation unconsciously reminds us of an earlier trauma, and triggers sensations that we regarded as dangerous then (but which are not at all dangerous now). Soon, we may begin to experience the same sensations in any situation that resembles the situation in which we have had this first panic. Gradually, more and more situations bring it on until we're paralyzed with fear at almost every turn. Because we are adults, our logical, analytical mind thinks there must be some reason in the present for our sensations, or else, why would we be feeling so panicky? So when we have these sensations, our mind scans the horizon for what must be dangerous, and we add thoughts like, "I'm dying; I have to get out of here; I'll never be happy again; My career is over; I'm going to be trapped in this train tunnel forever."

If we examine the situation, these thoughts often defy all logic. "I'm stuck in a subway tunnel, I know I'll get out in 15 minutes or half an hour, there's plenty of air in here, I have a good book with me, what's the problem?" Or perhaps even more disturbing, "I'm walking down the street, or sitting at my computer, and suddenly I feel like I'm under attack." The fact is, it's not the situation that we're afraid of. It's the sensations. So just as the only way to get through a situation and conquer it is to face it head on, we must face the sensations head on. How do we do that? By experiencing them as sensations, without adding meaning or interpretation to them. When we can simply be with those sensations and resist the urge to interpret them, they soon become nothing. They don't mean anything. We don't have to get rid of them. They don't have to stop us from doing anything. And before long, we regain the ability to have a life. If we've had a long history with these sensations, this may take a little while, but healing is often surprisingly quick.

I'll give you an example.

One client came to me because he had been unable to get on a subway for 10 years without being heavily tranquilized. When I asked him what happened when he tried, he said that his tongue would begin to go numb and he would panic and be terrified that it would escalate to the point where he couldn't stand it.

After talking about what panic is, and about how being with the sensations is the only way out, he agreed to meet me at the subway and take a ride with me.

When we met, I asked him how he was feeling. He said he was terrified and said that he might have to get off the train if he got too scared. I said fine.

We got on the train, the doors closed, and I asked him how he was doing.

"I'm terrified," was his reply. "My tongue is going numb." I asked him if he could be with the sensation in his tongue, and he said he was afraid it would keep getting stronger. I asked him, "What's stronger? Numb is numb. The worst that can happen is you won't feel your tongue at all."

He stayed with his tongue for a couple of seconds, and then said, "But my left leg is shaking uncontrollably." "Can you let it shake?" "OK." "How's your tongue doing?" "Oh that. Fine. But my carotid artery is pounding. Can you feel it?"

I felt his neck and said that although I couldn't feel it pounding I was sure he could. "How's your leg?" "Fine." "Just be with the artery."

All of a sudden he said, "I feel fine. I'm not nervous at all."

And we rode the subway, went over a bridge, missed a stop, backtracked, walked through a tunnel and rode around for an hour, all without his feeling a single uncomfortable sensation. He was fine.

Now here's the interesting thing. The victory is not that he feels fine. The victory is that he is able to go on the subway and have whatever sensations he's having and simply be with them. So the worst that could happen is he could go on the subway and have his pounding heart, his numb tongue, his shaking leg for 45 seconds each. Or even longer. They can stay as long as they want. Since they were designed to distract him from doing things that he, as a child, thought were dangerous (on a different level – he wasn't necessarily afraid of the subway as a child, but something in the experience reminds him of it) once he looks directly at the sensations and insists on staying with them, they lose their distracting purpose and often disappear.

But what does disappear actually mean?

At one point in the ride, I said that given the fact that there were years when I myself had been unable to get on a subway, I was amazed at the fact that I was feeling nothing. But then I stopped and realized that I was in fact feeling plenty being on that crowded train. I did have some pounding in my heart. When I walked up a staircase, my legs felt heavy, and I noticed that the thought flew through my mind that I might be having a stroke. I was having all that stuff, but I didn't care at all because I wasn't afraid of it, so I wasn't even aware of it.

It's like when I was doing Broadway Shows. I didn't perceive that I was nervous before every show, but if for some reason my schedule was interrupted, if I had an interview or a meeting right before a show, I'd notice that my hands were shaking.

So in order to overcome panic, all you have to do is be 100% willing to have it, whenever it arises. In this way, it becomes a non-entity, it becomes just the sensations you're feeling, and just like the marathon runner who will never not feel the fatigue and hunger and thirst one feels at mile twenty, but continues to run anyway, these sensations will cease to have any meaning and will not stop you from doing anything. Before long you will cease to notice them, and even if you do, you will not live in fear of them.

And strangely enough, those of us who have been through this become extra-strong, because we are able to tolerate tremendously powerful sensations and a great deal of fear that others often are incapable of staying with. And it is simply the ability to stay with sensations that allows you to do anything you want to do.

CHAPTER 25
I CAN'T/I CAN

This is a process that I often assign the whole class at the end of a Thought Exchange Group. I have found it to be extremely helpful in dealing with a specific challenge or issue.

When there is something you want to achieve or see manifested in your life, take a piece of paper, draw a line down the center of it from top to bottom, write, "I Can't" at the top of the left side and, "I Can" at the top of the right side. Then write the thing that you want under each heading. For example :

"I Can't"	"I Can"
Get a book published	Get a book published

Every time you come to some point of decision in the process, write what you would do if "I Can't" were true, and what you would do if "I Can" were true. So, on this subject your list might look something like this:

"I Can't"	"I Can"
Get a book published	Get a book published
Don't reread and edit manuscript.	Reread and edit manuscript.
Don't give the manuscript to others to read.	Give the manuscript to others to read.
Don't call that publisher.	Call that publisher.
Etc.	

What we're really saying is: "If I were a person who can't have this, then I would......." and, "If I were a person who can have this, then I would....."

I recently used this process with great success in purchasing a house. I had always dreamed of living in a country house in Connecticut, and when my partner became the Minister of Unity Center for Practical Spirituality, in Norwalk, we began to think it would be practical to own a home there as well as an apartment in New York City. We didn't know how we would pay for it, but we decided to open our minds and begin looking.

In very short order, we found the perfect home for us. Two-and-a-half secluded acres with a river flowing through the property just eight minutes from Shawn's Church, five minutes from three train stations and 45 minutes to New York City. It was a dream. The price was several hundred thousand dollars more than we felt we could afford, but we decided we would open our minds and see what might happen.

So I made a chart:

"I Can't"	"I Can"
Have my dream house	Have my dream house

The first issue that came up even before making an offer, was, would I be able to get a mortgage? I already owned an expensive apartment in New York City which I had bought seven months before, and although it had increased in value, I didn't know if my financial picture would warrant me being lent more money.

But since the object of the chart was to write on the left side what I would do if I can't have the house, and on the right side what I would do if I can have the house, I wrote the following:

"I Can't"	"I Can"
DON'T CALL A MORTGAGE BROKER.	CALL A MORTGAGE BROKER.

I picked up the phone and called my attorney to get the name of a mortgage broker she liked who had given me advice in the past, called him up, told him the specifics of my situation, and asked him to look into it.

He took some facts and figures from me and told me he would call me back after he had gotten my credit report. He called shortly thereafter and said, "Have you EVER paid a bill late? Your credit report is more than perfect!" With that, he said that if I put 20% down (I'm a musician so my income fluctuates a great deal) he was positive he could get me a no-income-check mortgage and could even give me approval that day.

I was thrilled. Except now I had to find a way to get the money for the down payment. My cash was all tied up in the apartment and in stocks, both of which could not be sold at this time.

The stocks were a long-term investment I had made and were down in value at that particular time. Although, due to the real estate boom, the New York apartment had probably increased in value by several hundred thousand dollars in the previous year, I knew that the law stated that I couldn't sell it before two years without paying an enormous amount of tax. I was willing to sell it, thinking I would rent something else in New York, but that would have to wait nine months. The challenge was to find the money for the down payment. Now.

My first conflict was whether to ask my father to help me. For reasons related to my relationship with my father, asking him for money had always been a very complicated affair. Sometimes it would come through smoothly, sometimes it would be a humiliating, rancorous and confusing experience. I doubted whether he would give me this kind of money.

But I was doing my chart, so I wrote down:

"I Can't"	"I Can"
DON'T ASK DAD FOR MONEY.	ASK DAD FOR MONEY.

I picked up the phone, and with some trepidation, told my father my situation. I told him I didn't have the money, that I realized certain stocks that were held in the family trust should not be sold, that I could sell the apartment in nine months and repay the loan; but for now I needed to find the down payment and was wondering if he had access to that kind of money.

He asked me a few questions about the house, the apartment and my financial situation and said, "Sure, I know I can find if for you. There will be no problem."

It was amazing. Can you see how if I had been living inside the thought "I can't," I wouldn't have even asked him? By simply moving to the thought "I can," I went and asked a difficult question and got the answer I'd been hoping for.

Now we had to move to the offer.

We knew that the house had been on the market for six months and that the couple that owned it had already built another house, so we assumed they would be anxious to sell. Since we could not, without the sale of our New York apartment, afford anywhere near their asking price, we thought about putting in a very low bid, about $200,000 less than the asking price. We were nervous about it, but I sat down with the chart and found myself writing:

"I Can't"	"I Can"
DON'T MAKE THE LOW BID.	MAKE THE LOW BID.

Our broker called their broker and verbally gave him the offer. He turned it down flat, saying, "They need an offer at least $100,000 higher." Our realtor reported this to us, and we figured we were out of the game.

That was the logical conclusion anyway, but since we really wanted the house, we decided not to judge by appearances, or as the actress Ruth Gordon used to say, "No matter what, never face the facts." So I went back to the chart and wrote the following:

"I Can't"	"I Can"
DON'T CALL THE REALTOR.	CALL THE REALTOR BACK.
DON'T CALL THE MORT-GAGE BROKER BACK.	CALL THE MORTGAGE BRO-KER BACK.

We made the calls and they both suggested that if we went up $100,000, the negotiation would end up at a price which would ultimately be too high for us. They suggested that we do a written offer for $50,000 more, even though the sellers had asked for $100,000 more,

I went back to the chart and wrote:

"I Can't"	"I Can"
DON'T OFFER $50,000 MORE.	OFFER $50,000 MORE.

We made a written offer. Our realtor called us back and told us they still would not budge, that their realtor said they were in no rush to move (which our information said was not true) and that they would not consider the offer. It seemed as though they were not going to jump into the negotiation. Since we weren't prepared to offer more, it looked like a dead issue.

But...we wanted the house. My partner and I had a talk and realized that if we were to have this house it would have to happen in some way that we could not predict. We had said that we wanted the house at a price we could afford, and Shawn pointed out that there were two ways that could happen—they could come down in price or we could suddenly afford more.

So we wrote down:

"I Can't"	"I Can"
GIVE UP.	HOLD THE THOUGHT THAT THE HOUSE IS EASILY OURS AT THE RIGHT PRICE.

We also realized that we needed to wish them well if we wanted to live in a world where people, including ourselves, get what they want, so we added:

"I Can't"	"I Can"
HOPE THEY CAN'T GET THEIR PRICE AND ALL THEIR DEALS FALL THROUGH.	AFFIRM ALL THE PROSPERITY IN THE WORLD FOR THEM.

Holding the thought that the house could be ours at a price we could afford, I decided to look further away from New York, even though we didn't want to live that far away, to see what we could find. I made an appointment with a realtor in a more out-lying town, but as soon as I got there, I realized that this was a futile endeavor. Not only was I not seeing anything that came remotely close to the house we loved in Norwalk, but I knew from the drive that I didn't want to live that far away from New York City. But I thought, "I'm living within the thought that it's possible for me to have the house I want, so there must be a reason for this trip."

The reason soon became apparent. While I was driving around, chatting with the lovely man who was showing me houses, we got into a conversation about my New York apartment. I told him about having to hold the apartment for nine more months, but I also mentioned that I had been living in it as a renter for seven years previous to my owning it. He said that he thought that as long as it had been my primary residence for more than two years, I didn't have to have owned it for that whole time. That was news to me. I picked up my cell phone right then and there and called my accountant. She verified that as long as it had been my primary residence for three out of the last five years, I was free to sell it without paying the taxes.

This was fantastic news. I now had the possibility of getting my hands on not only the money to buy the house, but the money to furnish and fix it up and maintain a rental in New York as well.

What to do next?

"I Can't"	"I Can"
DON'T CALL MY NEW YORK REALTOR AND PUT MY APARTMENT ON THE MARKET.	CALL MY NEW YORK REALTOR AND PUT MY APARTMENT ON THE MARKET.
HOLD OFF CALLING THE CONNECTICUT REALTOR.	CALL THE CONNECTICUT REALTOR AND ASK HOW HE CAN KEEP THE DOOR OPEN WHILE WE GET THE LAY OF THE LAND WITH THE NEW YORK APARTMENT.

I called the Connecticut Realtor. He said he would call the broker and tell him that we had a potential change in circumstance and would he please keep us informed. I then called the New York realtor who didn't call me back.

I noticed I was getting anxious, so I sat still, experienced the sensations I was having as sensations, and then I went to the list and wrote:

"I Can't"	"I Can"
PUSH AND FRET.	LET GO AND LET GOD BRING THE NEXT MOVE TO YOU.

The moment I put down the pen from writing this, the phone rang and it was the realtor. He said it was a very good time to sell, and we made an appointment to meet the next day.

I opened The New York Times the next morning and there was a big article about how Real Estate was finally starting to drop, especially in the area of two-bedroom apartments, which mine was. My heart sank. Even though mine was a spectacular apartment on a high floor with beautiful views in a great building, I began to feel nervous.

So I went to my sheet and wrote:

"I Can't"	"I Can"
BELIEVE THE ARTICLE.	JUDGE NOT BY APPEAR-ANCES.

I met with the realtor, and he said, "Yes, we should put it on the market a little lower than we had planned." But he also told me it was still worth way more than I'd paid for it a year and a half before, and we should have no trouble selling it. I told him I would think about it for a few days before signing the contract.

That day at lunch, my friend Mitchell told me a wonderful story about his father. He said that years ago his father had been doing a lot of investing and spending a lot of money on new ventures, when a friend called him up and said, "What are you doing? Don't you know there's a recession going on?"

To which his father replied, "Yes, I know, but I'm not participating in it."

That story gave me a laugh and the encouragement to "Judge not by appearances."

The next thing that happened was that the weather, which had been beautiful for the previous two weeks, suddenly changed. Day after day we had clouds and rain. Since this was a "view" apartment and pictures needed to be taken of the view, it was upsetting that we would not be able to take a good picture before the advertising deadline.

But I thought of my friend Mitchell's story, and wrote:

"I Can't"	"I Can"
FRET ABOUT THE WEATHER AND WORRY ABOUT THE REAL ESTATE BUBBLE BURSTING.	KNOW THAT I DON'T HAVE TO PARTICIPATE IN THE REAL ESTATE BUBBLE— IT ONLY TAKES ONE BUYER, AND MY SALE IS NOT DE-PENDENT ON THE WEATH-ER.

The next morning, I was reading the newspaper and there was a big article about how global warming was melting the Arctic Ice Cap. The article said that although, of course, in so many ways, this was not a good thing, an odd advantage was that suddenly huge oil reserves were being revealed and becoming accessible, just at a time when oil prices were through the roof (which was causing higher interest rates and economic worries, thus contributing to the downturn in real estate prices).

It made me think, in terms of the weather, that you never know why things happen or what effect they'll have, so I wrote in the book:

"I Can't"	"I Can"
WORRY.	LET GO AND LET GOD BRING THE NEXT MOVE TO YOU.

On Tuesday morning we called our Connecticut realtor and made an offer on the house.

The owners came back with a counter offer—not a large move—but large enough to put us into the game. Looking for our next move, I wrote:

"I Can't"	"I Can"
GIVE UP, OR MOVE RIGHT TO THEIR PRICE OUT OF FEAR THAT WE'LL LOSE THE HOUSE.	COME UP THE EXACT AMOUNT THEY CAME DOWN AND KEEP MATCH-ING THEM WITH THE IN-TENTION OF MEETING IN THE MIDDLE.

With that, we came up $15,000. They had come down $10,000 and to show good faith we came up $15,000.

They came back with a price right between the two of ours and we had a deal.

On the same day, we got a call from our doorman who had heard that we were putting our apartment on the market. I told him we hadn't done it yet but we were about to. He said he had someone who already lived in the building who was interested in seeing it. We told him to send her up.

A lovely woman who had actually rented our apartment years before we had, came up, and after one look said, "What are you asking?" I told her we had an asking price in mind, but that we were going to show the apartment at an open house the following Sunday to see what the market would bear. She asked what it would take to take it off the market. I named a price that was $160,000 above our asking price, and she said, "I'll take it. And I don't need a mortgage. I'll pay cash!"

(Interestingly enough, because of the rain the previous week, which I had regarded as "bad," I had waited before signing with a realtor. Be-cause of this, when this sale came through, I had no commission to pay, which saved me enough money to install a luxurious master bathroom in the new house.)

So, we went from desiring a house with no visible way to afford it, to having the house of our dreams and selling our apartment for a record price—all by exchanging the thought "I can't have what I want" for "I am allowed to have what I want," and then consistently taking on "I Can" thoughts and taking the "I Can" actions. This outcome always existed as one of the infinite possibilities in the Great Un-Manifested, and we were able to bring it forth quickly and easily by simply exchanging our thoughts.

I have found, when I do this process, that I automatically and effortlessly make the moves toward what I want. What this does is allow me to constantly and regularly exchange thoughts that reflect as failure for thoughts that reflect as success—as what I want to see. When you're performing actions inside the thought "I Can" they become easy, unconflicted, and bring about the desired result.

So, if you have something you want to manifest and you're not sure how to do it, make an I Can't/I Can list and see what happens.

NOTE: I think it's important to be clear that the I Can/I Can't technique, or any Thought Exchange technique for that matter, is not about controlling the world or making things magically happen. It's about holding a thought or possibility in mind, taking whatever action comes to mind, seeing what happens, and no matter what happens, continuing to hold the thought and move forward until the desired result appears. As Craig Ferguson says in his wonderful autobiography, American on Purpose, "I've taught my son that we keep on failing until we succeed." Inside the thought we're holding, we keep moving in the direction we're going, and this gives us the most possibility of getting where we want to go.

Had my father not given us the money, we would have continued to hold the thought, "I Can" and sought out other ways to manifest the money until one appeared. If we, on the other hand, had gotten discouraged and exchanged the thought for "I Can't," we would have given up on finding the money and thus not been able to buy the house. Even if this particular house had sold out from under us, or if the sellers had not met our price and no further funds had become available, by holding

holding the thought "I can have my dream house," we would have continued to take actions within that thought until our dream house (in this case, another house) appeared and was ours.

PART 7

BREAKING THROUGH THE "BIG STUFF" THAT HAS HELD YOU BACK YOUR WHOLE LIFE

CHAPTER 26
THE DARK NIGHT OF THE SOUL

"The ordinary way to contemplation lies through a desert without trees and without beauty and without water. The spirit enters a wilderness and travels blindly in directions that seem to lead away from vision, away from God, away from all fulfillment and joy. It may become almost impossible to believe that this road goes anywhere at all except to a desolation full of dry bones—the ruin of all our hopes and good intentions. The prospect of this wilderness is something that so appalls most men that they refuse to enter upon its burning sands and travel among its rocks.....

And yet, strangely, it is in this helplessness that we come upon the beginning of joy. We discover that as long as we stay still the pain is not so bad and there is even a certain peace, a certain richness, a certain strength, a certain companionship that makes itself present to us.....

Then, as peace settles upon the soul and we accept what we are and what we are not, we begin to realize that this great poverty is our greatest fortune. For when we are stripped of the riches that were ours and could not possibly endow us with anything but trouble, when we rest... from that activity of knowing and desiring which still could not give us any possession of our true end and happiness, then we become aware that the whole meaning of our life is a poverty and emptiness which, far from being a defeat, are really the pledge of all the great supernatural gifts of which they are a potency."

Thomas Merton
    "Seeds of Contemplation"

Many advanced Thought Exchange students have commented that rather than getting easier, Thought Exchange can get harder and harder to do as we go along. At first this might seem strange, but upon examination, it makes perfect sense.

The more we do Thought Exchange, the more willing we become to experience the sensations that have stopped us. When we begin, we will often start with smaller issues and find, to our surprise, that we're able to tolerate these sensations and have breakthroughs. But as we work more deeply, we begin to tackle the "big guns," moving toward situations and memories that generated the sensations that we've been running from our whole lives. Even though these sensations, like all others, are harmless, they may scare us more than others, because they were so scary when they originally happened, and we may find ourselves shrinking from them or avoiding them altogether by going back to our old "protective" thoughts and behaviors.

I created the following exercise when my Advanced Thought Exchange group was finding themselves getting stuck in resistance. Although it seems simple, this is actually a powerful process that can reveal and dismantle the whole defensive structure you have built for yourself. As such, you may come in contact with sensations that you have been defending yourself against since you were a small child. It is in contacting and experiencing these sensations that true healing happens, but this process can be painful and even frightening, so if you choose to do it, hang onto your hat!

Take a piece of paper and draw a vertical line down the center. On the left side, title the column "'Negative' Thoughts That I Habitually Hold." (I put "Negative" in quotes because as I've said before, there is no such thing as a negative thought. A "negative" thought is merely a thought that produces a result that you don't happen to want. Somebody else might view the same thought as "positive.")

After you've labeled the left column "'Negative' Thoughts that I Habitually Hold," label the right column, "Exchanges."

Now, in the left column, make a list of all the "negative" thoughts you can think of that you habitually hold, that have always seemed like they are "just the way it is, facts of your life, etc." If you're anything like me, and you really do this, you may be amazed at the quality and quantity of thoughts that you carry through your everyday life without even questioning them.

Here's the list I came up with:

> I'm not allowed to have what I want.
> Ask and you shall not receive.
> I am bad.
> I can't have what I want.
> Everything gets taken away at the last minute.
> I am not the real thing.
> My dreams do not come true.
> I can't be rich.
> I'm talented and respected but can't have a hit.
> I'm a steamroller and I have to be stopped.
> My power will kill people or get me killed.
> I don't know what I'm doing.
> Therapy can't work.
> It is impossible for me to be happy.
> If I let down my guard, everything will fall apart.
> I have great principles but they don't work for me.
> I always want the wrong things.
> I can never get ahead.

Amazing, isn't it? To think that each of these thoughts is a staple of my everyday thinking. Kind of disturbing, but also very revealing. No wonder the mirror of my life shows up with so many unwanted, difficult reflections.

Once you've listed all the thoughts you can think of, read over the list again. Don't judge it, just notice it, experience it, let yourself feel what that feels like.

As strange as it may seem, although this list may look like it would be

255

upsetting, you may find that you feel surprisingly comfortable with it. The reason for this, of course, is that each of these is a protective thought that you took on to not feel the sensations you experienced when you took on the opposite thought.

I'm sure you can see where we're going. If each of these thoughts is the opposite of a thought that generated sensations that you found intolerable, imagine what's going to happen when you begin exchange them all.

I wasn't kidding when I said, "Hang onto your hats!"

So now that you've got your list, go through it and exchange each thought for one that would be more likely to reflect in the world as what you would like to see there. You don't have to believe the new thoughts. You don't have to feel good about them. (In fact, most likely you won't.) Just exchange them.

My list of thoughts and exchanges looked like this:

"NEGATIVE" THOUGHTS I HABITUALLY HOLD (that don't produce the results I desire)	EXCHANGES
I'm not allowed to have what I want.	I'm allowed to have what I want.
Ask and you shall not receive.	Ask. It is already given.
I am bad.	I am good.
I can't have what I want.	I can have what I want.
Everything gets taken away at the last minute.	Things always turn out fine in the end, so if they haven't turned out fine, It's not The End.
I am not the real thing.	I am the real thing.

My dreams do not come true.	My dreams can come true. All I have to do is let them.
I can't be rich.	All the money in the world is already mine, readily and easily available to me.
I'm talented and respected, but can't have a hit.	I can have a hit as easily as the next guy.
I'm a steamroller and I have to be stopped	What I want, and any success I have, is good for everybody.
My power will kill people or get me killed.	My power enlivens me, enlivens people and enlivens the world.
I don't know what I'm doing	I know exactly what I'm doing.
Therapy can't work.	Therapy can work.
It's impossible for me to be happy.	It's possible and available to me to be happy at every moment.
If I let down my guard, everything will fall apart.	When ever I let down my guard, everything falls into place.
I have great principles but they don't work for me.	My principles work, so if my principles, aren't working it's because I'm not living them.
I always want the wrong things.	I'm allowed to want and have whatever I want.
I can never get ahead.	It's possible for me to make <u>way</u> more money than I spend.

Over the next few days, whenever you're having a problem or something isn't going the way you want it to, refer to the left side of this list, and see if you can identify which habitual thought you are thinking that is reflecting as this problem. If you find it, exchange it.

If none of the thoughts on your list seem appropriate, stop and ask yourself, "If I am seeing this issue before me in the mirror of the world, what must I be thinking?" When you identify the thought that is being reflected as this particular problem, add it to your list and exchange it. Here are some of the present-day thoughts I found I was holding that gave me real insight into lifelong issues:

I was sitting with my partner Shawn, who happens to be a Unity minister, talking about a problem I was having with my stock portfolio. I was very worried about money and seemed unable to relax about it. He works a lot with willingness, so he asked me if I was willing to experience myself as prosperous, no matter what the apparent condition I was seeing before me was.

To my surprise, I realized that I was unwilling to experience myself as prosperous, and that to even think about doing so made me feel uncomfortable and endangered. None of the thoughts on my list seemed to cover that, so I looked deeper, and uncovered a thought that I didn't know I was holding. The thought was, "It is dangerous for me to feel prosperous." This actually made sense to me since, in my childhood, I had often had things taken away or withheld from me if I let it be known that I wanted them, or worse, if I expressed a confidence about my ability to have them.

I exchanged that thought for, "Feeling prosperous is feeling prosperous. Period!" In that way, I was letting myself know that in all the endless possibilities that exist in the Great Un-Manifested, one of them is that feeling prosperous does not have to lead to resistance or loss.

A few days later, I was dealing with another issue, and my prayer partner asked me if I could ask God for guidance. When I asked myself that question, I realized that I didn't want to do that. This led me to uncover the thought, "God always gives me the wrong answers." Now obviously that thought had to do with a history that I had of getting wrong answers from people who were supposed to be taking care of me, answers that served them rather than me. But I was applying this to spirit, to the universe, to God, and thus, in my way of thinking, to my own internal voice. Whatever the source, I had a thought that prevented me from trusting intuitive, internal guidance. Having uncovered that thought, I exchanged it for, "All the right answers are available to me right this second."

Several more incidents occurred that revealed habitual thoughts that I wasn't aware I was holding, and the final additional list (or should I say, the list up to this moment, since this is a continuous process and I'm sure I'll find new additions as I go through life) looked like this:

It is dangerous for me to experience prosperity.	Experiencing prosperity is experiencing prosperity, Period!
I'll never get it.	I've got it already.
If I want it I won't get it, so I'm not allowed to want anything	I'm allowed to want whatever I want fully and deeply, and wanting something does not cause me to not get it.
God gives me wrong answers.	All the right answers are available to me right this second.
What is there to be grateful for?	I have everything.
I always miss the boat.	There's always another boat for me to catch.
I have the wrong instincts	My instincts are excellent, if I just follow them.
People want to resist what I have to offer.	People want what I have to offer.
When I need something, it's withheld from me.	I always have and always will have everything I need.
I do all the work and don't get any payoff.	I am willing to experience the payoff.
I can't have what I want.	The world is at my service at all times, giving me exactly what I ask it for in thought.
I can't think good thoughts.	I can think any thought I want to, anytime
I'm on a treadmill moving backwards.	I can get off the treadmill any time I want to.

THE "FORTRESS OF PROTECTIVE THOUGHT"

So I had my list of all the "negative" habitual thoughts I could think of, and I'd exchanged them all. You would think that by unearthing all these long-held "negative" thoughts and exchanging them, I would get happier and happier, more and more comfortable, more secure, more sure of myself, etc. (Well, YOU wouldn't think that because you've read this book, but many people practicing many forms of "positive thinking" would think just that.)

But here's the result of doing this exercise that was very surprising to me at the time. In fact, I began to notice that the more I did this process, the more anxious I got. I actually began to think, "Thought Exchange doesn't work. It just leads you into trouble, upset, frustration and disappointment."

I brought these thoughts to my Special Thought Exchange group, and the results of working on them were revelatory.

As we began to work on my thoughts, we noticed that every suggestion that a member of the group offered was met by me with a reason why it wouldn't work. No matter what they said, I had a reason why, in my particular case, there was no way out of the problems I was in. Here was "Mr. Thought Exchange" himself, unable to exchange a thought, actually making a case for why, in my particular case, nothing could work.

As we looked at this, we began to realize that I had developed an incredibly circular, impenetrable system of thoughts which seemed designed to prevent me from ever breaking through, breaking out or finding a solution. I had actually allowed most of these thoughts to develop into beliefs, which made it impossible to exchange them (remember, a belief is a thought we think is true and thus, by nature, cannot be exchanged) and also made them manifest (since belief is the stage just before manifestation in the Thought Exchange circle.)

Taking note of this, we then asked the question, "Why might I have developed this "fortress of thought?" What was it protecting me against? (Remember, EVERY thought we take on, no matter how "negative" or destructive it may seem, we take on for a good reason — to protect ourselves from experiencing a sensation.)

Since the fortress was designed to protect me against knowing something I was afraid of knowing. it was not readily apparent to me what it was I was afraid of. But it was clear that because we had brought to light many of the thoughts that made up the "fortress," and had exchanged them, the fortress was getting shaky, as though someone had begun to lower the drawbridge over the moat of the castle, allowing the possibility that the "enemy" could get in.

We decided to go at it by seeing if we could find a thought that would go outside the system set up by the "fortress." People began suggesting things like "admitting I was powerless, letting go and letting God, etc." My question was, "What thought would allow me to do that?" I came up with the thought, "There are things outside of what I know that could be solutions to these issues." Another possible way of putting this was, "I don't know everything."

Since part of the issue was that I was convinced that if I let down my guard and allowed the fortress to crumble, terrible things beyond my control would happen that would swamp me, it was difficult for me to even think those thoughts, as thinking them brought up many sensations that were difficult and painful to stay with. But in staying with them, I began to realize instinctively, that there must be a good reason to have these sensations, even though they were painful. I then realized that it was the particular upsetting things that were happening in the present that were bringing up those sensations, which gave me insight into why I had kept on repeatedly generating the same kind of upsetting situations throughout my life. Perhaps my healing was in being able to feel those sensations that had been too overwhelming for me to feel when I was a child. So I decided to look for a thought that would allow me to stay with the sensations that came up, no matter how frightening and painful they were.

The thought I came up with was, "Bring it on!" "Bring on the pain if that's what's coming! Bring on the failure if that's what's going to happen! If I'm going to lose all my money then I'm going to lose all my money! If I'm going to lose the house, then bring it on! If I'm going to live in the street, then I'll live in the street! If I'm going to feel unbearable emotions, bring 'em on!"

As I took on this thought, very interesting things started to happen. First of all, I realized immediately that if one of the basic premises of metaphysics is "what you resist persists," then my resistance to failing, to things falling apart, to losing everything, had actually been keeping those very things in place. I realized that my whole life had been being lived as though there were things that must not, at all costs, happen, and my resistance to them had actually supported their happening. By acknowledging that it was, of course, always possible that these failures could occur, I was able to let down my resistance to them, which immediately contributed to their not persisting. Having had this realization, I now became willing to lose everything, and the grip that this resistance had on me loosened.

As a result of this, the next thing that happened was that I began to feel sensations. Lots of them. This was very difficult, because what I was feeling was the impossible pain from my childhood that, at that time, had had no way of being felt or resolved. I talk about this more specifically in Chapter 27 as the "Impossible Double Bind," but suffice to say here, it was extremely painful to feel what I felt.

As I had this realization and this willingness to feel my deepest pain, the next thing that happened (or should I say, the next thing that appeared in the mirror as a reflection of my thought) was a series of devastating failures. On the same day that I found out that a show that had been a principle source of income for me for twelve years was closing, I sustained an enormous and shocking loss in the stock market which put me below what I considered my "safety" margin (made up by me, of course) and I went to a concert of a famous star where I was supposed to hear one of my songs sung and he didn't sing it. Then I went on a teaching trip where several important Thought Exchange teaching commitments fell through because people hadn't bothered to plan them properly, and then I came home to find out that a project that was very important to me (in fact, it was this book, in a much earlier stage) had been surprisingly rejected out of hand, and my agent, who had loved the project, had dropped me as a client.

THE DARK NIGHT OF THE SOUL

All of this was enough to send me into what I have heard called "The Dark Night of the Soul." I felt totally humiliated, lost all ambition, all willingness to go on, and lived with a sense that whatever I started would only end in failure, so why start anything?

I gave up. I surrendered. I stopped trying.

I even wrote a song, the first I'd written in a long time, that seemed to perfectly express the fury, humiliation and helplessness I felt at being in this "impossible" situation.

This was the lyric.

GIVE UP
(David Friedman)

I HAVE TRIED EVERYTHING I COULD
AND I DON'T KNOW WHICH WAY TO GO
I HAVE REACHED, I HAVE RUN
I HAVE GRABBED FOR THE SUN
AND THE ANSWER HAS STILL BEEN NO

I HAVE GIVEN IT ALL I'VE GOT
AND I'VE DONE EVERYTHING I SHOULD
I HAVE WORKED, I HAVE TRIED
I HAVE PRAYED, I HAVE CRIED
AND IT HASN'T DONE ANY GOOD

NOW I'M AT THE END OF MY ROPE
AND I FIND I'M GIVING UP HOPE
CAUSE I FEEL SO EMPTY INSIDE
BUT THERE'S ONE THING LEFT THAT I HAVEN'T TRIED

GIVE UP, GIVE IN
IT'S CLEAR THAT I JUST CAN'T WIN
LET GO DON'T FIGHT
STOP TRYIN' TO MAKE THINGS RIGHT

EVERYTHING THAT I'VE TRIED HAS FAILED
EVERY PLAN THAT I'VE HAD FELL THROUGH
NOW THERE'S NOTHING TO GIVE
ME A REASON TO LIVE
AND THERE'S NO MORE THAT I CAN DO

SO I'M WONDERING WHY I'M HERE
AND I'M ASKING WHY I SHOULD STAY
IN A WORLD THAT ABUSES ME
BATTERS AND USES ME
BADLY DAY AFTER DAY

BUT THE ANSWER'S NOT IN MY MIND
WHEN I SEARCH THERE ALL THAT I FIND
IS A FUTURE BASED ON THE PAST
AND IT SAYS TO ME, SURRENDER AT LAST

GIVE UP, GIVE IN
IT'S CLEAR THAT YOU JUST CAN'T WIN
LET GO DON'T FIGHT
STOP TRYIN' TO MAKE THINGS RIGHT

GOD, I OFFER MYSELF TO THEE
GOD, IF SOMEONE IS GONNA COME THROUGH
IT'S GONNA BE YOU, NOT ME

I GIVE UP, I GIVE IN
IT'S CLEAR THAT I JUST CAN'T WIN
I LET GO, I WON'T FIGHT
I'M THRU TRYIN' TO MAKE THINGS RIGHT
IF YOU WANNA MAKE THINGS RIGHT
THEN DO IT, BUT I WON'T FIGHT
I GIVE UP

I was experiencing agonizing pain, but I realized, somewhere in the corner of my mind, that I was now, at last, feeling what I had avoided all my life—the "impossible" combination of anger, sadness and frustration that certain childhood incidents and their resulting sensations had generated. These strong feelings (anger, sadness and frustration) had been my effort to get away from those sensations, but at the time of the originating incident or incidents, there had been no outlet, no chance of resolution for them, so in order to avoid feeling them, I had spent my life diverting them into physical symptoms which gave me an excuse for stopping myself from trying and achieving things I knew I could achieve. This tactic might seem ridiculously self-defeating, but it served to keep me away from situations that might generate the sensations of which I was terrified.

At the same time, however, I was, constantly bringing up situation after situation that would generate the original sensations so that I could experience them, be with them, and have an opportunity to master them. But the moment they would come up, they would seem to be too much to bear, so I would sidestep them. Now I was feeling them, and I thought I might die.

This realization resulted in an unconscious exchange of thought (from "It is impossible to be with these sensations" to "It is possible to be with these sensations") which immediately reflected in the world as people saying things to me that assisted me in moving through and staying with the emotional journey on which I had placed myself. These things had, perhaps, been said to me before, but within my new thought (which I was unaware of at this point) I was able to hear them.

There were several things that people close to me did that were helpful. My partner Shawn, finally "got" how in pain I was, and instead of trying to fix me or snap me out of it, just said to me, "This is an important healing. I'm here. I'm with you. Feel away. And, by the way, know how much I love you and how good you are."

My friend Mitchell said that when he had been in a similar crisis he had made it through by holding the thought "There is something after this."

My prayer partner, Hami, suggested that I do the open inquiry of simply asking the question "Why am I here" without attaching myself to results.

I also held onto the thought, "Bring it on!"

My therapist pointed out that as a child, not only had I had these enormous sensations and the resulting feelings thrust on me, but somehow the situation had been so repressive that I couldn't even allow myself to know I had these sensations. So it would stand to reason that having them come into my awareness would be terrifying and bewildering and feel endangering to my very life. He then went on to point out other times when I had thought I would die if I came into awareness, and in fact didn't (like the years I'd thought that if I found out I was gay I couldn't go on, only to eventually become extremely comfortable with, and in fact, happy about, being gay).

Two more things that Shawn said also proved extremely helpful. When I was in such pain that I felt that I couldn't go on, he quoted the axiom, "Stick around for the miracle." He also pointed out that, just as had been the case with the founders of Unity, with Edwene Gaines, with Ekhard Tolle and with so many other mentors I admired, my own healing would be the catalyst for really doing my work on a large level, and only when I was able to walk through the fire of my own healing and come out the other side would I really be able to take my message to a larger audience.

All these things helped me to continue walking forward, doing whatever was in front of me without hope or enthusiasm, but nonetheless, doing.

EXPERIENCING AND BEING
WITH THE SENSATIONS

Just at this time, in one of my Thought Exchange classes, someone brought up an issue that gave me an important key to what I was going through. Melanie (not her real name) said that her problem was that she could not allow herself to love someone she really cared about. If she had one foot out the door or was ambivalent, she could date someone and show affection, but if she really cared for someone, it was too dangerous. When I asked her what the danger was, she said that she could be hurt. When I asked her what would happen if she was hurt, she said she would have to kill herself. I found that response curious, interesting and unusual.

I asked her about her childhood hurts, and got a story of major abuse and rejection, both physical and emotional. When I asked her what her reaction had been, in her childhood, when she had been so abused, she again said, "I always thought of killing myself."

A thought came to me, and I said to her, "I've had this thought out of left field, so reject it if it doesn't apply to you, but it occurs to me that if you were so abused, it must have generated an enormous amount of helpless anger that had nowhere to go. Is it possible that the reason you thought you'd have to kill yourself is that if you were to be in touch with your anger you would kill someone else?"

She burst into tears of recognition and said, "That's totally it."

So I asked her, "If you were hurt and were extremely angry, what would you have to do." Her immediate response was, "Kill myself."

I then asked her, "If you were hurt and extremely angry, and you didn't have the option of killing yourself, what would you do?" And she answered, "I'd have to kill someone else."

I then asked her, "If you were hurt and extremely angry, and you didn't have the option of killing yourself, and didn't have the option of killing someone else, what would you do?" And she answered, "I guess I'd have to disassociate from the feelings."

And I then asked her, "If you were hurt and extremely angry, and you didn't have the option of killing yourself, didn't have the option of killing someone else, and didn't have the option of disassociating from your feelings, what would you have to do?"

Melanie thought for a long time, as if stumped. Then the light bulb went off and she said, "I guess I'd have to feel my anger." There was a new light in her face, and I knew at that moment that even though she was potentially in for a rough ride, she had started on the path to healing and recovery.

This incident in class helped me to understand that I too had to feel the sensations that lay under my tremendous anger, frustration and humiliation. As I went through the next few weeks, I would notice that at times, my anger and thoughts of humiliation would be so great that I would think about killing myself. At those times, I would remind myself that one of my options was to simply feel the sensations that I was using that anger to avoid, and I would move back into them. Then I would sometimes notice that I was thinking about killing all the people who had hurt and disappointed me. When I'd notice these thoughts, I would remember that one of my options was to simply feel my sensations, and I would move back into them. At times, I would be in such pain that I wanted to take tranquilizers or sleeping pills to just stop being me and disassociate for a while. When this happened, I would remind myself of Melanie and remember that one of my options was to simply feel my sensations and notice my thoughts of anger, frustration and humiliation.

I stayed in this state for several weeks, barely getting by, just doing the basics, still without hope or enthusiasm. During this time I couldn't even exchange thoughts, or should I say, I refused to exchange thoughts, because I was so angry and feeling so hopeless that it seemed futile to do so. So I just stayed where I was and felt it.

But in the corner of my mind, I wondered why I was unable to simply exchange thoughts, why I had to insist on staying in this darkness. There must be a good reason.

A conversation with Pat Brody, my best friend since childhood and now a brilliant therapist, revealed the answer.

Learning To Take "No" For an Answer

Pat, who of course knew what was going on with me, called me to find out how I was doing. I told her that I was in this place where my world was falling down around me, nothing seemed to be going right, and I was so hooked into it that I couldn't even seem to exchange any thoughts. In some way, I was insisting on being in it. Together, we decided to look at why that was.

Pat had been my friend since childhood, and as such, had been present throughout those years to see first-hand what they had been like for me. She pointed out to me that one of the main things that was said to me as a child was, "You have to learn to take no for an answer." What this actually meant, when it was said to me, was, "When you get a no, you are not allowed to express any feelings about it, you have to just bury it." At the times when I didn't do that, when I dared to express dismay or upset or anger at getting a no, I was physically hit and things that were important to me were taken away from me.

Thus, every "No" generated powerful sensations that produced big feelings that had no way to be expressed, and the threat that if those feelings were expressed I would be in physical and emotional danger.

Very quickly, I began to not even let myself know that I had those sensations and feelings. By the time I was five I developed a tic disorder and an inordinate panic about death. By the time I was eleven I developed heart palpitations that prevented me from running or overexerting myself. (I had been the fastest runner in my class up to that time, something I was very proud of.) By fourteen I was in a relationship with a girl (even though I was clearly gay, something I could not let myself be aware of.) By twenty I was married to her, and within a couple of months I was in a mental hospital. All to avoid the sensations I would get when I would hear the word "No."

Throughout my life, I noticed that the pattern had been that I would move toward something I wanted, and then, when I got close, my anxiety would overwhelm me and I would, in some way, walk away from it just as I was about to get it. In the context of Pat's and my conversation, I realized that I was always avoiding the possibility of "No" because the combination of gigantic sensations and repression that "No" caused seemed too much for me to bear.

The other thing I knew about my life was that time and again I would bring up situations where I could feel that "No," only to shrink from it. I suddenly realized that the whole point of my getting myself into the situation of closed doors and complete frustration that I was in now was to give me the opportunity to feel and be able to tolerate, or as I like to say, withstand, the complex and difficult sensations and feelings that "No" brought on.

The next night, in our Thought Exchange Group in Connecticut, I realized, in a flash, that the Thought Exchange I had recently made had been, without a doubt, the most important one I'd ever done. For the first time in my life, instead of trying to get away from that "No," instead of trying to make something appear that would allow me to sidestep or overcome the "No," I made a thought exchange that plunged me right into it.

Without being aware of it, for my whole life since childhood, I had held the thought, "It is impossible to take no for an answer." Since every endeavor in life potentially involves some form of "No" making the possibility of receiving a "No" ever-present, this made it impossible for me to achieve the things I wanted to achieve, impossible to stay the course in navigating difficulties, and ultimately impossible for me to have anything important to me, because the threat of having it taken away was always there, and the sensations and feelings that might come with that take-away seemed impossible to bear.

By exchanging the thought, "It is impossible to take no for an answer" for, "Bring it on!" I was, for the first time, facing what it felt like to be in my initial childhood predicament. In doing that, I was reclaiming my ability to feel those "unfeelable" sensations and feelings and thus reclaiming my ability to move toward my dreams and tolerate whatever happened on the way to them.

Knowing this, I understood the brilliance of how I had engineered an all-doors-closed situation for myself and brought myself to a place of complete frustration and hopelessness in my life. It was only in this place that I could truly feel these sensations and feelings, with no escape, and have a chance to heal.

I sat still and resigned myself to just feeling as angry and hopeless as I felt for as long as I felt it. Suddenly, I became aware that small disappointments generated huge hopelessness, and I just sat and felt that. I noticed the sensations I was having. I noticed how angry I was. I didn't judge it. I didn't act it out. I didn't try and get rid of it. I just felt it.

Coming Out The Other Side

Gradually, as I stayed in this state, some realizations began to dawn.

By staying inside the "Fortress of Thoughts" that I had built and refusing to exchange them, I experienced a life filled with failure and pain and thwarted ambitions. Gradually, as I looked at this, I began to connect with how much power I was wielding by being in this "Fortress of Thoughts." I looked at my life and realized that through my thoughts alone, I had actually been able to project a life that made my every ambition turn out wrong, that made me not have things I said I wanted, that made me fail time and time again, and that superseded my talents and my ability to use them. Even though the situation seemed completely negative, when I was able to stay with my "negative" thoughts, I was able to experience how powerful my thoughts were, and how unerringly they were appearing in the mirror of my life. I didn't yet feel ready to exchange them, but at least I was connected to the system and how it works.

Fortunately, through this whole time, I was teaching Thought Exchange, so I was constantly being exposed to the principles. And since life is nothing more than an exact reflection of our thoughts, guess which issues kept coming before me time and time again? Mine!

271

After one session, I suddenly remembered that if the world was just a reflection of my thoughts, then the serious failures and rejections I'd been experiencing had to be simply reflections of my thought, and were not being done to me. At this point, although the events were still painful, I was able to say "thank you" to the people who had perpetrated them, because I realized that these people were merely reflecting back to me the thoughts of failure and lack of self worth that I was holding, so that I could see them and have an opportunity to exchange them.

Resigned to stay in the sensations that the big "No" I had put myself in were generating, I began to notice, over time, that I was getting more accustomed to them. The sensations didn't change, but my ability to tolerate them did. When you're a child, a ten minute wait may seem intolerable. As an adult, we have the ability to wait ten minutes. The wait isn't any shorter, and our feelings of irritation may not even be any less, but we have the ability to tolerate them, usually to the point where we don't even notice them or where they don't affect us. A child might be unable to allow him or her self to wait on a line that long, while an adult can easily do that if what's at the end of that line is something he or she wants. Same situation, same sensations, more ability to tolerate them.

So, with all hope gone, with a complete willingness to tolerate the "impossible" sensations that I had resisted all my life," and with no more resistance to failing or losing everything, I had nothing to lose. I didn't feel good, I wasn't excited about anything, I couldn't see how any of my dreams could come true, but I was able to live in and tolerate (or withstand) all of that.

GENTLY HOLDING THOUGHTS

My life in the outside world still looked as hopeless and bleak as ever, and every time I tried to do anything to change that, or even tried to think of doing something to change that, the pain would come up and the outside world would continue appearing as it had. Knowing that no matter how I feel, thoughts are what cause the outside world, I wondered, "How can I take on and hold the thoughts that I know will produce the results I want, when the moment I take them on I experience such pain and such "negative" thoughts?"

I realized that the only way to do this was to separate the thoughts from what I was presently feeling, what I was presently believing and what I was presently seeing manifested in the "outside" world.

Often, when we take on a thought, we then keep looking at our sensations or into the "outside" world to see if it's "working." The very act of doing this is an act of doubt, so that doubt immediately shows up as a reflection in the world, because you can't fool a mirror. We also often try to use thoughts to "fight back" against what's happening in the world, but that would be like fighting against our own reflection in the mirror. If we did that, our fight would immediately be reflected back to us, and that's what we would see in the mirror. So I decided that the only way to deal with this, to get back on the path of thinking thoughts that would be reflected as what I wanted to see in the world, was to just "gently hold the thoughts," without expecting results, without checking results, and without hoping for anything or trying to feel better. In other words, while all my pain was happening, while all the failure was happening, all I would do would be to "gently" hold the thoughts of what I wanted to see in the world.

The day after I'd made this decision, my prayer partner, Hami, asked me what my prayer for the day was. The best I could do was to say, "I pray for the willingness to be willing to be willing to hold new thoughts while experiencing all that I experience when I hold them." This was a fragile but important step. I wasn't even ready to be willing, or ready to be willing to be willing. But for the first time, I was on the path to holding the thoughts I wanted to see manifested in the world, no matter what I was presently feeling or seeing in the world. I had isolated thought from sensation, belief and manifestation.

What happened in this state was that I took my attention off the "hopeless" outside world, and even, whenever I could, off my sensations, and began to focus exclusively on the "inside" world of thoughts. I thought to myself, "Well, I can't seem to make anything happen in the outside world, so I might as well just think thoughts for the sake of thinking them."

I decided to start off each morning thinking through a list of thoughts that I wanted to see manifested, no matter how I felt when I woke up. I would "gently" think these thoughts, not trying to make them happen, not trying to change my sensations, not checking to see if they were being effective. I would just think them.

<u>Some examples of the thoughts on my list were:</u>

- I'm allowed to have what I want.

- It's possible to have what I want.

- All the money in the universe is available to me right now.

- There is something after this.

- My Thought Exchange book is published by a major publisher and is a best seller, no matter what circumstances look like at this moment.

- The shows and CD's I'm working on can be extremely successful, no matter what has happened in the past.

- It is possible for my dreams to come true.

- What has happened in the past has nothing to do with the next thought I choose and what happens in the future.

- Now, is all there is.

For those times when I really felt overwhelmed, I decided to choose one thought that would encompass all these thoughts. That thought was:

- Anything is possible.

As I'd go through my day, when I would come across a thought of lack or of impossibility, instead of going to the outside world for evidence as to why that thought was "true," or trying to act in some way to keep myself from feeling what I felt when I thought that thought, I simply felt the sensations that went with the thought, and exchanged the thought in my mind, without expecting a result in the outside world or even paying any attention to the outside world.

Freed from the burden of having to see or make things happen in the outside world, I was now working solely in the realm of thought. This looked, in many ways, the same as the process looked before I had gone through my "dark night of the soul," but there was an important difference.

In the past, I would take on a thought that I thought would manifest as what I wanted to see, and immediately my "impossible" sensations would come up. Being unable to tolerate those sensations, I would be unable to stay with the thought, and would quickly exchange it for a thought that would ease my anxiety, but would not result in what I wanted to see in the world.

Now, when I took on such a thought, I would still come across my "impossible" sensations. In fact, I would even "expect" them. But when they came up, I could say, "Oh, there are those sensations again," feel them, notice that I was holding the thought that everything was hopeless, and exchange the thought back to the thought I wanted anyway.

So I was just holding thoughts and allowing the universe to be however it was, my life to be whatever it was, and my sensations to be whatever they were.

I was working in pure thought.

Although I was not paying attention to the outside world and not expecting anything from it, I began to notice, out of the corner of my eye, that things were happening. I had wanted to increase my coaching practice, but for the past year it had just sat at one or two clients a week. I'm not quite sure how it happened, but somehow I was now seeing 9 or 10 clients a week. Yes, I had been sending out emails, offering private coaching sessions, and being pro-active, but I had only been doing whatever came to mind, and not doing anything I didn't feel like doing.

I began to get braver, and remembering that we always have the choice to think any thought, I let myself think thoughts that completely flew in the face of what I was seeing in front of me. I had been having some difficulty getting my book published (not more than most people have had finding an agent and publisher, but remember, I had been a person who couldn't take "No" for an answer) so I just took on the thought, "My book is published and a best seller" without at all concerning myself with how that would happen.

Again, out of the corner of my eye, I began to notice that people were coming up to me with suggestions for agents, people in my classes were spontaneously talking to me about how they got their books published, and I began running into best-selling authors and other people who could help me.

I took on the thought, "It's possible," and completely stopped watching the stock market. Of course, this involved me being able to tolerate that I might lose all my money, in addition to tolerating my thoughts that nobody is taking care of me, but with my new-found willingness to tolerate those thoughts and sensations, and my willingness to lose everything ("Bring it on!) I could do that. My stocks began coming back.

I took on the thought that all the shows and CDs that I was working on and that had been so stalled, could be produced and successful. Meetings about those shows began appearing. With those meetings came all my sensations that I had been interpreting as anxiety and hopelessness, and my thoughts that I wasn't allowed to have anything, that everything was a ruse, and that it would all be taken away from me at the last minute. I was able to tolerate those sensations, and keep exchanging my thoughts back for those I wished to hold, without looking at or caring about results. And since I wasn't focusing on the outside world, but on the inside world, if this was all a ruse and everything was going to be taken away from me, then so be it. With that in mind, I could hold the thoughts that these projects could be successful, and feel the sensations that came along with those thoughts.

This was a completely different life, lived on the inside, where our lives actually take place. As I allowed myself to take on any thoughts I wanted, free of resistance to the outside world or to the sensations my thoughts provoked, the outside world, of course, began to mirror those thoughts, and my life began to look as I had dreamed it would look. But I wasn't even concerned with how the outside world looked, so I didn't even celebrate or get excited about those things. I began to know that they were just reflections of the internal world of thought, where life is really being lived, and that's where I stayed. Life, which had always been a roller coaster, became calmer, more serene. I began to feel like an artist, sitting in front of blank canvas, deciding what I wanted to paint and painting it.

This journey not only brought me to a healing of life-long issues, but deeply and thoroughly answered what has always been, for me, one of the most complex questions about the whole "positive thought" movement. For years, in book after book and seminar after seminar, we've been told that our thoughts control what we see in the world, that "laws of attraction" are the way of the universe, that if we think "positively" then "positive" things will happen. We all know this and yet time and again, year after year, we don't put it into practice.

In going through my "dark night of the soul" I got to know, first hand, why we have such trouble holding the thoughts we want to hold, and what it actually takes to hold those thoughts and heal. The thought will assuredly bring about the result, but with it comes all the sensations and other thoughts that must be experienced while holding the thought, and this can often require great bravery and perseverance. But the thing that I learned during this "dark" period was that no matter how difficult it may seem, no matter how frightening and discouraging it may feel, IT CAN BE DONE. Now there's a thought!

So whenever you're ready, make this list, and step onto the roller coaster that may scare you, may lead you through "the valley of the shadow of death," but will ultimately let you off with a freedom and healing that you have never before allowed yourself to experience.

CHAPTER 27
YOUR INNER CHILD
WHEN THE OLD THOUGHTS AND SENSATIONS PERSIST

As we've seen throughout this book, when we begin to exchange our thoughts that are reflecting as manifestations we don't wish to see in the world for thoughts that might reflect as what we do wish to see in the world, sensations that we experience as upset and anxiety often arise. We know that the key to allowing our thoughts to move around the circle into Belief and Manifestation is to be able to tolerate or withstand these sensations, so we do our best to stay with them and keep exchanging any other thoughts we have around them for the thought we would like to see appear in the world.

Sometimes, however, the sensations are so strong and so persistent that we have great difficulty staying with them, no matter how hard we try. Along with them, we notice that our thoughts keep returning to thoughts of fear and anxiety, and we feel like we're losing our ability to exchange those thoughts for the one we want, because the one we want produces so much upsetting sensation.

In my Thought Exchange Workshops, person after person has reported that they go through life with the same underlying anxiety, panic or thoughts of unworthiness, and no matter how many workshops they take, no matter how many positive affirmations they repeat, no matter how many successes they have, these sensations, thoughts and internal voices persist.

If you're continuously having thoughts and sensations of anxiety, upset, fear and unworthiness that seem extremely out of proportion to the situation or that have persisted throughout much of your life, and these thoughts and sensations have seemed to stop you from being able to function as a successful adult, it's most likely that they are a child's thoughts and sensations.

If you think about a little child having a tantrum, or a little child who has been hurt, you realize that the child cannot be reasoned with, cannot be talked out of its sensations, and that forcing the child to just face things or barrel through or "be strong" will only serve to damage the child. Furthermore, if you are irritated with the child, or if you abandon the child so that you can go about your business, the child has no way of dealing with the issues at hand other than to either scream louder, or suppress the sensations, go inward, and as a result, never deal with them. As this child goes through life, this unresolved hurt will come out as panic, upset, physical symptoms, inappropriate attempts to get attention, and failure.

Many of us, as children, were treated just that way by our parents, not necessarily because they meant to hurt us, but often because they themselves had unresolved childhood issues. As a result of this, we are walking around with screaming, un-cared-for inner children. I know, for myself, I often feel that I'm on a plane, conducting an orchestra or teaching a class, with a screaming infant constantly distracting and up-setting me. For years, I didn't know what to do about it. If I tried to ig-nore it, it would appear as physical symptoms. If I tried to let myself be the infant, I would become non-functional. Nothing seemed to work.

BEING WITH THE PHYSICAL SYMPTOMS AND SENSATIONS

With the realization that the anxiety and the physical symptoms we experience are the child in us trying to get our attention, I set out, in a Thought Exchange Workshop, to explore ways in which we might be with, deal with and assist the child.

I began by asking everyone in the group to close their eyes and notice their physical sensations, zeroing in on one uncomfortable sensation that seemed most prominent. If any thoughts arose, I asked them to simply notice them and go back to focusing on experiencing the sensa-tion. After a short while of just being with the sensation, I asked people to open their eyes and continue being with the sensation.

After describing the sensation (in physical terms—buzzing, tingling, pain, pressure—as opposed to "feeling" terms like angry, sad, hopeless) I asked people to take on the thought of something they really wanted, something they dreamed of being, having or doing.

When they had that thought in mind, I asked them what had happened to the sensation. In almost every case, the sensation had escalated, had gotten "worse," had gotten stronger. This was surprising to many people. So often people think that if they take on a "positive" thought, they will feel better, but this is often not the case. In fact, it is my contention that this escalation of symptoms when we take on the thought of what we want, is the number one reason why we don't hold onto that thought.

So we had to look at why this happens and ask the question, "What is the purpose of these symptoms?"

THE PURPOSE OF PHYSICAL SYMPTOMS

When we take on the thought of what we want, and immediately begin to experience an escalation of anxiety and physical symptoms, our complaint is often something like, "Why do I have to have these sensations? Will they continue for the rest of my life? How do I 'get rid' of them?"

So we asked ourselves, "Why are these sensations here? What is their purpose? What does having them accomplish?" We realized, from retracing the experience we had in the meditation, that what these sensations did was prevent us from (or at least try to interfere with) our taking on the thought we wanted to take on. Why would they do that?

BECAUSE THE THOUGHT WE'VE TAKEN ON WAS DANGEROUS TO US AS A CHILD, and our inner child, who has the memory of the consequences of having had that thought, is doing everything in its power to get us not to think it. And the only way it can get our attention is through physical symptoms and anxiety.

For so many of us, in our childhoods, we got into trouble, were punished or were ignored, when we "dared" to be too excited, too happy, too full of ourselves, too expressive of our feelings. The child inside us sees us doing this in the present, and it sees danger, even though there is no danger to the adult. And we, so often, think that it is the adult that is afraid, or think that there is some real danger because of the sensations we feel, which are really the child's protestations. And we exchange away our thoughts of excitement or possibility for ones that will prevent us from going in the direction of these things that we desire.

So these sensations are like a child standing by our side, pulling at us, telling us that it's afraid to do something. Let's say a child had been hit by a car while crossing the street. You now want to cross the street with that child, and he or she is screaming, "Don't do it. I'm afraid. We're going to get hurt." It's a child. It doesn't know that adults have ways of crossing the street that are safe. It only knows that it was hurt.

What would you do with that child? Ignore it and let it scream? Be irritated because it's preventing you from crossing the street comfortably? Tell it it's ridiculous, there's nothing to be afraid of and drag it into the street kicking and screaming? Lock it in the closet? Put a pillow over its head? Can you see that if you did this, the child's anxiety, panic and screaming would have to escalate? But this is what we do with our own sensations (inner child) all the time.

So what do we do? One way to get the child to stop screaming is simple, and we often do it. We just say, "OK, we won't cross the street." The child will now be temporarily relieved and will probably calm down, BUT WE DON'T GET TO CROSS THE STREET, and this will leave us, the adult, in a state of stoppage and frustration. Another thing we do is say, "I'm too anxious to cross the street. If only I didn't have that sensation, I could do it, but because that sensation is 'attacking me' I can't." It seems like the sensations are punishing us, but they're not. They're the child warning us of what it has perceived (and truly experienced) as danger.

So what do you do with the child? What any good parent or caretaker would do. You sit with the child, you hear it, you honor it and understand how it feels. And then, you gently hold the child and take it across the street, knowing that its feelings are legitimate, based on its experience, but also knowing that there is a safe way to cross the street. And just because you did it once wouldn't mean the child is now fine. You might have to do it a lot. But the object would be for the child to learn, THROUGH ITS OWN EXPERIENCE, SUPPORTED AND HELD BY YOU, that it could handle things, handle how it feels to cross the street, handle what it takes to look both ways and then cross when it's safe. And the child would learn.

So the way to allow the "child" of our sensations to "grow up" is to simply be with these sensations. But since these sensations remind us of a time when we were in danger, we often instantly jump away from them into "protective" thoughts ("I can't do it, this will never happen") or into explanations of why we can't do it. To not do that is to put down the "drug" of protective thought and to be with "the pain" which, for an adult, though possibly uncomfortable, is handleable.

Once we are able to be with the sensations, we have complete freedom to hold whatever thought we wish to hold, and thus to see anything we desire manifested. One member of The Thought Exchange, who often gets a sensation in her stomach that she interprets as upsetting, impossible and life-stopping, came up with the thought "I can stomach this." Within this thought, something that she has, in the past, interpreted as life-stopping, becomes merely a tolerable sensation, so she is free to take on any thought. The ability to do this is what leads us to true liberation from the past (by incorporating it, not getting rid of it) and freedom in the present.

THE INNER CHILD MAKES A SURPRISE APPEARANCE

A surprising occurrence at the end of one of our workshops gave me some important keys as to how to handle and heal this Inner Child using Thought Exchange.

We were near the end of a Thought Exchange workshop, and were struggling to find a thought exchange for one of our members who was experiencing a lot of abuse at work. Suddenly, another member, we'll call her Karen, interrupted and said, "I'm sorry, but I'm feeling so activated, I have to speak." This was a very unusual occurrence, so we asked the person working if he was willing to be interrupted for a moment, and he said it was alright.

Karen then proceeded to tell us that she was so upset by the problem this person was having that she felt she needed to fix it for him. I pointed out that what she was saying was that in order for her to be comfortable, someone else had to not have a problem. This quickly led us to understand that in Karen's childhood, her caretakers were so fragile and undependable that she had to try to fix them and keep them in good shape if she was to have any hope of being taken care of by them. This, of course, is not what parental caretaking should be, and spoke of a condition where, when her little child was in need, she was essentially "parentless."

I suggested that Karen might look at what her own internal issues of fear were, rather than trying to fix something outside herself, and immediately she began weeping uncontrollably, writhing, stuttering and exhibiting neurological twitches in her face and neck. She began screaming that it was too painful, that it hurt too much, that she couldn't take it.

It was apparent that what we were seeing was a young child without any parent to contain it, and the pain was enormous. I said to her, "I'm talking to a child, aren't I" and she responded, "Yes." I gently told her that I could see how much pain she was in, and I asked if I could speak to the adult that I knew was also sitting there. At first she said "No, I don't want you to," and I realized that to her, an adult must be her mother, and given her history, she had no desire to have her mother present. I told her that we saw her, and asked, gently, once again, if I could just speak to the adult for a moment. She said OK, and in one second the twitching stopped, the facial expression completely changed, and there was a fairly composed adult sitting in front of me.

I asked the adult if she knew that the child was so upset and she said, "Yes, but I have trouble contacting the child." At this point the child burst out and said, once again, how painful it was, as the neurological symptoms returned. I asked for the adult again, and the adult immediately reappeared. At that point she said something like, "God, everyone's going to think I'm so crazy."

I asked the class, "Who identifies with what they were seeing before them?" and every single hand shot up. Although it might not always appear so dramatically, everyone in the room had the sense that there was a child who had upset emotions and great fears occupying the same space as the adult they appeared to be.

I then asked Karen, "If you were to see a child in the kind of pain your child is in, suffering the kind of abuse your child suffered, what would you do?" She immediately answered, "I would know exactly what to do. In fact, I saw a child on the subway who was clearly being talked to in an abusive manner, and I thought, 'Give me that child for a couple of months and I could heal it.'"

I asked her if she could tell her child that, and she again said, "I'm having such trouble contacting her." It was clear that I had a multiple personality on my hands, but unlike some multiples, at least the child and the adult knew about each other. But the child was keeping her distance from the adult because the child feared the adult, and the adult was keeping her distance from the child because of the pain the child held which the adult preferred not to know about.

I suggested that the adult just tell the child, "I can take care of you. I know exactly what to do for you." After some hesitation, the adult said that to the child. Immediately, the child appeared and, although still apprehensive, seemed calmer.

I told the child that she was not alone, that she had a mommy who was in the same body as her and who was always here to help her and who could not be separated from her. It was clear that the damage we were dealing with here was very early, from a time when a child shouldn't even have had to know that her source of nurturing was separate from her, so that the child, who was helpless, could not have even thought that there was a possibility that she could not be taken care of.

My telling the child that there was a mommy with her all the time who was inseparable from her seemed to calm her even more, so I asked for the adult again and the adult readily appeared. Since the adult had said that she knew what to do for the child, I asked her what she might do at this moment to nurture her. She said that after class she would go buy the child a big cookie and they would go home and watch a Ricky Schroeder movie together.

EXCHANGING A CHILD'S THOUGHT FOR AN ADULT'S THOUGHT

As we were leaving class, one of our long-time members commented that what we had just experienced seemed to shed a whole new light on the core of what Thought Exchange work was.

I thought about the significance of the Adult/Child relationship, and came in the next week with some new exercises to test how this might apply to Thought Exchange.

I began the class with the usual meditation where I asked everyone to remind themselves that they are in and part of The Great Un-Manifested, asked them to look around and choose one thing they would like to see manifested, move toward it, occupy the same space as it, and open their eyes knowing that even with their eyes open they were still in the Great Un-Manifested, occupying the same space as that which they desired, with Everything that was invisible still around them.

I then asked people to write down what it was they saw as the thing they wanted to see manifested. We went around the room, and each person read theirs aloud. (As always, I gave people the option that if for any reason whatsoever they chose not to share what they had picked, they could simply pass.) We heard the usual assortment of thoughts about health, achievement, relationship, etc.

I then asked each person to write their thought at the top of the page, and write below it all the thoughts that came up when they thought that thought. We then went around the room, and as expected, most of the thoughts were thoughts of fear, anxiety, "This can't happen; Who do I think I am wanting this?" etc. There were also some thoughts like, "This could be fun, I can do this;" and some mixed thoughts like, "I'm scared but also excited."

I then asked everyone to go down their list of thoughts and put an A next to all those thoughts that were an adult's thoughts, and a C next to all those thoughts that were a child's thoughts.

As we went through the thoughts, it was apparent that all the anxious, worried, self-deprecating thoughts were a child's thoughts, based on experiences the child had had or things the child had been told. Some people thought that some of their worried thoughts were adult thoughts, things like, "You'd better get a move on if you want to have success," or "If you're going to be lazy you're not going to get anything done." But as we looked more carefully, we realized that these thoughts were based on things that had been said to us, as children, by people who we deemed to be adults, but who were actually talking from their own wounded child place. We made the distinction between "Adult" and "Big Person," or "Grown Up," one being a person who actually was an adult, the other two being people who, although they were in big bodies, were functioning from their own child place.

There were some thoughts like, "Ooh, this is fun" or "I can't wait to do that," that seemed to be child's thoughts. When we looked carefully at them, we realized that these were, in fact, thoughts that we had had as children that had been nurtured and supported so that we could bring them into the present. With this in mind, we labeled them adult thoughts that we had kept with us from childhood.

I then asked everyone to go back to their original thought, the thing they had spotted in the Great Un-Manifested that they would like to see manifested, and write down any adult thoughts they could come up with that pertained to it. Each person then read a list of adult thoughts that included nurturing thoughts like, "I know you're frightened of organizing the apartment, but I know how to do it, so let's go buy some plastic bins and we can sit down together and decide what goes in each of them," or, "You don't have to do it perfectly," or, "You have the skill to do that," or even just, "You're good."

We suddenly realized that when we do a Thought Exchange, we are invariably exchanging a Child's Thought for an Adult Thought. The Child's Thought is always a protective thought, taken on to keep the child (and us as adults) away from a sensation that the child has deemed to be intolerable and dangerous. This Protective Child's Thought has been producing the same result that the un-parented, unhealed child got when the original trauma or upset occurred. In order to see a different result, we have to exchange that thought for an Adult's Thought which is unfettered by the trauma. That adult is always present in us, but so is the child.

So here's the revelation. Up until now we had been exchanging our old thought for our new thought and trying desperately to hold onto the new thought, hoping the old thought wouldn't come back. Invariably we would find that the old thought kept returning, and so we learned that every time we saw the old thought, we would simply exchange it for the new one. But with our new insights into the presence of a child and the Child's Thoughts, we now realized that there had to be a constant "Exchange" between the Child and the Adult so that the child could "Grow Up," be healed, and become incorporated into the adult.

For instance, if you had a child who was afraid to cross the street, you could give it the thought, "It's perfectly safe to cross the street." But that thought would not suddenly allow the child to cross the street, and certainly would not allow the child to cross the street without fear. You would have to recognize the child's fear, gently take it by the hand, tell the child it's safe, put your arm around the child and walk it across the street. The child might be very afraid, but that fear would not make you afraid, nor would you have to have the child not be afraid. You would recognize the child's fear and, with your thought and your holding, help the child to cross the street. Once the child had crossed, the child might still feel fear, and you might have to repeat this process a hundred times. At some point you might say, "Are you ready to try crossing alone?"

You would hold the thought that it's perfectly safe, the child might now have some of that thought, but not all, and you would stand at the curb and watch the child cross. The child might get scared and run back to you, in which case you would hold it, repeat your Adult Thought that it's perfectly safe, and send the child off again. After a number of tries and a gradual letting go, with you always holding the thought that it's safe, the child would eventually let go of the thought that it's unsafe, be an experienced street-crosser, and take on once and for all the adult thought you gave it.

As we discussed this, people in the group started to report experiences in which their child had been ignored by their parents. Someone related that when he had learned to swim, he had simply been thrown in the water and told to figure it out. He had, in fact, learned to swim, but swimming was always associated with a feeling of trauma and fear. In another case, someone's mother had sat across the room, refusing to help, as the little boy had to figure out how to tie his shoes. The mother thought she was making him strong, and in fact, he did learn to tie his shoes all by himself. But tying shoes always had an element of abandonment and pain attached to it, something he wasn't consciously aware of, but which appeared as "free floating" anxiety or tension.

So when we see something in our lives that we don't like, and we experience anxiety when we choose a new thought, we know that we have been holding a Child's Thought. In order to see something we want, we know that we must exchange that Child's Thought for an Adult's Thought. When that Adult's Thought produces fear and anxiety, we know that that is the fear and anxiety of the child. So we go back and forth, noticing and acknowledging the Child's Thought as just that, a Child's Thought, choosing our Adult Thought, noticing our sensations, acknowledging what part of the Child's Thought is still there, exchanging it for an Adult's Thought, and back and forth.

This understanding gives a new meaning to the term "Thought Exchange." Not only do we simply exchange one thought for another, but there is a constant and ongoing exchange of thoughts between the adult and the child. As we continue to make this exchange, the child "grows up" and heals from trauma, and our sensations (or, more accurately, our perceptions of those sensations) begin to match our thoughts more closely. This makes for smoother, easier manifestation, and more importantly, for the healing of childhood wounds.

WRAPPING OUR CHILD'S THOUGHT IN ADULT THOUGHT

With this understanding in mind, I set out to create a chart that would be the map for how this new kind of exchange occurs. By following the steps here, we have a new and powerful way to tolerate and heal sensations and thoughts of anxiety and fear that come up. I will use an actual example that came from a private Thought Exchange session.

A client was setting out to do a creative project that she had dreamed of doing but on which she had procrastinated for a long time. When she looked at what was in front of her, she saw the thought, "I can't do it. I'm not good enough."

She exchanged that thought for:

NEW THOUGHT
"I can do it"

This thought immediately produced the sensations that were interpreted as anxiety and fear.

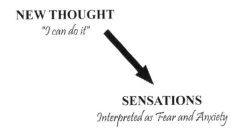

NEW THOUGHT
"I can do it"

SENSATIONS
Interpreted as Fear and Anxiety

My client noticed that immediately a new thought appeared. That thought was, "I can't do it. My mother would kill me." It became clear that she had taken on that thought to quell the anxiety that was brought

290

up by the thought "I can do it." If she couldn't do it, she wouldn't have to take any steps that might lead to her experience whatever anxiety she had experienced when she had tried to take similar steps as a child.

So the chart now looked like this:

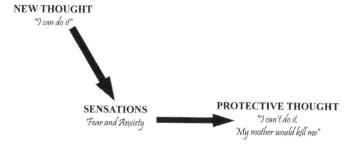

If we stay with the protective thought, the protective thought will generate new sensations that are perhaps more comfortable (since we're not asking ourselves to step into territory that was previously perceived as endangering to us.) These sensations would lead us to the belief, "I can't do it," and the Manifestation we would see would be, "I can't do it."

It would look like this:

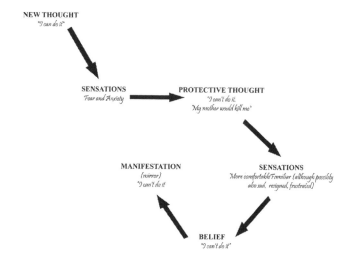

The way to not have this new circle be formed is to notice that we've exchanged the new thought, "I can do it" for the protective thought, "I can't do it. My mother would kill me," and exchange the protective back for the thought we wish to hold.

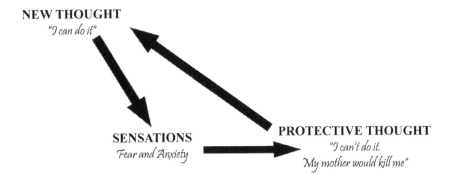

NEW THOUGHT
"I can do it"

SENSATIONS
Fear and Anxiety

PROTECTIVE THOUGHT
*"I can't do it.
My mother would kill me"*

Hopefully, as we kept doing this, we would become more and more able to tolerate the sensations that came up, and be able to move on through the circle to Belief and Manifestation.

However, if we go around the triangle a few times and find that the anxiety continues and we can't seem to hold the new thought, we know that we have to do more work with the Child's Thought. So we take the Child's Thought and we "surround" it with Adult Thoughts. It's like asking the question, "If this child had a group of adults surrounding it, helping it, what would the adults be saying?"

Our chart might now look like this:

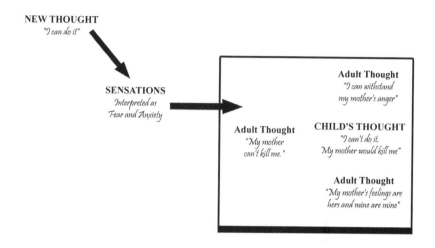

As these Adult Thoughts dialogue (or "exchange") with the Child's Thought, the child begins to feel safer. You then can move this whole box into the position where the sensations are, and gradually, with the help of the Adult who is not simply obliterating and replacing the Child's Thought, but is listening to and holding the Child's Thought, the sensations will become more and more tolerable, and it will be easier to move on through the circle through Belief to Manifestation of the thought "I can do it."

So the end result would look something like this:

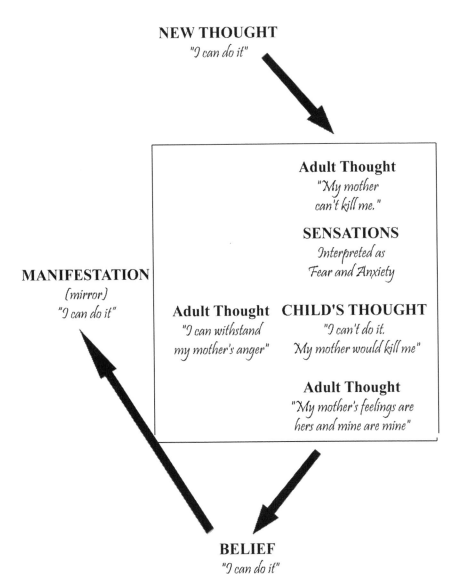

WHEN YOU'RE WORRIED ABOUT THE FUTURE, LOOK TO THE PAST

There is an axiom in psychotherapy, that if you're worried that something terrible is going to happen in the future, it has to be because it has already happened. Otherwise you wouldn't know to worry about it.

Sometimes, when something upsetting happens, we find ourselves having thoughts like, "I'll never make it, I always fail, I'm not allowed to have money."

If we look at these thoughts, we can immediately see that they can't be true. We have no way of knowing what's going to happen in the future, no matter what has happened in the past. So why do we choose to take on thoughts like these?

Perhaps it's because these upsetting occurrences remind us of upsetting occurrences that happened in the past. Those occurrences brought up sensations that we were afraid to feel, and at the time, probably couldn't have tolerated feeling. In an effort to heal, we've spent our lives generating situations that bring up the same sensations, only to run from them because we think we can't tolerate them. These are often big sensations, sensations that bring on thoughts of terror or isolation or panic. If they weren't, we wouldn't have run from them, and we wouldn't continue to run from them today.

So we take on a thought that points us toward the future, away from the past where the sensations were. The future is something that still has hope, we still have the chance for it to be different, while the past and the sensations it contained, has already happened in the past and can't be changed. The fact that the past has happened, the "damage" has been done and can't be undone, may seem like a hopeless situation, but the healing is in being able to experience those sensations, not avoid them, not set them aside, not lament why they shouldn't have happened, not try to overcome them, just feel them. Once we are capable of simply being with the sensations from the past, even if the same things happened to us again, we would be able to experience the sensations, handle the situation, and move on. If this were the case, we would not be afraid of the future in the same way, because we would know that we could handle it.

So the next time you find yourself having a fearful thought about the future, try exchanging that thought for, "What I'm experiencing is a memory." Then ask yourself, "What happened? What happened that I'm remembering, that I felt this way about at the time?" Think about that, and feel the sensations you felt as it was happening. Not your thoughts about it, but your sensations at the time. Then think about what it would have been like to have an adult present to hold you or comfort you or listen to you as you had those sensations.

The amazing thing is, in my experience with numerous people who have done this work, that the moment we truly begin to consciously experience the sensations from the past, our adult steps in and holds us. Automatically. And as the adult holds us, those sensations get felt, and we heal.

The other wonderful thing that happens is that when you know that the anxiety and fear that you're feeling are from the past (triggered by the present but not about the present) and your adult is helping your child deal with the sensations from the past, the present and the future become a level playing field. By that I mean that suddenly your level of anxiety is appropriate to the actualities of the present situation, and you become aware that no matter what has happened, there are infinite possibilities open to you. You get to use your adult capabilities and function as an adult.

By being aware that it is a child's memory that is experiencing the anxiety, and by really allowing that child to feel those sensations in the presence of and with the support and empathy of your Inner Adult, you "grow up" that child and integrate it into your adult self. You are now looking at the world from the present, not through the filter of trying to avoid old sensations that keep coming up.

Feeling Sensations means
FEELING Sensations

When I began working on this book, I had been in psychotherapy, on and off, for several decades. In that time, I had uncovered and worked on many traumatic incidents from my childhood. I had analyzed them, I understood why they'd affected my life as they had, I'd made the connection between what those incidents had taught me and how I lived my life today, I'd cried about them, I'd hit pillows, I'd complained about them, I'd struggled with them, I'd spoken up to my parents about them, I'd done EMDR, Somatic Experiencing, Bioenergetics and other trauma-releasing techniques, I'd read books and taken seminars, and yet, I was still not free of them. I was still repeating and repeating situations in which the same sort of things were happening to me, I was still depressed, and I still had a bleak and limited view of the future based on the past.

In the course of doing this work, I suddenly realized that the problem was that I was trying to get away from the sensations connected with these incidents, trying to "release" them, trying to get over them, trying to get rid of them. I was doing everything except just experiencing them. I realized further that the reason for this was that I was still holding the underlying thought that these sensations would swamp me, overwhelm me, or even kill me if I were ever to feel them.

From the child's viewpoint, this was perhaps true. So it could be said that I was still living my entire life from the perspective of the child who had been injured. As I began to go back to these incidents in a new way, I realized that the point was simply to FEEL them.

So, for instance, my mother's death had been something that I'd never processed. Try as I might, I couldn't feel much of anything for her. I attributed it to her emotional distance, to ways in which she hadn't protected me as a child and, in fact, had even supported situations that caused me to be physically and emotionally endangered. Another factor in my avoidance of experiencing my mother's death was that it came so closely on the heels of my long term partner suddenly leaving me. I was still feeling overwhelmed with those sensations, and thus felt that I couldn't allow these additional ones in. But even with all this, the fact is, I loved my mother, and yet I could feel nothing.

When I went back this time, to the day she died, I just closed my eyes, went through the day, and felt what it felt like to suddenly be called to the hospital, to find that my mother was behind a curtain being intubated for two pulmonary embolisms. I could hear the nurses yelling at her to stop resisting. I could hear her choking, but I couldn't see her. Shortly thereafter, my mother went into a coma and she died 9 hours later without my getting to speak to her. As I looked at her lifeless body, I wished I could stand there and speak to her for an hour, but nurses were there, my father was anxious to go, and I didn't get the time. As I went through the eyes-closed experience of being back there, I felt the sensations that I would have interpreted as panic, overwhelming sadness and the feeling of rage, all of which I had suppressed in order to "get through" the traumatic event.

As I stood there, in my mind, looking at her lifeless body, I began to cry, and the thought, "I'm sorry" came to mind. I suddenly experienced, first hand, the sense that I always had to take care of my mother, that I had to take the brunt of any anger that was directed at her, that I had always felt sorry for her and felt helpless to help her. I felt what it felt like to have a mother who I felt sorry for. It wasn't about the words, it wasn't about the explanation, it was about the experience of the sensations that went along with those thoughts.

I was finally feeling the sensations that I hadn't felt at her death, and that I had immediately suppressed in order to take care of my father and in order to feel like I could go on. I was now feeling them in the presence of an adult, my adult, inside of me, and I was able to tolerate them, have them, have compassion for them, and know that I could feel these sensations and be alright.

After this, I began to go through many other incidents, some from the recent past, and some from my childhood, and just sit in the sensations that came with them. I realized that it was the fear of experiencing those sensations that kept me from moving forward in my life, into other areas where those sensations might arise. By going back and actually experiencing them, and realizing that I could simply be with them, I was not afraid to encounter them in the future.

So, after years and years of therapy, I realized that what I had thought was feeling my feelings (or more accurately, my sensations) had actually been talking about them, analyzing them, and trying to run from them or get rid of them. I was finally going about the business of reclaiming my sensations, making them part of me, incorporating them. The word incorporate, which comes from a combination of in and corpus, which means "body" seemed particularly apt. I was taking back parts of me that I had separated and split off from myself. I was becoming one integrated being, with less and less mysterious feelings that I had to split off from, avoid and not know about. I was putting my sensations back into my body, into the same place as the rest of me.

So when you have thoughts of fear about the future, and you go back to see what incident in the past it actually refers to, try just sitting with the incident, eyes closed, not talking about it, not analyzing it, just feeling what your body feels like, feeling what your psyche feels like, and experiencing the physical and emotional sensations as pure sensation.

This is what an adult does. A child complains about them, wishes they hadn't happened, tries to wriggle out of them, tries to make whatever it perceives to be the outside cause of them stop happening, and then continue with and tries to find ways not to feel them or to never go near situations that might bring them up again. An adult simply feels them and incorporates them into his or her experience, thus always returning to a state where anything is possible.

It's not the analysis, not the understanding that provides the healing. It's the ability to simply experience and tolerate the sensations. And with an inner adult, an adult who has the awareness that all thoughts exist and that we are capable of choosing any of them, you can experience and tolerate these sensations, and heal in ways you may have never imagined.

AN EXAMPLE OF THE "IT'S A MEMORY" PROCESS

Ellen (not her real name) is an actress who was struggling with an inability to get herself to go to auditions. She exchanged many fearful thoughts for thoughts like, "It's just an audition, I can do this," but she always experienced so much anxiety that she couldn't stay with those thoughts, and would exchange them back.

I asked her to write, on a piece of paper, the thought, "I go to a Broadway audition."

I then asked her to write down all the thoughts and sensations that came to her when she had the thought, "I go to a Broadway audition."

Most of the thoughts were thoughts of fear and anxiety and self-hatred. A few were thoughts like "This could be fun" and "I can do this."

I then asked her to look at each thought and sensation and ask herself, "What happened that I felt this way about in the past that is the source of my having this thought and sensation?" She came up with many things that had happened with her mother, things she had been told as a child, upsetting experiences where she had been neglected, deserted or criticized.

We were doing this Thought Exchange at my house in the country, so I asked her to take her list of things that had happened and walk around the property and notice how she felt when she read that list.

When she came back, she reported that she felt a deeply disconcerting sense of being nowhere, of not having her feet on the ground, of not being "here." It was a sense that she always had tried to avoid, by being ambitious, by taking on thoughts of fear about the future and then trying to conquer them, and by failing at things or not being able to do them.

The amazing thing she reported was that after a few moments of feeling this very upsetting sensation, another part of her came in and said, "I'm here. We're right here. Wherever that is." This she recognized as her adult self.

With all this anxiety placed properly in the past and being tended to by her adult self, she noticed that when she thought about going to an audition, she had the natural amount of concern and anxiety about it, knowing that it might go well, it might not, it might be scary or it might be fun, but whatever it was, her life was not in danger, and she could handle the outcome.

She was now on a level playing field, and could do what she wanted to do and have whatever experience she might have.

FINDING YOUR INNER ADULT

Sometimes, when the Inner Child is extremely activated, we feel like the adult isn't there. I once said to a therapist, "I can't find the adult. What if the adult isn't there?" to which he responded, "You can read, can't you? You can drive a car? You can dial the phone?"

The fact that there is a being present who can do these things is a sign that there's an adult there. The Inner Child would be too young to know how to read, write, or perform other adult tasks.

Another way to find your inner adult is to call him or her up on the phone. I had a client who was always "reaching out" to people, making phone call after phone call for advice in an effort to feel better when he felt emotionally activated or thought he might be in trouble. I suggested he keep two phones on his desk, and when he felt the need for support or advice, pick up one phone and call himself on the other. Putting one phone in one ear and one in the other, I suggested he ask for advice in one phone and see what advice he gave in the other phone. (You don't have to actually make the call. You can just hold the two phones, or one hand to each ear for that matter.) He was very surprised to find out that when his Inner Child called his own Inner Adult, the Inner Adult had everything the child needed. And unlike other adults (and as is often the case, when he was making these calls, he was often finding other people's child selves at the other end of the line) his Inner Adult was always with him, always available, and was an interested party in everything he was experiencing and everything he ever had experienced.

Because our Inner Adult is capable of being with sensations that the Inner Child has been unable to be with, our Inner Adult has access to all the thoughts that are possible in the universe. Without having to feel a certain way or believe them, our Inner Adult can search the Un-Manifested for whatever thoughts might be helpful to hold the child. They are always there. The anxiety and panic are what the child is feeling. The adult does not have these same interpretations of circumstances and sensations, so no matter what is going on with the child, the adult is capable of holding these thoughts and experiencing, with the child, what the child is experiencing.

WHEN YOUR INNER CHILD IS UPSET, SPEAK TO IT AS THE PARENT IT NEVER HAD

Children, properly heard, properly mirrored and properly supported, grow up. If your Inner Child is upset or frightened or "unable to cope," it can only be because the child did not have adequate adult support when he or she encountered situations that were too hard to handle for a child alone. It's too late for that child (now in an adult's body and an adult's circumstances) to get outside adult support, but as we've seen, there is one adult who is always with the child and has the inside track as to what that child has been through, what that child is feeling, and what that child needs. You.

Think about a child in pain. If you encountered one, you would know exactly what to do and what to say to soothe it. You would hold it. You would tell it you were here. You would tell it that everything is going to be OK. It's amazing how easy it is to do that for another child, and how difficult some of us find it to do for our own Inner Child. So if you're having difficulty finding the right words to say to your Inner Child, think about what you might say to another child, and then say it to your own.

Settle the Inner Child in your arms, and tell it things like, "I'm listening; It's OK sweetheart. You're safe. I'm here. You are not alone. I'm here and I know. You've got my attention." Keep talking until you find the thought the child needs. You'll know you've found the right thing to say or do when you experience the child calming down. You'll know you've found it when the child calms down.

EXPERIENCING SENSATIONS WITH THE CHILD

I think it's a point worth stressing, that when the adult is caring for the child, he or she is experiencing sensations <u>with</u> the child. Not <u>as</u> the child. Not <u>for</u> the child. When the child is crying, the adult is not just watching and holding. The adult is crying along with the child. An adult can do this without becoming a child, so the child can know that it is being safely held while at the same time knowing that its sensations are being felt in the adult, which helps the child to feel real and feel that he or she is being seen.

SENSATIONS – THE LINK BETWEEN THE ADULT AND THE CHILD

When a child is frightened of something that the child could actually do if he or she weren't frightened, what the child is really frightened of is the sensations associated with doing that thing. The child experiences a sensation, and the sensation signals the child to stop doing something, to not go near something, to be afraid of something.

For instance, if a child has been frightened by an oncoming car, the child might respond by being afraid to go near the street. If a child has been burned on the stove, the child might respond by not going near the stove. If a child has been unreasonably or painfully thwarted when he or she asked for something, the child might, for the rest of his or her life, even as a grownup, never ask for things in the same way again.

It's not that the grownup could not figure out how to cross the street, or learn to use a stove without getting burned, or ask for something and either tolerate the "no" or learn how to negotiate until the "no" turns to a "yes."

It's the child within the grownup that remembers the sensation and thinks that it must be avoided at all cost, even though the sensation is now harmless.

A good analogy for this is the Invisible Fencing that pet-owners often use to keep their dogs within the boundaries of the property without using a real fence. The perimeter of the property is wired with an underground electrical fence that sends a mild shock to a collar worn by the dog as the dog gets closer to the edge of the property. This shock is not at all dangerous, but the dog has learned to shy away from it as a sign that there is danger in going closer to the fence.

There are dogs who learn to tolerate this sensation, and these dogs simply run right through the fence. And once they do it once, and have the experience that there is no danger there, they can easily tolerate the sensation, and can no longer be contained to the perimeter of the property. They are free, by virtue of the fact that they were able to tolerate a meaningless, albeit uncomfortable sensation, and move forward anyway.

In order to be able to break through to doing things we've been afraid to do, the only thing we have to be able to do is tolerate the harmless, meaningless sensations that come with doing those things. The question is, "How does a child, who has come to believe that these sensations are dangerous, learn that these sensations are, in fact, harmless, and learn to tolerate the discomfort?"

The answer is, the child has to be taught this by an adult. And, the best way this can be done is for the adult to take the child's hand and say, "See, I'm feeling the same sensations that you're feeling, and I can do this while feeling them. While holding my hand, so can you."

So whenever we, as an adult, see ourselves reacting to situations as though we were a child, we must know that it is the child within us, the child who remembers history as a child, who is really having that reaction. And we, as the adult, must go to the sensation that the child is afraid of, the sensation that the circumstance generates, mentally take the hand of the child, and say, "See? I can take this. Let me lead you.

Let me go through the experience with you to show you that it's OK."

The problem originally developed because when we were traumatized as children, no adult took our hand and told us this. Because of this, that part of us remained traumatized, adapted in the only way a helpless child could adapt (by avoiding the sensations and any situations that might create them) and never grew up.

But the situation is far from hopeless. We can grow it up now, with our own adult self doing this for the inner child. And it's the best way to do it, because our adult self is always with the child, and has actually experienced, first hand, everything the child has ever experienced.

So whenever you experience being unreasonably frightened about something, know that it is actually your Inner Child that is frightened, not your adult self. Take the child's hand, experience the sensations with the child, and you will soon see that childhood part of you grow up and merge with the adult, who you actually are in the present.

OUR INNER ADULT AS "GOD"

As I watched people work and did my own work with exchanging Inner Child thoughts for Inner Adult thoughts, I was struck by the resemblance between the qualities of the Inner Adult and the qualities that both New Thought and traditional religions attribute to God. Whether God is thought of as inside us or outside us, God is often described as the One who knows our every need even before we do, and can give us whatever we wish for if we just ask. In New Thought, God is located inside each person. It occurs to me that if Thought is the cause of what we see before us, and all you have to do is Exchange a thought to see whatever you wish appear in your experience, then your Inner Adult is, in a certain sense, your inner experience of God. With every possible thought available to us, with nothing being impossible, perhaps when we contact our Inner Adult we are actually contacting our experience of God. Like God, our Inner Adult is an ever-available source of comfort and healing, having the same omnipotence for our Inner Child as parents have for young children and the concept of God has for so many people.

PART 8

STORIES, METAPHORS AND POINTS OF INFORMATION

CHAPTER 28
HELPFUL HINTS, IMAGES AND REMINDERS

As I've taught Thought Exchange and walked through my own life, I've encountered numerous stories, situations and images that I have found helpful in clarifying the approach to life that I've discussed in this book. Some of them came through me, some through others. Here are a few of the ones that have been most helpful to me.

At times, they may seem to be repetitive or to be saying the same thing, but like religions, which are all basically different ways of leading us to the same place, I have tried to offer as many angles of understanding as possible. Any time you're experiencing a circumstance where a new way of looking at things might be helpful, browse through them and see if one or two of them might offer you a fresh insight into the situation.

MONEY CAN ALWAYS BE FOUND IN UNLIMITED SUPPLY (IN THE GREAT UN-MANIFESTED)

As I said earlier in this book, we are all part of the Great Un-Manifested. Some things, like us, are showing, and others are not and need to have the light shined on them to be revealed. One of my favorite images I use when I want to feel abundant, is the image of wading through piles and piles of money. Money is all around me, up to my waist, so much so that it's almost difficult to walk through it. This is more than just an image — it is actually true.

There is an unlimited supply of money in the universe, equally available to everyone. Like thought, nobody owns money, it appears temporarily in the hands of those who have the thought that they can have it, and then it goes back into the Un-Manifested, to reappear elsewhere.

ORDERING OFF THE MENU

Another way of describing the Great Un-Manifested, where all things already have been created and exist, is to use the image given from the bible of "A table has been set before you." I was using this image in a class I was teaching, describing how there is a table with everything you could ever want and not want, and all you have to do is order anything you want and it is there. A very funny actor who was taking the class, raised his hand and said, "Waiter, I'm ready to order. I'll start with one bad relationship, and then, as soon as I finish that, would you bring me another? On the side, I'll have some poverty and maybe a little bit of illness, and that will be fine for now." We all found that hilarious, but in fact, that's what we often do. We can order anything we want, and through our thought, our orders often look very much like that.

THE BOAT DOCK

When I came across the idea of the Thought Exchange and personified it as a store, I began to construct a whole town in my mind. In addition to the Thought Exchange, where you could go 24 hours a day and return any thought, no matter how long you'd had it or how worn out it was, and exchange it for any other thought, I began to think, "What else is in this town?" I realized that of course there was a bank with unlimited money available, for the taking, to anyone who asked. And I also realized there was a boat dock where at every second there was another boat leaving to every destination to which you might want to go. If you "missed the boat," you simply got on the next one.

NEVER LOST

The boat dock was inspired by an experience I'd had at Hertz® Rent-a-car in Dallas, several years before. I was renting a car in Dallas and they were in the early stages of testing the Global Positioning Systems that are now standard in so many cars, so they offered us a free trial of the "Never Lost" System. The way it worked (as most of us now know) was that you had a little computer screen, and you punched in your desired destination, and what route you wanted to take to get there. (scenic, shortest mileage-wise, most highways, fastest, etc.) The machine would then draw you a map, and would actually talk to you out loud, saying "get in your right lane, get off here, turn left, etc;" guiding you until you reached your destination.

This, in itself, was amazing at the time, but the most extraordinary part to me was that if you went off the path, a voice would say, "You are off the path." When this happened, you simply pushed a button and the machine reset to show you how to get to your destination from where you now were. There was NO SUCH THING as not being able to get where you were going, no matter HOW FAR off the path you had gone. This, philosophically, was an exciting and enlightening concept to me. It meant that no matter how much I'd tried and failed to reach my destination, no matter how lost I had gotten, there was ALWAYS a way to get where I wanted to go. How comforting!

You're On A Chessboard

This image, that elucidates the Never Lost idea in another way, came to me during one of the Thought Exchange workshops. If we think of the world as a large chessboard laid out on the floor (sort of like the one in the first Harry Potter movie, but with an infinite number of squares) we can see that we are standing on one square, and the goal we are moving toward is on another square, perhaps just a few squares away, perhaps on a square way across the board at the other side of the room. Although there is a clear, straight path from the square we're on to the square across the room, we don't have to know all the steps, we just have to take the next one. So let's pick a goal, like say, to get a book you've written published. Here's what the chessboard might look like:

				GETTING A BOOK PUBLISHED		
	WHERE I AM NOW					

Now, looking at this, can you see that from where you are, there are eight possible moves you can make? (Actually, the number of moves you can make is infinite, but for the visual purpose of this example we can see eight.

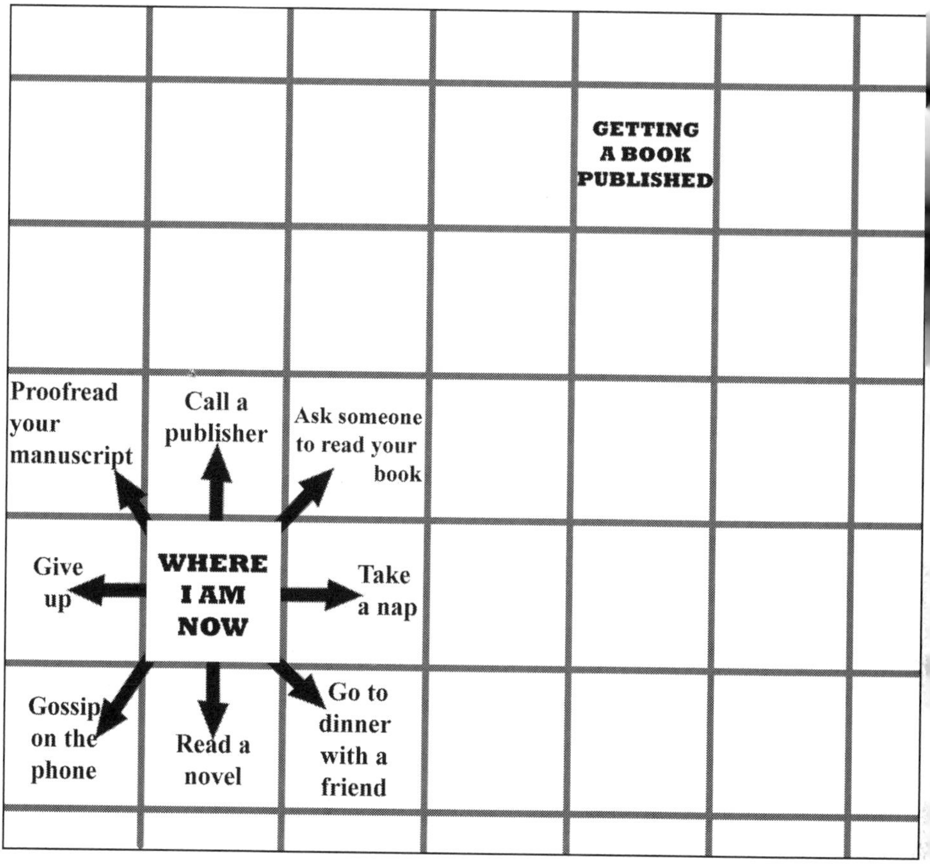

GETTING
A BOOK
PUBLISHED

Proofread your manuscript

Call a publisher

Ask someone to read your book

Give up

WHERE I AM NOW

Take a nap

Gossip on the phone

Read a novel

Go to dinner with a friend

Some of these moves may appear to be moving "toward" the goal, some of them "away" from it. But can you see from this diagram that every time you make a move, you now have eight more choices (actually infinite) to make, and that there is never a time when you can't get to where you're going from where you are, even if you've made a million "wrong" choices?

So the way your path might ultimately look could be something like this:

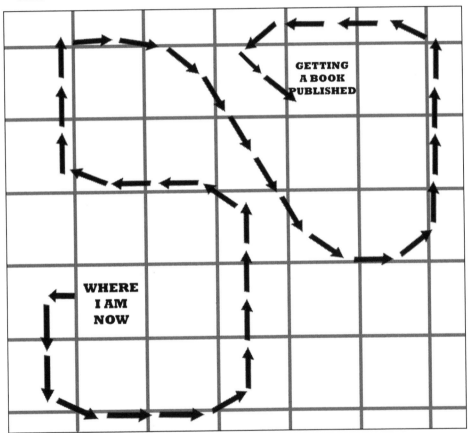

Isn't it comforting to know that you don't have to know the whole path? You can just take one step at a time, see where you are, notice the infinite steps that are available to you, take the next step, and no matter how many "mistakes" you make, you can always get to where you're going by simply holding the thought and taking the next step within that thought.

WHAT YOU WANT ALREADY EXISTS

When you're having trouble coming up with a thought that is a statement of truth, not just a wish for something to be true, you can always acknowledge that what you want already exists, in possibility, in the Great Un-Manifested. The best and most common use for this is when dealing with illness. So often, we affirm "I'm already healed." I've always had trouble with that. I think, "If I'm already healed, why do I still have the condition? Am I ignoring it, pretending it's not there?" It's never made sense to me. But what I know is true is that the cure for my condition already exists in the Great Un-Manifested. So if I take on the thoughts, "The cure for my condition already exists; The cure for my condition is already here; My condition is already cured in the Great Un-Manifested," all of those statements are true and allow the light to shine on the cure and bring it forth.

IT IS POSSIBLE

Another version of this is, "It is possible." Whenever we have trouble knowing that we can do or have something, we can always look in the Great Un-Manifested. Since EVERYTHING exists there (even though we don't see it) we know that what we're looking for is there, and thus know that it is possible that it will be revealed. You can always exchange a thought that contains "It is not possible" for a thought that contains "It is possible," knowing that this is not just a wish, but that it is truly already there in The Great Un-Manifested.

Recently, I had a wonderful opportunity to use "It is possible" at an airport. I arrived an hour before my flight, checked in at the curb, and was told by the skycap, "You'd better get to the security line as quickly as possible. It's long." I walked into the terminal, and was dismayed to see a line that snaked back on itself six times and then extended the whole length of the terminal, around the corner and all the way to the back of the building. As I reached the end of the line, I realized that it might take up to two hours to reach the front. My plane was departing at 10:59, which was about 40 minutes away. At that moment I "knew"

I was going to miss my plane. I began thinking, "This damn airline. I always have trouble with them. Now I'm going to miss my flight. How am I going to reschedule? I wonder if maybe I should just go home and cancel the concert." (I was flying to Birmingham, Alabama to participate in a benefit concert for an organization I had performed with the year before.)

Suddenly, I remembered The Thought Exchange. "OK," I said to myself, "If the world in front of me is a mirror of my thoughts, what am I thinking?" And I had to admit, all the thoughts I was thinking were thoughts that would be extremely likely to appear in the world as my missing my plane.

Looking into The Great Un-Manifested, I of course realized that it had to be true that there were many ways, already in place, to make my plane. I immediately exchanged all the thoughts I was having for, "It is possible for me to make my plane."

About two seconds after I thought this thought, a representative of the airline walked by, announcing, "Who is on the 11:10 to Memphis?" I said, "I'm on the 10:59 to Birmingham." He said, "Come with me," and proceeded to escort me and several other people to the front of the line and through security. I easily made my plane.

I couldn't have known that this was how this would happen, but by holding the thought, "It is possible," I left myself open to all the possible ways in which I could make my plane. Had I been holding my thoughts about missing the plane, it's possible I would have heard the airline employee say Memphis and not spoken up, since I was going to Birmingham.

It was a wonderful lesson in how immediately our thoughts are reflected in the mirror of our lives.

IF YOU THINK YOU CAN'T....YOU CAN'T

The following exercise is a simple yet powerful demonstration of the power of a thought to stop us from doing even things that are easy for

for us to do.

Try this. Sit down, think the thought, "I can't stand up." Refuse to exchange that thought for the thought, "I can stand up, "and while thinking "I can't stand up," try to stand up.

Amazing, isn't it! You cannot stand up while thinking the thought I can't stand up. In order to be able to stand up, you MUST have the thought, "I can stand up."

If you were able to stand up, it's because you exchanged the thought for, "I can stand up." If you did that, try it again, and really refuse to exchange the thought.

If we can keep ourselves from standing up by simply thinking a thought, imagine how many other things we're perfectly capable of that we're keeping ourselves from doing simply by holding the thought that we can't.

The next time you find yourself "unable" to do something, look at what you're thinking, exchange the thought, and see what happens.

You Can

Years ago, I was spending some time performing in Los Angeles, and I was miserable. I was at a club I hated, living in inadequate quarters, newly coming to terms with my homosexuality and feeling terrified in the promiscuous Los Angeles environment, and in general, having a breakdown. My New York therapist at the time happened to be in Los Angeles, and after having a session with him, I drove him to the airport. He was returning to New York and I was staying in California for two more weeks. As we pulled up to the terminal, I stopped the car, turned to him and said, "Ed, I feel like when you get out of this car I won't be able to go on." He looked me in the eye and said, "I know.............Bye."

He got out of the car, and I drove away and went on. It was a fantastic lesson. What he was saying was, "I know you're having a sensation, and based on that sensation you're taking on the thought that you can't go on, but thinking that you can't go on doesn't mean that you can't go on. You and I both know that you can go on. All you have to do is be willing to have that sensation." He didn't tell me not to feel the sensations or not to have the thoughts. He didn't tell me I was ridiculous for having either the sensations or the thoughts. He simply acknowledged that I had the thought, and that it was just a thought, not the truth. It was a wonderful way for me to experience that sensations are just sensations. When one takes on a new thought, it's important to remember this, and just have the sensations you have, while also knowing that it is not the sensations that are determining your abilities or your actions. I had a strong sensation that I was interpreting as, "I can't go on," but that in no way prevented me from going on.

ANY INCIDENT CAN BE PART OF ANY OUTCOME

Jane (not her real name) is a successful actress who had been out of work for some time. When we explored the thought she must be holding in order to be seeing that reflection in the world, she realized that she had been holding the thought "This is not for me."

She exchanged that thought for the thought, "This is for me," and inside that thought, began to get the sense that she was going to do well at auditions and that her next job was right around the corner.

Things seemed to be going along well, until one night she called me, distraught, to tell me that her manager had just informed her that because she had not been getting jobs lately, he was dropping her.

Jane had all sorts of thoughts about this: that she wasn't good enough, that her temperament or her excess of enthusiasm in the past had caused her to make enemies, that she would now have to start to push and shove and work overtime to get work, that she would never work again, etc. We made an appointment to meet the next day and work on it. When Jane came in, I said to her, "Let me tell you two stories."

Story #1: You're holding the thought that you're going to get a lot of acting jobs, and the next thing that happens is your manager drops you. You exchange the thought, "This is for me" for "I am not good enough and cannot get what I want." Inside of that thought, you begin pushing, writing letters, fighting your way into auditions, giving people the impression that you are desperate, and alienating those who thought you were too pushy to begin with. You get no work and you quickly run out of money and are forced to give up your apartment and live in the street. Homeless and destitute, you soon have to turn to prostitution to support yourself, become addicted to heroin, and six months later, you die a horrible death from an overdose.

(Sound familiar? I notice that sometimes I can go from, "I missed an appointment" to "I'm going to lose my house and die" in about 3 seconds.)

Story #2: You're holding the thought that you're going to get a lot of acting jobs, and the next thing that happens is your manager drops you. You notice that you've exchanged the thought, "This is for me" for "I am not good enough," and you exchange it back for "This is for me." Inside of this thought, you realize that you're exhausted from the whole ordeal, so you decide to relax, not push, and in fact, take some time off to go to Canyon Ranch. At Canyon Ranch, you run into a director you haven't seen in 20 years who says, "I'm so glad I ran into you. I'm doing a new Broadway show and you would be perfect for the lead." You audition and get the part, and you win a Tony Award for it. Out of that, you are tapped to star in a T.V. series, you and the producer of that T.V. series fall in love, you get married, and live happily ever after in a mansion in Beverly Hills with your gorgeous, loving husband, your beautiful children and your houseful of acting awards.

Jane saw that both of those stories, plus a million others, were totally possible out of the same incident. When you're holding a thought, often things will happen that appear negative. If you understand that these "negative happenings" are simply steps along the path, you will know that whatever is happening, it's all part of the process that is leading you toward the manifestation of whatever thought you're holding.

Inside of the thought, "This is for me," Jane was able to relax, knowing that her getting dropped by her agent was neither an intrinsically good or bad thing, but could be one step along many paths leading to many possible outcomes, depending on what thought she was holding. In fact, her manager releasing her could, in many instances, be exactly what was needed to get her where she was going; just as a boyfriend, girlfriend, husband or wife leaving you might be the first step toward finding true love; or getting fired from your current job might be the first step to having the career of your dreams.

WHEN YOU TAKE ON A NEW THOUGHT
THE UNIVERSE BEGINS TO MOVE
(OFTEN IN WAYS YOU DON'T LIKE OR ARE AFRAID OF)

In working with countless people on exchanging their thoughts, I've observed that one of the reasons we have difficulty taking on a new thought is that when we take one on, especially one that we've been afraid to think, the mirror of the physical world immediately begins to move to reflect it. If, on the natural path to the reveal-ment of that thought, there is something that we're terrified of or reluctant to experience, we will take on protective thoughts to keep us away from that particular experience and the sensations that accompany it. These protective thoughts may keep us away from the experience we're afraid of, but they'll also keep us away from the thought that will generate the experience we DO wish to have.

So how do we allow ourselves to take on the thoughts we want to have, knowing that they hold the potential of being reflected as things we don't want to see?

The first and most important instruction is: YOU MUST NOT TRY TO FEEL OR TO BELIEVE THE THOUGHTS. JUST TAKE THEM ON.

People think that if they "think positively" they're supposed to feel great. That couldn't be further from the truth. As I said before, when you take on a new thought, things immediately begin to happen to reflect that thought. Often, the reason you haven't taken on that new thought is because you didn't want those things to happen. So when you take on the new thought of being willing to have love in your life, your current love may leave you, or you may realize that you, yourself have to leave. When you take on the new thought to finally write that book, you suddenly have to do the work, you might have to spend time away from your family, go on a book tour, be in the public eye. When you take on the new thought that your career fulfills you, you might have to leave your current job, get fired, go through a financially challenging period, go back to school or move to another city.

So, if one lives by the premise that the thought will be reflected, one takes it on but does not try to feel or believe anything. That will come later. The thought will generate that. But we must simply take on the thought and let it generate the result as reflection. The way to walk through all those challenges is to KNOW that thoughts can only be reflected in the mirror, so no matter what it seems like, what it feels like, if you are thinking that thought, returning to it constantly, that is what MUST show up in the mirror of your life.

To reiterate. If you go back to the Thought Exchange Circle diagram, the only thing we have choice over is our thought. We can't choose sensations, because sensations are generated by thoughts. We can't choose beliefs, because beliefs are generated by the combination of thoughts and sensations, and are by definition un-exchangeable (since beliefs are thoughts that we think are true.) And we can't choose what we see in the mirror of our life, because that is simply a reflection of thought, sensation and belief. Often, when I demonstrate the fact that you can choose any thought and think it, I ask people if they can think "I am good." Especially in a church group, people immediately say "Yes." I then ask people to think, "I am bad.'"

There are always a few who say "I can't, because I know I'm not bad." And I say, "I didn't ask you to believe it or to feel it, just to think the thought." They then realize that they can think a thought that's contrary to their sensations or beliefs, and often that thought will bring up sensations they didn't expect.

SENSATIONS AREN'T CAUSE

Often, when people begin to understand Thought as Cause, they go through a period where they become nervous and superstitious, thinking, "I'm holding that thought but I notice that I'm anxious or frightened or feeling 'negative' things. Does this mean that those negative things are going to manifest?"

When I understood, as a Broadway conductor, that the orchestra was always playing my thoughts, I became a much more powerful conductor, because I was now in touch with the real source of why the orchestra played what I wanted them to play. I was able to simply hear what I wanted, allow my arms to move, and lo and behold, the sound in my head came out of the orchestra.

But there was one thing that puzzled me about this. I noticed that I still had a lot of fear that the orchestra wouldn't play, and that the process of letting go and taking the "risk" that they would play what I heard in my head produced sensations of breathlessness, pounding heart and shakiness.

I began to wonder why my fear did not affect their playing. I could stand there and hear what I wanted, and even though I experienced a lot of fear and anxiety, they still played what I wanted them to play, as long as I was thinking it.

When I began to create The Thought Exchange, the answer to that question became clear. SENSATIONS ARE NOT CAUSE. They are effect, and as such, sensations do not cause manifestation. Thoughts do.

This was a wonderfully freeing revelation. I realized that I could still feel scared, frightened, or angry, still shake and sweat, experience a pounding heart, whatever, and see the manifestations I desired, as long as I didn't choose thoughts based on those sensations.

As we've discussed before, when we take on a thought that will most likely manifest in the mirror of the world as what we want to see there, we often feel sensations that we may interpret as fear and anxiety. The reason for this is that sometimes the events that that thought causes, although necessary to the ultimate manifestation of that thought, might be events that we associate with events that we were afraid to have happen when we were children. Often, we take the sensations these events generate to mean that there is something dangerous about the event happening now. Actually, as I've said throughout this book, it's not the events we're afraid of, but rather the sensations that the thought of these events produce. The avoidance of those sensations was the very reason we didn't take on the thought in the first place.

In short, when these events happen, they generate sensations. Understanding Thought-as-Cause allowed me to know that it was perfectly OK, in fact, necessary, to feel those sensations, as long as I didn't take on protective thoughts to get away from them. So when I take on the thought, "The orchestra is always playing what I'm thinking," and when they actually do it, I feel frightened and panicky, my fear and panic will not in any way effect the orchestra playing what I want them to play. But if, based on that panicky feeling, I choose the thought, "The orchestra won't play what I'm thinking," I might then manifest that result.

So, if we take on the thought, "Sensations are just sensations and do not cause manifestation," it is possible for us to easily hold whatever thought we're holding, and also have our sensations, without fear that they will manifest as what we don't want.

Exchange "I Am" for " I Feel"

So many times we hear ourselves say (and thus hear ourselves think) "I am sick. I am tired. I am unhappy. I am hungry." In many spiritual traditions, the words "I Am" are used as the name of God. Since, in Thought Exchange work, we do not necessarily use the word God, but instead describe all that God is or has given as The Great Un-Manifested, then it would follow that "I Am" could be considered another word for the Great Un-Manifested, for all that is or ever potentially could be.

You've all heard the admonition, "Don't take the Lord's name in vain." Shawn Moninger, my partner and the minister of Unity Center for Practical Spirituality in Norwalk, Connecticut, points out that if "I Am" is the name of God, then saying "I Am sick" is using the adjective "sick" to describe God, implying that God is sick (or in our terms, that sick is all that the Great Un-Manifested contains.) This would be tantamount to taking the Lord's name in vain, since it couldn't possibly be true that sick is all that God is, or, in Thought Exchange terms, that sick is all that is contained in the Great Un-Manifested.

If you exchange "I am" for "I feel," you have not only stopped "taking the Lord's name in vain," but more importantly, you have exchanged a thought (I am sick) for a sensation (I feel sick.) As we just described above, sensations are not causative, they are merely the effect of thought. So while the thought "I am sick" might reflect in the mirror of the Manifested world as sickness, "I feel sick" is just describing a sensation you're having, and thus does not promote illness. Once you have exchanged "I am" for "I feel," you can then zero in on "I feel sick" and actually describe the sensations you're having in more accurate detail. Rather than describing them as "sick," you can describe them as pain, tingling, hotness, coldness or nausea. When you can simply experience these sensations without adding thoughts to them, you are then free to choose any thought, and can choose thoughts that would be likely to appear as health, rest, joy or satisfaction of hunger.

A fascinating side note is that certain languages often seem to understand and express this concept better than English does. In French and Italian, rather than saying "I am hungry," they say "I have hunger." Rather than saying "It is cold" they say "It makes cold." Rather than saying "I am afraid" they say "I have fear."

So whenever you hear yourself making an "I Am" statement that contains pain or lack, exchange it for an "I feel" statement, locate the exact sensations you're experiencing, and see what happens, both in what appears in the mirror of the world and in your ability to work with it by exchanging other thoughts around it.

"FEELING" BETTER

Although people go into therapy or seek a spiritual path for many reasons, the most basic one seems to be the desire to feel better. Most of us gauge how we're doing in life by how we feel. When we don't feel "good" we try to do something to change that feeling. It's an odd paradox that sensations (which are really what we're talking about when we use the word "feelings" in this context) are experiences that come unbidden, as the effects of thoughts, and yet so many of us judge some sensations as good and some as bad, and try to change the sensations we don't like by working on them directly or running away from them.

If thoughts are the cause of manifestation, and sensations are a natural (and uncontrollable) byproduct on the way to those manifestations, then it seems that the only way to be able to feel "good" while allowing ourselves to stay with the thought that will manifest the result we want, would be to be able to feel whatever sensations we're having and feel comfortable with them, not labeling them good or bad.

One of the members of our workshop put it beautifully. "If you want to feel better, you have to learn to _feel_ better.

SAME THOUGHT/DIFFERENT MEANING

One of the members of The Thought Exchange had decided to leave her day job, and had picked the date on which she was going to give notice. The day before she was going to give notice, she showed up at The Thought Exchange Workshop. She was very excited at the prospect of starting a new life, but as she spoke, she also revealed that she was very anxious. As we explored her anxiety, she realized that the reason she was anxious was that she was thinking, "What if I never work again? What if I never have any money?"

I asked the question, "What would a person who thought that was going to happen, who saw the world as being a place where once you left your job it was all over and you'd never have another opportunity, have to be thinking to have that reflected in the mirror of their life?" After some conversation she came up with, "It's not possible for me to make a mistake." That rang very true to her—the notion that she was not allowed to make one mistake, and if she did it would all be over.

As we discussed that, she of course realized that in all the infinite possibilities always existing in the Great Un-Manifested, that was not true. She realized, in fact, that there's no such thing as a mistake. Everything you do simply leads you to the next thing, and there are infinite possibilities at every moment as to what will happen next.

Her face lit up as she suddenly realized that rather than "It's not possible for me to make a mistake" being a "negative" thought, the truth was that the thought that she actually wanted to take on was "It's NOT possible for me to make a mistake " (meaning, "It's absolutely impossible for me to make a mistake no matter what I do.") She went to the Thought Exchange and exchanged, "It's not possible for me to make a mistake" for, "It's NOT possible for me to make a mistake." Same thought, new meaning.

One version of this idea has been very useful to me. Being someone who experiences many sensations before I go on stage, I've exchanged the thought "I'm anxious about going onstage" for "I'm anxious to get onto the stage." The word anxious, which I used to interpret as "nervous," I now interpret as "excited."

So often it's our thought about a thought, or our interpretation of what that thought, or a word in that thought means, that determines how we hold it.

WHEN YOU HAVE A THOUGHT YOU DON'T LIKE, KNOW IT'S NOT TRUE

It is very important as a first step to exchanging a thought, to know that whatever thought you're having, it's not TRUE. It is not true that you can't have something. It is not true that you can either. Both are true and both are not true. Whatever you think, appears, not because that thought is a fact, but because any thought can appear out of the Great Un-Manifested. So, when you have a thought like "I can't have money" or "I can't get well," first know that that isn't TRUE. The condition has just been held in place by your continued thought, and the condition could change instantly if a new thought were to be substituted.

RUNNING THE MARATHON/ CLIMBING MT. EVEREST

As I've said over and over, the main key to being able to keep choosing a thought that will appear in the mirror of the world as something you want to see there, is to be able to "withstand" or tolerate the sensations that come with having that thought.

A good metaphor for this is running the Marathon. In lectures and Thought Exchange workshops, I often ask the group, "What is the first thing you need in order to be able to run the marathon?" Some people say, "Great shoes." Some say, "Months of training." Although those things are important, there is definitely something you need to have in order to run the Marathon that must come before either of those.

In order to even be able to consider running the marathon, you must take on the thought "I can run the marathon." Inside of this thought, you train, you enter, you buy good running shoes, and do all the things necessary to prepare for the marathon. You then start to run the marathon. If, somewhere along the way, your legs begin to hurt, your breath becomes short, or your body begins to ache, these are sensations that must be tolerated in order to continue running the marathon. Even experienced runners who win marathons, experience and tolerate these sensations. Should you decide that these sensations are intolerable, the easiest way to get them to stop is to exchange the thought, "I can run the marathon" for "I can't run the marathon." The "I Can't" thought will cause you to stop running, and the sensations will go away. Of course, you won't get to finish the marathon. But the pain will stop. Winning marathon runners may notice, that when they encounter these sensations, they might momentarily exchange the thought "I Can" for "I Can't." But it is the exchange of the thought back to "I Can" that allows them to complete the race.

What this demonstrates clearly is the reason we choose "negative" thoughts. These thoughts protect us from some sort of pain that we might have to experience were we to hold onto the thought that will give us the result we desire. So the next time you notice yourself having an "I Can't" thought, ask yourself what sensation it's protecting you from experiencing. Then ask yourself if you are willing to experience that sensation in order to get what you want. If the answer is yes, exchange the thought and keep going.

Another example I like to use is climbing Mt. Everest. You decide to take on the thought "I can climb Mt. Everest" and inside of that thought, you begin your climb. Then you hit freezing weather, lack of oxygen, and pain in your legs. The easiest way to get rid of these sensations is to exchange the thought "I can climb Mt. Everest," for "I can't climb Mr. Everest." That will stop the pain, but will also stop the climb. To climb Mt. Everest, you must not only hold the thought that it's possible, but must be willing to experience whatever sensations you experience inside the thought. The ability to do that will allow you to climb Mt. Everest, or do anything else you want to do.

THE PLAYING FIELD IS ALWAYS LEVEL

If you tossed a coin 5000 times and it came up tails 5000 times in a row, what are the odds that it will come up heads on the next toss?

Most people, when confronted with this question, instinctively say something like "5000 to 1." In fact, the odds are 50/50. No matter how many times you've tossed the coin, and how many times it's come up tails, on each toss there is a 50% chance of it coming up heads and a 50% chance of it coming up tails.

Of course, we can understand why, had you just tossed tails 5000 times in a row, you might have some thoughts about your inability to toss heads. You might think, "I'm a tail tosser" or, "It'll never come up heads," or something like that.

But the fact is, we are always playing on a level playing field, and what has happened in the past in no way affects the odds or diminishes the infinite possibilities that are always available to us in every moment. So when you've had things not work out the way you'd hoped, or had a series of what you would call failures, take a look at the thoughts you're holding based on those experiences, look at the truth, which is that life is always a level playing field where all possibilities exist, and exchange your thought to reflect the possibility that anything can happen, no matter what has happened in the past.

WHAT MUST OPRAH BE THINKING?

When you uncover the thought that is reflecting as what you don't want, and are at a loss to find the thought to exchange it for, often it's useful to ask yourself a question like, "What must Oprah be thinking?" Find a person who personifies and has reflected, in his or her own life, what you would like to see reflected in yours. Ask yourself, "What thought must they be having that is reflecting as what they see in the mirror of their life?" So, for example, let's say you wanted to have great success and notoriety in your career and were not seeing that.

Looking in the mirror of your life and asking yourself what thought that must be reflecting, you might uncover that you are having the thought, "I have nothing to offer people." You might then think to yourself, "Who is someone who has the kind of success that I want?" Oprah might come to mind. Asking yourself, "What must Oprah's thought be on this subject?" you might come up with, "I always have something important and valuable to offer people." Or, "I live in a world of endless possibility, and I am allowed to have anything I want." Or, "No matter what my past is, my present can be anything I desire it to be." When you come across the thought that you think would reflect as what you want in your life, take it on. Of course, we can't know exactly what Oprah is really thinking, but we can see, by looking at what is being reflected in the "mirror" of her life, that she is holding thoughts that are reflecting as manifestations that we would like to see in our own lives. So, since we know that all thoughts are there for the taking for any of us, we can imagine which thoughts Oprah must have taken on, and take them on for ourselves.

I spoke before of the writer who was afraid of criticism, who when asked to think of someone who is criticized all the time and is extremely successful, thought of Madonna and exchanged, "It is intolerable to take criticism" for, "Who gives a shit?"

I know that my friend Kathie Lee Gifford always lives in beautiful homes, so when I went to buy a home, I exchanged "I am not allowed to have what I want" for what I assume Kathie must be thinking, which would be something like, "The abundance of the world is open to me and I am allowed to have what I want." Doing this, my dream house came to me "out of the blue," at the perfect price.

ALLOW IT TO BE INSTANT

Have you ever noticed that when you step in front of a mirror, it takes absolutely no time or effort on your part to have your reflection appear there? The mirror is also never inaccurate. It never moves when you don't move, it never leaves anything out of the reflection, it never adds anything to the reflection. It just passively, effortlessly and exactly mirrors what is standing before it. Instantly, with no time lag whatsoever.

Practice exchanging a thought and instantly noticing the change. Especially if you're dealing with a lifelong thought, notice that the exchange of that thought produces instant results. For example, I have often held the thought, "Everything will be taken away at the last minute." Inside of this thought, as I approach the end of something, I become very anxious, start to feel bad and worried, and often feel like I can't go through to the end. The moment I can know that that thought is not "true," is not a fact, my body feels different, I have a different sense of enjoyment of my life, a different feeling of security, and events turn out differently. Just as it takes NO TIME for your reflection in a mirror to change when you move or change something, it takes NO TIME for a new thought to take effect.

THE MIRROR HAS NO OPINION

Have you ever stepped in front of a mirror and had it say, "Ugh, you look terrible" or "Why are you wearing that?" or "That outfit is so awful, I refuse to reflect it!" Or, for that matter, has the mirror ever said, "You look gorgeous today." Of course not. That would be ridiculous. The mirror, and the universe, reflect exactly what you're thinking, without opinion, without bias, without judgment. The mirror is merely here to let you see what you are thinking. What you do with that, what you think of it, what you feel about it, are totally on your side of the equation, not in the mirror.

THE MIRROR IS ALWAYS REFLECTING EXACTLY WHERE YOU ARE NOW

Thoughts do not take time to manifest, just as the mirror takes no time to reflect what's in front of it. If you have a dream or a wish, and you exchange your thought, it's not that it takes time for your thought to appear in front of you, but rather that the mirror is always reflecting exactly where your thought is at the moment.

So keep looking in the mirror of life on a moment-to-moment basis, and whatever you see there, acknowledge that this is exactly how far your thought has come, so far. Work on exchanging it, again and again, until the reflection shows you that you have actually taken on the thought you want. Insisting, "But I'm being positive and it's not appearing before me," is not only ludicrous, but counter-productive. Always get yourself to the point of power by acknowledging the thought (or complex group of thoughts) that is being reflected in the mirror of your life. Once you are clear as to what those thoughts are, you are in a position to take a little shopping trip to The Thought Exchange and exchange them for thoughts that will reflect as the results you desire.

THE WORLD IS <u>NEVER</u> OPPOSING YOU

So often, we hear people say things like, "I affirmed that good was coming to me and then the world gave me something bad." Or, "I prayed for something and it didn't happen." If this were true, that would mean that the universe has the power to oppose us or to not reflect what it is we're thinking.

That would be like saying that the mirror has the power to oppose us or to decide on its own not to reflect what's standing in front of it. It would be like looking into a mirror and seeing a different outfit than the one we're wearing. Or moving up and seeing our image in the mirror move down. I think we would all agree that that's impossible. And yet, so often, we think of the world as opposing us rather than reflecting us.

The next time you're with a friend, do this little experiment. Ask your friend to reflect, in movement, exactly what you do. Give your friend a big, confident smile, and notice that your friend's face immediately reflects that back to you. Now put an expression of doubt on your face, and notice that doubt immediately appears on the face of your friend. In this exercise, it's clear that your friend is not creating doubt, just reflecting yours. But can you see that if you were unaware that you were showing doubt, you might think that you were being opposed by your friend?

Now "put up your dukes." Put two fists in the air aimed at your friend. Immediately, you will see two fists coming back at you. Is your friend opposing you? You're seeing two fists coming at you, but I think, again, it's clear that those two fists are merely an exact reflection of what YOU are doing.

So, in the world, even when you see "two fists" before you, if you are aware that the world is always cooperating with you by reflecting you exactly, you have the power to change those "two fists" by simply putting your own "fists" down. The world is NEVER opposing you, only reflecting you.

EVERYTHING IS ALREADY HERE

Know that everything you could ever want is already here. It can't not be. Everything, good and bad, wanted and not wanted, has already been created in possibility, just waiting to be revealed. When something's not coming through, an important first step is simply to know that it's here (because everything is here, in the Great Un-Manifested). Just knowing this allows you to more confidently put yourself in a position where you can exchange your thoughts and reveal what you want.

It's like when a woman is nine months pregnant and someone says, "The baby's coming soon." The baby is already in the room. It's not visible, because it's inside the mother, but it's not coming from any-where—it's already here.

In Thought Exchange groups, I sometimes demonstrate this point by asking the group to look at my face. I then ask them, "Is my face here? Is my face in the room?" They all, of course, say, "Yes." I then put my jacket over my head, covering my face completely, and ask, "Is my face in the room now?" The answer, of course, is still "Yes." People can readily see that my face is still in the room, it's just not visible at the moment. To make it visible, all they'd have to do is know it's there and simply remove the jacket from in front of it. So it is with every-thing we're looking for that we don't see. It's here. It's just not visible at the moment.

A TABLE IS WAITING

The image of a table set with everything you could want and not want is often helpful to people. When you want something, picture a table with it, and everything else, on it, and pick up what you want. Remember, just because something is on the table doesn't mean you have to use it, so there's no need to rail against it or get it off the table, just don't pick it up. You don't put pepper in a cake, but it's not a problem that it's in the kitchen. It's there to be used by you for something else, or by someone who wants it. In fact, if you wanted to put pepper in a cake you could do that too. Everything is available, nothing is impossible. NOTHING!

100 WAYS TO SEE WHAT I WANT APPEAR

Often, when I have no idea how something is going to manifest, or when I think that the possibility is very farfetched or remote, I sit down and make a list of 100 ways in which what I want to see might possibly appear. I use this technique to remind myself that there are unlimited ways in which anything can appear.

So, for instance, if I want to see $1,000,000 and I have no immediate prospects for earning $1,000,000, I say to myself, "In what ways could $1,000,000 appear?" Then I write a list, including things that seem possible, things that seem ridiculous, things that are illegal, things I might never do. So my list of how I might receive $1,000,000 might include:

- Write a hit song.

- A relative I never met dies and leaves me $1,000,000.

- I find a paper bag on the street that has $1,000,000 in it.

- I win the lottery.

- Someone rings my doorbell and hands me $1,000,000.

- I make a speculative investment in the stock market that pays me $1,000,000.

- I buy real estate and it appreciates amazingly.

- I do a favor for someone and they tithe me $1,000,000 in gratitude.

- I rob a bank.

- I marry someone extremely wealthy.

- One of my wealthy friends decides to give me a gift.

- I buy something that seems worthless at a garage sale and it turns out to be worth $1,000,000.

- I start a new career and am extremely successful.

- I write a #1 best-selling book.

- I am surprisingly cast in a movie or a hit T.V. series.

You see the point. Some of them are unlikely, some of them unseemly, some of them not so farfetched, but at any rate, they open my mind to the notion that there are many ways in which $1,000,000 could appear. I might even actually try some of them. (Don't worry. I'm not going out to rob a bank. Not today, anyway.)

THE "NEGATIVE" THOUGHT AS THE SOURCE OF YOUR POWER

One of the challenges I have found with the new thought/positive thinking/affirmation culture is the fear of the "negative" thought, the unwillingness to acknowledge that we are having those thoughts, and the effort to make something happen by plastering a "positive" thought over a "negative" one.

The cornerstone of Thought Exchange work is getting in touch with and connecting to the concept that what we see before us in the "mirror" of the world, is a reflection of our thought, not the cause of our thought. The only way you can connect to that is to go to what you are seeing in your life right now, and then see what thought MUST be being reflected for you to be seeing what you see in the mirror. When people bring up something that they regard as negative, then refuse to acknowledge the thought they're having, and instead try to think of a positive thought, or profess to be having only positive thoughts, they're as disconnected from their life, and their power to create it with thought, as a person standing in front of the mirror looking at the reflection of a particular outfit and refusing to admit that they have that outfit on.

Can you see, that if you're looking in the mirror and seeing a blue shirt there, and refusing to acknowledge that you're wearing a blue shirt, the reflection in the mirror will NEVER change? If you see an outfit in the mirror that you don't like, the only way to get the reflection to change is to change the outfit. If you're not willing to admit that you have the outfit on, you're not going to change it. You can stare at the mirror, yell at it, complain about it, fight it all you want, but it's not going to budge until you acknowledge that you are wearing what you see. Once you have acknowledged this, you have total power to change the reflection, because changing the outfit is something that is well within your power. By the same token, once you recognize the thought and acknowledge that it is you having the thought that is being reflected in the mirror, you are empowered to exchange that thought, like an outfit, and only then will the reflection change.

In this paradigm, one can see that there is no such thing as a good thought or a bad thought. There are just thoughts. To further the kitchen analogy that I spoke of earlier: Some people like pepper, some don't. Some want to eat snails, some can't stand them. Once you get to the point where you're not judging thoughts, you can look at the ones you're having, and even if you regard them as "negative," you can see that the point is that your thoughts are appearing in the mirror of your life, you're connected to that way of looking at things, you're wielding your power at ALL times, and thus you have the freedom to reveal anything you want in your life by simply exchanging your thought, rather than by trying to work on what's before you (which is impossible since it's nothing more than a reflection of the thought you're having.)

It's like people who say, "You need to have more faith." In fact, we have all the faith we're ever going to have. The question is simply, "Where is that faith being directed?" It's amazing how we can squelch our talents by believing we can't do something, how we can fail at something because we have complete "faith" that we can't succeed, or how we can never reach for a dream because we "know" we can't have it." I once said to a therapist of mine, "I'm just not a good manifester," to which she replied; "Are you kidding? You've managed to take a world-class musical talent and squoosh it into a mediocre career for the past several years. Do you know how much faith and belief and talent at manifesting that takes?" It was an eye opener. So we are ALWAYS manifesting, ALWAYS exercising our faith, and ALWAYS exercising our choice of thought and watching it appear.

Knowing this, what is it that continually makes us actually choose the experiences we're having, only to complain that they are not what we want? What is it that keeps us from easily choosing the thoughts that will bring us the things we desire in life?

We Never Sabotage Ourselves

So often we hear people say, "I wanted something but I sabotaged myself." In hearing this over and over, I had to ask myself, "Why would we do that? Why would we stop ourselves from getting something we want?"

In doing Thought Exchange work, I've come to understand that when we take on a thought that will reflect in the world as something we want to see there, if that thought is accompanied by frightening or difficult sensations (because of past experiences) we will often exchange that thought for one that will not get us what we want in order to protect ourselves from sensations that seem threatening or that we might perceive to be intolerable.

This being the case, we are not sabotaging ourselves at all. We are, in fact, protecting ourselves.

Exchanging the word sabotage for protect allows us, first of all, to have compassion for ourselves instead of beating ourselves up, and secondly, to then look, see what it is we're protecting ourselves from, identify it as a sensation, and gradually develop our ability to tolerate that sensation while holding the thought that will reflect as what we want.

So the next time you think you are sabotaging yourself, check and see if you are, in fact, actually protecting yourself. Remember, we always take on "negative" thoughts for good reasons.

THE OLD THOUGHT IS ALWAYS
AVAILABLE TO YOU

As I've said throughout this book, when you return a thought that you don't want to The Thought Exchange, you can be sure that there are many people who will want it. The reason for this is that we often take on "negative" thoughts to protect ourselves from feeling sensations we don't want to have, or to prevent ourselves from taking actions that we're afraid of taking. It's those very thoughts that keep us stuck, but nonetheless, they do offer us a strange kind of protection.

I was working with a woman who was struggling with an eating disorder. After several months of work, she came to me one day and said, "I now completely understand why I'm not eating, I know it's because I'm saying no to outside intrusions that I now know I could be saying no to in other ways, and yet I'm still not eating." I thought for a moment and said, "You are aware that you can always go back to not eating? It's always there for you, available to you, even after you have eaten." With that thought she immediately began to eat.

She needed to know that the thought that had protected her would always be there should she need it. Once she began eating again, she no longer needed that thought, but she knew that she always had the option to go back to it. She also knew that she always had the option to choose a new thought that would give her more health and happiness.

THERE'S NO SUCH THING AS "SET IT AND FORGET IT"

When we look at successful people, or people who have things in their lives that we wish we had, we often think that they have permanently found some thought, completely solved some problem, and are irrevocably and forever destined to be having the success they are now experiencing.

In fact, it's important to remember that at every moment we are choosing thoughts, and those thoughts are being reflected in the world. All thoughts exist at all times, and all thoughts may be chosen at any time. Someone may have chosen a thought that has reflected as success for 20 years, but that doesn't mean that they couldn't, at any moment, choose a thought that reflects as failure and immediately see failure in their lives.

If this seems scary, or negative, remember that it works both ways. You can have been choosing thoughts that have produced failure for half your life, but that doesn't mean that thoughts that produce success are not available to you right at this moment.

It's like standing at a buffet table that has every food in the world on it. You can eat steak for 10 years and never touch the liver, but the liver is ALWAYS available to you. After 10 years of eating steak you might try the liver. If you like it you can eat more of it. If you don't like it, the steak is still there, and you can always return to eating it.

So know that Thought Exchange is a lifelong, moment-to-moment process, not something you do for a little while and then forget about. Whether or not you're aware of it, your thoughts are always manifesting, so you might as well take the reins and see what you want to see appear in your life. People who are consistently successful, are people who have gotten into the habit of choosing thoughts of success, no matter what the circumstance.

DON'T GIVE IT A THOUGHT

One day, as I was doing this work, I suddenly heard the common expression, "Don't give it a thought" in a new way.

We often make the mistake of thinking that our thoughts are caused by the events in our lives, instead of visa versa. When we think this, we will often choose our next thought based on what just happened, instead of thinking of what just happened as a reflection of our thoughts, knowing that any and all thoughts are available to us at every moment.

When difficult or shocking things happen, or when we have sensations that feel unpleasant or remind us of old sensations that were troublesome to us at one time, it is almost unavoidable that our old or habitual thoughts will pop into our head. When we have a failure that looks like other failures we've had before, usually the first thought will be something like, "I always fail," or "I can't get what I want." Knowing that all thoughts are available to us, we can quickly exchange those thoughts for ones that will allow a different result to appear in the future.

At times like this, in order to avoid taking on those thoughts that don't bring about what I desire to see in my life, I look at the incident that has just occurred, and say to myself, "Don't give it a thought." The incident has already happened, but the choice of whether to give a thought to it—and thus perpetuate it—is mine. By not giving it a thought that supports it, I leave the way open for the new thoughts that will reflect as different results.

CREATING AN ENEMY THAT ISN'T THERE

The other day, we were in the middle of a Thought Exchange Workshop when our cat, Mercer, an extremely high-bred Blue Point Himalayan, made a rare public appearance. She stepped into the room, jumped up onto the couch, and sat down on a piece of paper belonging to one of the members of the group. There was a pen on that paper, and within a few moments, Mercer began glaring at it suspiciously, as though it was threatening her. Then, she began batting at it with her paw as though it was attacking her and she had to defend herself.

I pointed out to the group that Mercer was giving us a wonderful demonstration of how, when we have a sensation we don't care for, we sometimes look around for something to blame that sensation on so we can attack it and get rid of the sensation. It was clear from Mercer's behavior that she was taking an inanimate object that had no ability to move or think, and certainly no ability to attack, and treating it as though it were the aggressor. Although we laugh when we see that behavior in a cat, how many times do we do it ourselves? I invest in the stock market, and the other day I opened my computer to find that my stocks had gone down a considerable amount. The next thing I knew, I was screaming out loud at the stock market, asking it why it always had to punish me, why I wasn't allowed to make money, and why, whenever I wanted something, it stopped me from getting it.

In the middle of my tirade, I suddenly stopped and said to myself, "Now I KNOW that the stock market doesn't think, doesn't DO anything to me, and has no ability to respond to me consciously. So why am I choosing to construct it in this way?"

As I sat with it, I realized that my viewing of the stock market promoted sensations in me that were exactly the sensations that I couldn't tolerate in my childhood. Being in the bind of having "someone" do something to me that caused me great pain, and having that "someone" absolutely not respond to me except to make sure that if I had a desire it was thwarted, was a very familiar position to me, one that I had been in very frequently in my childhood. I had come to understand that throughout my life, I had often turned down career opportunities and avoided risks so that I wouldn't have to feel those sensations.

Knowing this, I now began using the stock market's fluctuations as a chance to learn to feel and tolerate those sensations, rather than taking on a thought based on them that would cause me to either fight or give up. By simply experiencing my sensations, rather than "giving them a thought," I was able to reconnect to the fact that I have the freedom to choose whatever thought I want, no matter what sensations I'm feeling, and thus to have any outcome I desire appear.

Once I began to choose thoughts of prosperity and success (and to experience the sensations that went with them) the stock market turned around for me. Whenever I would notice it going the other way, I would not fight it or struggle with it. I would just look at my thoughts and exchange them. (And of course, experience the sensations that went with them.)

Now I want to be clear that my thoughts are not "controlling" the stock market. But by my knowing that all I'm seeing in the stock market is a mirror of my thoughts about how prosperous or non-prosperous I am, not only will the stock market's fluctuations cease to have the devastating effect on me that they've had in the past, but I will have, at every moment, the opportunity to choose to go through life considering myself prosperous whether the stock market is up or down. As I hold the thought of prosperity, that thought will be reflected in the conscious and unconscious choices that I make. The result of this will be that I will begin to see the places that already exist in the world of infinite possibility where prosperity exists for me, and in this way, prosperity will come into manifestation. It might be from the stock market. It might be from elsewhere. That doesn't matter. What matters is that I will be living an internal experience of prosperity, which MUST appear, in reflection in the world, as "external" prosperity.

So the stock market, like EVERYTHING ELSE IN THE REFLECTED WORLD, is neutral. It doesn't think, it doesn't care, it just reflects whatever it is I'm thinking. If it seems like an enemy, it can only be because I'm creating it as such.

You Have 1/4 of a Second

Research has shown that we have about 1/4 of a second between the time an incident occurs and choosing our next thought. That may seem like a very short time, but once you begin to notice it, it's more than enough.

Often, when I ask someone who is afraid to sing "What do you think about your singing?" they'll tell me that the reason they can't sing is because someone told them, when they were young, that they had a terrible voice. This is not actually the reason they can't sing. The reason is that each time they are about to sing, they take on a thought based on what that person told them. The thought they're currently choosing to take on is what's causing their problem with singing, not what the person told them.

If I told a person who was twenty that they were forty years old, they would not take on the thought, "I'm forty years old," because they would not believe it. Some people, when told they can't sing, don't believe it, and don't take on that thought. It is always our prerogative to take on any thought at any time.

So, the next time something difficult or upsetting happens, try to notice that 1/4 of a second you have in which to choose a thought. See if you can choose one that supports what it is you want. And of course, as always, the thought you choose may come with sensations that may be uncomfortable.

CATCHING THE SENSATION THAT PRECEDES THE CHOICE OF THOUGHT

George (not his real name) one of the members of The Thought Exchange, decided to work on his issue around finding a life partner. George was an extremely attractive, successful, smart, kind man, so it seemed amazing to the group that he would have any trouble meeting someone. The only conclusion we could draw is that George must be holding thoughts that were preventing him from doing so.

In exploring George's thoughts, we came across many that fit that bill. George realized that he held thoughts such as, "There will always be something wrong with a person I meet; I'm not good enough for anyone who would be good enough for me; It's impossible to find a partner," as well as numerous others.

We worked through those thoughts and came up with the simple exchange. "It is possible for me to have a partner with whom I am happy and who is happy with me."

George took on that thought, and when I asked him how it felt to think it he said, "Great!" And then, five seconds after that he said, "Wait a minute. The other thought just came back in."

I asked him what had happened, and he said, "The other thought just reappeared." I asked him if anything had happened in between his taking on the first thought and the second thought reappearing.

In exploring it in detail, he realized that there had been a split second in which he had felt a sensation which he associated with fear, followed immediately by his taking on the old thought.

Even though it appeared to George, at first, as though the old thought had simply come back, in fact there had been a moment of sensation that he didn't want to feel, followed by his choosing to exchange the thought. It is crucial to recognize that split second of sensation, because it allows us to see that the taking on of the old thought is a choice. In this way, we are not the victim of thoughts, but actually notice that we are choosing them. Knowing this, allows us to choose the thought we want, over and over again, no matter what sensation we're experiencing.

WHEN YOU ASK PEOPLE HOW THEY FEEL, THEY USUALLY TELL YOU WHAT THEY THINK

Ask someone how they feel and they'll usually say things like, "I feel like I'm going to die. I feel like I'll never find the love I want. I feel that I've been ignored." Or, "I feel hopeful. I feel like I'm in love. I feel successful." These are not feelings. They are thoughts. They are interpretations of what physical sensations mean.

Point this out to that person and they'll then say things like, "I feel angry, I feel sad, I feel hurt." The interesting revelation for me was that although we've always called these statements feelings, they too are actually thoughts about sensations.

If we ask the question, "How do you know you're angry? What tells you you're sad? What gives you the signal that you're hurt?" we begin to realize that we are having physical sensations about which we are making interpretations. In many cases, the interpretations are ways of trying to get around or get rid of the sensations. If we know we're "angry" we can yell at someone and "get the feeling out." If we know we're "sad" we can get comfort to "get over" our sadness. These are all valuable things to do, but they're not the same as FEELING sensations.

In Thought Exchange, we've come to redefine "feelings" as physical sensations, things that are felt rather than things that are thought. Tingling, burning, coldness, shaking, tightening, bubbling are all sensations. As we've worked on being with our sensations, we've discovered that these sensations are actually what we often have trouble staying with, since they remind us of sensations we had when we were in traumatic situations earlier in life. To get away from these sensations, we take on thoughts, but it's actually in our ability to simply experience the sensations as they are, that the healing comes. Once we can experience our tingling, burning, pounding, trembling, etc. then we can once again move into and through situations in which these sensations occur, without stopping these situations off for fear of feeling those sensations.

So the next time you "feel" something, try just sitting with the sensation without describing it or taking on any thought about it. If you notice thoughts coming in, just go back to the sensation. See if you can refrain from even calling sensations good or bad, comfortable or uncomfortable. Just experience them as sensations.

In working with this, we have found that sometimes we don't have words to describe these sensations directly, so don't try, just feel them. One therapist friend of mine coined the phrase "Unnamed Sensation" to describe these sensations. As you sit with these "Unnamed Sensations," you will begin to notice that they are just that, sensations. And when you understand this, things you thought you couldn't tolerate are actually quite tolerable.

YOUR THOUGHTS ABOUT YOUR SENSATIONS

Close your eyes and take a few moments to notice your body. Notice the sensations you're having. A tightness in your stomach…A tingling in your head….A pounding in your heart….A pain in your back…Or, comfort, relaxation. Whatever you notice. Just linger for a moment, or for as long as you want, on each sensation that presents itself to you. After a few minutes, begin noticing what thought you take on in response to each sensation. You might feel a pain in your back and take on the thought, "I'm dying of cancer." You might feel a tightness in your chest and notice you've taken on the thought "I'll never be able to do my career." You might feel relaxation and take on the thought, "There must be something wrong. I have to find it." Just notice that with each sensation you take on a thought about it.

Now focus on one particular sensation, feel it, and notice the thought you take on about it. When you're clear on what that thought is, ask yourself, "What other thought could I take on about this sensation?" Exchange the thought you were holding for the new thought. After thinking this thought, ask yourself, "What other thought could I take

346

on about this sensation?" Exchange the thought you were just holding for that new thought. Then, again, ask yourself, "What other thought could I take on about this sensation?" And exchange the thought again.

The point of this exercise is to notice that when we have a sensation, we almost automatically take on a thought about it, and we often think that that thought is true. It's actually just a thought that we have chosen, and we have the ability to choose any thought. Remember, you don't have to believe any of the thoughts or feel a certain way when you think them. The thought is not there to change anything or to get rid of this sensation, but thinking a new thought will change your experience and ultimately your reality.

When people in workshops did this exercise, they found that a pain could transform from something that threatened their life, to something that could have healing properties, to something that felt comfortable, depending on what thought they were holding about it. They found that a sense of anxiety didn't mean they couldn't speak in front of a crowd or make that fundraising call or ask that person out on a date. They found that a tingling sensation or a tight feeling didn't mean they were going to fail or that they shouldn't pursue what they were going for. These were all just thoughts they had chosen in response to a mere physical sensation.

My favorite example of this is when someone says to me, "I'm feeling hot all over, I'm shaking, I'm breathing fast, I'm sweating, my heart is pounding and my head is spinning" and I ask them, "Are you having an orgasm?" Can you see how the same set of sensations, in a different context, can be perceived as positive or negative, depending on the thought we take on about it?

So the next time you have a sensation that feels uncomfortable, notice that you've taken on a thought about it, and notice that you have, as always, the choice of thinking any thought in the world. Keep exchanging until you find a thought that works for you, one that allows you to do what you want to do and be how you want to be.

Your First Thought in the Morning

When I'm going through difficult times, I often find that when I wake up in the morning, I feel fine for a few moments until I start to think. As I lie in bed, I notice that I start to worry, ruminate, and think thoughts based on fear of whatever current situation I'm in. I've found that it's a wonderful practice to start exchanging thoughts and choosing the thoughts I'm going to hold for the day while I'm still in bed in the morning. When I've got them, I can get up and spend the day living inside them.

Right Now

Generally, when we are anxious, it is about the past or the future. We are worried about how we are going to handle some event, remembering how things went in the past, and we focus our thoughts on that. This often happens first thing in the morning, or when we are lying awake in the middle of the night. One of the thought exchanges that can be really helpful in times like these is to exchange any thought we're having for "Right here, right now, everything is fine."

This morning, I found myself worrying about how I was going to be able to do certain things in my day. I suddenly realized that at this very moment, I was lying in a comfortable bed with two wonderful dogs and a cat, in a beautiful home, stretching and relaxing. In this very moment, everything was fine. That is actually always the case. It's just our worry about the outcome, often based on history, that causes our discomfort. So try exchanging any and all thoughts for, "Right now I am here and I am fine, and at any moment in the future I will be there and I will be fine."

A New Attitude About Gratitude

"An attitude of gratitude
Is more than just a platitude
In fact it gives us latitude
To get much more from life"

My partner, Shawn, is a Unity minister, and as such, was giving me a lecture on gratitude. I was going through a difficult time, and he said, "I don't know what to tell you to do, but I do know that you have to be grateful for everything."

Some really upsetting things were happening, and my response to him was, "How can I be grateful for losing a fortune in the stock market? How can I be grateful that my show didn't get produced? How can I be grateful that I didn't get chosen for that job?"

The usual explanations like, "You never know what God has in store for you," or, "You can't see where this is leading but it's leading somewhere good" seemed weak and Pollyanna-ish. It almost always irritates me when people say things like "All is in divine order" or, "This is part of God's plan." I get it, but it just doesn't seem like something I should be grateful for. It seems like a copout or a way of justifying and not feeling upsetting things.

In an effort to find the answer to the question of why I should be grateful for everything, I began reviewing what I know to be true. God (or whatever we call the law of the universe or the way things work) does not give us things and take things away, because everything has already been given and exists in the Great Un-Manifested at all times. God is not aware of itself. God does not punish us (or reward us for that matter.) God just is.

Suddenly, I got it. My explorations of thought exchange had taught me that the world is nothing more than a mirror of our thoughts, and that our real life takes place in our thoughts, not out there in the mirror of the world. So whatever I'm seeing in the world is a mirror of my thoughts, there simply to reflect back to me what I'm thinking so that I have the opportunity to see it and exchange it in order to have a different experience inside. This exchange of thought also reflects in the world, but the reflection is not the point. What's going on inside is.

So the world is constantly, vigilantly standing there for one purpose and one purpose only. To reflect back to me what I'm thinking. When I'm thinking thoughts of great lack, the world reflects them back to me in the form of a loss of money in the stock market so that I can see those thoughts and exchange them. The world is doing me a favor which, if I choose to see and accept it as such, will always lead me to greater happiness and fulfillment.

For this I can always be grateful. "Thank you for showing me I was thinking thoughts of lack so I can exchange them. Thank you for showing me that I was thinking I can't have my dreams. Thank you for showing me that I'm thinking I'm not good enough."

Since these are only thoughts, and can be exchanged, and since what we see in the world is not hard and fast but just a reflection, I can be endlessly grateful that I have this perfect friend who always, at every second, stands before me with a mirror and reflects back to me, without judgment, without criticism and without punishment, what I'm thinking, simply so that I can see it and exchange it for something I would prefer to be experiencing.

Who wouldn't be grateful for that?

OUR LIVES ARE HAPPENING IN OUR THOUGHTS – NOT IN THE MIRROR

If there is one principle that must be understood in order to grasp The Thought Exchange, it is the idea that our lives are really happening in our thoughts, not in Manifestation. Manifestation is the mirror of our thoughts, it's the reflection, not the object. When we have the thought that something is here for us, it is reflected in the Manifested, but it is not the reflection that gives us the joy. It's the thought that gives us joy.

If we can grasp that, we can grasp that we have the ability, at any moment, to be happy and fulfilled and abundant, by being happy, fulfilled and abundant in Thought, no matter what's in front of us. It follows, that as soon as we choose thoughts of happiness, fulfillment and abundance, we will see the manifestation of those thoughts in front of us. Thought is the cause, and all thoughts are directly available to us at all times.

Begin to really know that your REAL life takes place in thought, and you grasp the power to see everything you could ever want appearing in your life, right now.

THERE'S NO "OTHER PERSON" YOU'RE ONLY SEEING YOUR OWN THOUGHT

Once we understand that the world we see is nothing more than a reflection of what we're thinking, designed to refer us back to our own thoughts, where all creation and change takes place, we begin to see "relationship" in an entirely different way.

There is no one "out there." There is no one "else."

Anything that we "see" happening to us is actually happening, invisibly, within us. What we're seeing is just a reflection of our thought. What is "happening," is only happening in our experience."

With this new perspective, we come to understand that our partners do not make us happy. They are simply a reflection of our happiness. (Or, for that matter, of our misery.)

When relationships are not working, look to your thoughts, not to the other person. See where you're thinking you can't have something, or that you must be treated a certain way.

When you do this, and make a change in thought, one of two things will happen. Your partner will change, or your partner will disappear and be replaced by a partner who reflects your new thought. Either way, you have what you wanted, just, perhaps, not in the form you expected it.

When people are first confronted with this idea, they often express deep disappointment at the notion that they're "all alone," with no one else out there. Well it may be true that no one is out there, but that's because everyone is "in here," living in the same, invisible, infinite, Un-Manifested world of experience.

So, to our surprise, when we're willing to go in, that's when we feel a real communication and unity with the rest of the souls in the world, that is much more real and satisfying than trying to communicate with the rest of the bodies in the world.

The old way is like trying to have a relationship with a mirror. (I believe, in psychological terms that's called Narcissistic damage.) The new way is having a relationship with everything that's in front of the mirror. (i.e. Everything.)

Much more satisfying, wouldn't you say?

LOOKING IN THE MIRROR OF YOUR LIFE BRINGS THE UNCONSCIOUS INTO THE CONSCIOUS

One of the biggest challenges in psycho-therapeutic or emotional work is dealing with the unconscious. It's common knowledge that our behaviors and the outcomes they produce are often dictated by thoughts we're unaware of on a conscious level. So often, you will hear someone say, "I'm affirming, I'm thinking positive thoughts, I'm doing everything I think I'm supposed to, and yet I'm not seeing the result I desire."

If a thought is in the unconscious, we have often placed it there because we don't want to know about it. It might scare us. It might bring back upsetting memories. It might be a thought that doesn't match who we think we are. Whatever the reason, if a thought is running our life, and we're not conscious of what that thought is, we are disconnected from our ability to deal with our circumstances in ways that will bring about what we consciously desire.

The Thought Exchange is a perfect way to bring unconscious thoughts into conscious awareness, where they can be exchanged for thoughts that will reflect in the world as the conditions and things we want to see there. If we understand that the world we see before us is nothing more than an exact reflection of our thoughts, it would follow that we can see all our thoughts by simply looking in the "mirror" of the world.

The only requirement for doing this is that we understand that the mirror cannot lie. It cannot reflect something that's not there. So when we see something in the mirror, whether or not we are conscious that we are having the thought that is producing it, we must assume that if it's in the mirror, it's in our thought. Then we can look through our thoughts and find the thought that is being reflected as what we see before us. Even if we are unaware that we are having that thought, the mirror has proven that we are. Thus, our unconscious thought has been brought into consciousness, simply by our looking into the mirror of our lives. We are now in a position to exchange that thought and see a different reflection in our lives.

THE MIRROR PEOPLE

Did you ever notice (I'm sure you have) how certain events in our lives keep happening over and over and over again, in different places, in different situations, in different guises? No matter how hard we try to avoid them, they just keep coming up.

Often, when this happens, we begin to use these events as "proof" that we can't do or have something.

In fact, all that's happening is that we are seeing a reflection, over and over again, of a long-standing thought that we've been holding. And the purpose of our seeing that reflection is so that we can realize we're having that thought, exchange it, and experience the sensations that go with the new thought that we've been avoiding for years. When we can do this, not only do we heal, but the mirror of the world appears differently.

When we understand this, we begin to realize that these events are here to help us, and that the more we try to avoid them and change them, the more strongly they'll appear, until we see them, experience them, and learn the lesson they're here to teach us.

One thought exchange member came up with the idea of "Mirror People." She said, "It's like there are these people who are following me around, and their only job is to reflect my thoughts to me so I can see and exchange them, no matter where I am. It's as if they say, 'OK, everybody. She just went to work. Let's run over there and reflect her! Quick, she's out on a date. Let's get over there! She's on the subway!' Their only job is to do this for me, and they never fail."

If you think of it in this way, you can become grateful for every one of these events. Think of how hard these mirror people are working to get you to see something. They tirelessly and unfailingly are here to SUPPORT you in seeing what you have to see.

So the next time you walk into one of those events, look at the people in it, see them as the mirror people, and try taking on the thought:

NO MATTER WHERE I GO, THE MIRROR PEOPLE ARE ALWAYS THERE TO HELP ME.

And welcome the event as a chance to see your thoughts, experience your sensations, and heal.

Take Out the 't - Exchanging "Can't" for "Can"

If you've uncovered the thought you're thinking and you're having trouble coming up with the thought you want to exchange it for, start by looking to see if there's a "can't" contained in your original thought, and see what happens if you change it to a "can." For instance, "I can't write a book" is exchanged for, "I can write a book." "I can't have what I want" is exchanged for, "I can have what I want." In the Great UnManifested it is both true that you <u>can't</u> have what you want, and that you <u>can</u> have what you want, depending on which thought you choose. Often the most powerful thought is found by simply taking out the 't.

The "Unknowable" Veil Between the Invisible and the Visible

The whole premise of Thought Exchange is based on the notion that our invisible thoughts in the Un-Manifested world cause visible things to happen in the manifested world. We think, "I want to pick up the glass," and our hand moves and picks up the glass. We hear a note or a word in our mind, and our voice sings or speaks it.

The question arises, "How does something pass from the world of thought to the world of manifestation?" And the answer has always been, "I don't know."

Scientists will tell you that when you have a thought about picking something up, a chemical gets secreted that moves your arm. But why does that happen? The answer is, "We don't know."

But fortunately, we don't have to know. We just have to apply the principle and watch it work.

When we do this, we realize that where we live is 100% in the Un-Manifested world of thought and experience. In fact, as I've stated earlier, we can NEVER get into the manifested world. We don't live there. We can only watch it reflect our thoughts. And as such (and this can the hardest thing to wrap our minds around) IT IS IMPOSSIBLE FOR US TO EVER DO ANYTHING1

When I say this to people, they say, "What do you mean? I do things all the time."

NO YOU DON'T!!!! You THINK things all the time and watch them be reflected as doing.

If we can really understand this, we begin to see that every "doing" is really just a thought being reflected. For example, when someone is trying to sing a note, if they think it's too high, their body will reflect that by contorting their mouth so that the note will be squeezed and under pitch. When you tell them to stop doing that, they can't, because it is happening based on their thought that the note is too high. They're not doing it. Their thought is causing it. When you can get them to go into their thoughts and simply hear themselves hitting the note without knowing how, the contortions immediately stop and the body takes the position necessary to hit the note they want to hit. They are ONLY hitting the note on the inside and seeing a reflection of that on the outside.

Begin to see yourself as ONLY thoughts, thoughts which are easily and effortlessly exchangeable. Work on ANY issue you see in the world in this way, and you will discover a power beyond anything you can imagine. All events become phantoms, reflections, and ways of reminding you to return to the place where you already have everything and where you always have full control. It's freaky, but it's the truth, and knowing this truth gives you access to infinite possibilities of experience at every moment.

"PHYSICAL" SENSATIONS ARE NOT REALLY PHYSICAL

Although we often experience sensations as being located somewhere in the body, it is important to know that sensations are actually non-physical, invisible experiences that take place inside our consciousness. As such, a sensation may be perceived as energy, as a rush, or as a "sense" of well-being or of non-well-being (both of which are merely interpretations of the sensation and not the sensation itself.) As an invisible energy, sensations act as the bridge between the non-physical world of thought and the visible physical world, the force that penetrates the veil between the unseen and the seen.

SALAD IN MY TEETH

A very subtle distinction between this work and many other kinds of metaphysical work is that in this work we are clear that we're not "causing" anything to happen. We are simply seeing a reflection of our own thoughts. So you didn't cause your cancer, because there is no cancer to cause. It's just a reflection of your thought. It's not there to be fought or gotten rid of. It's there so you can see your thought.

Often people will say, "But I wasn't thinking that! Why did it appear?"

The point is, the mirror often shows you what you've been unconsciously thinking, even if you're not aware of it. We often see things in the mirror that we weren't aware of, like dirt on our face, or smudged makeup, or messy hair. When we see these things, we would never say, "Why is it reflecting that? I didn't see it before I looked in the mirror." We'd say, "Glad I looked. Didn't know that was going on. Now I can fix it."

My favorite example of this is what I call "Salad in my teeth." How often have I been out to lunch, eaten a delicious meal and then gone and taught a class or attended a social event, smiling and talking and thinking, "I look great," only to go to the men's room, look in the mirror, and see that I've had big green pieces of salad in my teeth the whole time.

I had NO IDEA that the salad was there, and I was behaving as though it wasn't. And all the time, I had big pieces of green stuff in my teeth, and everyone I talked to with confidence and wit could see them. But the reaction I was getting from the world might not have matched the thought, "I'm really cute, I'm really sexy, I'm making a powerful impression here," because what people might have been seeing or thinking was, "Ugh, what a disgusting pig," or "Isn't he silly," or anything in between

Once I see the salad in my teeth reflected in the mirror, I can immediately remove it, and people will instantly see me differently (without salad in my teeth.) But I couldn't remove it before, because I didn't know it was there.

Trust the mirror. Its not just that it never lies. It is INCAPABLE of lying. So if you see it there, it's there, even if you didn't know it. Like salad in your teeth.

What Play Are You In?

I was working with a Thought Exchange group that was predominantly made up of actors, and I thought of this analogy.

When you're acting in a Broadway play, you go to the theater, you put on your costume and makeup, and the play begins.

Perhaps you're playing a young girl who starts out in impoverished and difficult circumstances. You are born into a poor family, where you are beaten and abused. You run away at 15 and get taken in by a man, who continues to abuse you. To save your own life, you murder that man, and you are tried and go to prison. You are in prison for 20 years, and in that time you begin to seek out others who have been abused as you have been, and you help them. 20 years later, at the age of 37, you are paroled, and you begin an organization that works with people who were battered as you were. You begin to get national recognition, you soon become a television star, and in the course of your work, you meet a wonderful man who adores you and who treats you with love and respect. You have beautiful children and live a happy, balanced, fulfilling life. In the end, you win the Nobel Peace Prize, and the world recognizes that you have triumphed over adversity and are a shining example of happiness, commitment and success to all.

The play ends, you take your bow, you go back to your dressing room, change out of your costume, and the experience is over. You probably have the thought, "Whew, that was intense!" because you have spent the past few hours going through poverty, abuse, murder, prison, redemption, hard work, love, and reward. You have actually experienced those things in the past few hours, even though it's just a play. They seemed real to you and to the audience.

It occurred to me that this is exactly what our lives are like. We step into our lives, into a set of circumstances, we battle with them, we ride them, we work with them, we have particular issues and challenges, we achieve some things, we fail at others, and then it's over. Perhaps, when my life is over, I will get to the other side and say, "Whew, what a ride!" I will say that because I've just experienced my childhood, my struggles and successes in becoming a musician, my travails and triumphs in the areas of love and friendship, dealing with finances, mortgages, buying and renovating my house, working, writing songs, being accepted, being rejected, health issues, traveling, developing the Thought Exchange, writing this book, and all the things that happened after that I don't yet know about. And all of it seems so real, so permanent, so true.

And yet, perhaps, it's like a play. When you're in it, you can't step out of it. In the first act, when perhaps all the trouble is happening, the actor doesn't stop and say "I can't stand this, I don't want to experience this." It's all part of the story, and the difficult parts are there as part of the story leading up to the triumph. Or the tragedy. Or a combination of both. If you stopped in the first act, or kept repeating the first act, you'd never get to the second. And the events in the first act could lead anywhere. Even though, as an actor, you know the end, since the play has been written by the playwright, there is suspense, there are times of fear, there are times when the play seems to not be going in the direction you wish it would go, and in fact, if you're a good actor, you forget what the end is going to be because you are caught up in the moment. But the end is there, it's written, the play is a triumph or a tragedy, the outcome is already in place.

Robert Yarnall, a very talented member of the Thought Exchange who often comes up with brilliant ways of putting things and framing things, said, "Perhaps then, when we're experiencing adversity, we should ask ourselves, 'What play am I in? Am I in the play where I meet adversity and then have success in the end, or am I in the play where I meet adversity and go down the drain?"

Can you see that no matter what circumstance we're presently in, that circumstance could be part of any play and could be part of our ending up at any outcome?

So if you are an author trying to get a book published? and you get rejected, you can ask yourself, "What play am I in? Am I in the play 'David gets his book published and the book is a best seller?' or am I in the play 'David fails?'" How many times have we heard about an author or a songwriter who had their work rejected by many major publishers only to, in the end, have it accepted and have it be a bestseller or a hit? And how many times have we heard about people who were rejected and ended up never having anything published?

I suggest you experiment with being the author of the play you're in, by writing it with your thoughts. When some event happens that feels upsetting or seems to be not something that would move you toward the outcome you desire, you may notice that you've taken on thoughts like, "I can't do this," or "I can't have this," or "This will never happen." When you notice those thoughts, ask yourself "What play am I in? The one in which I fail to get what I want, or the one in which after many twists and turns and challenges the result I desire appears?" You'll start to notice that it's your choice. Exchange whatever thought of failure you're having for the thought, "I am in the play where I get what I want," or "I am in the play where I am successful," or whatever thought works for you, and watch what happens.

(For movie buffs or those who see things cinematically, the question "What movie am I in?" works equally well.)

LOOKING IN THE
UNMANFESTED 'WANT ADS'

Two of the most frequent issues that come up in Thought Exchange workshops are finding a job, and finding a romantic relationship. When people are encountering failure and frustration in these areas, and find themselves searching and searching to no avail, I stop and ask them, "Where are you searching for these things?" The answer is invariably, "In the world. I'm trying to date. I'm putting in job applications. I'm 'getting out there.'"

But remember, if the world is nothing more than an exact reflection of our thoughts, if nothing is really going on in the world any more than something is going on in a mirror, then if we're not finding what we want in the world, what we know is that we're thinking we can't find it. So we have to look for these things where they actually are. In the Un-Manifested.

So, when people get stuck, I ask them to spend the week looking in the "Un-Manifested Want Ads." I tell them, "Go into the Un-Manifested (where everything exists.) Open the Want Ads or the Personal Ads. Look for the job you want. Is it there? Look in the column under the salary you want, and find all the jobs in that salary range. Are they there? Are there more there? Now find the location. Is it there? If you're looking for a girlfriend or boyfriend, go to the listings and find the right look, the right age, the right personality, the right qualities, the right location. Are they there? Of course they are. They must be."

Just stay with this, constantly focusing on the Want Ads instead of on the outside world or the result. In this way you are coming at the world knowing that what you want is already here, and since the world is just a mirror, it must reflect that.

But make sure you don't go out into the world to check to see if it's "really there." The minute you do that, you are going out with doubt and thoughts of lack, and the mirror must reflect that. Just stay inside, and you will notice that you have the contentment and sureness that you were seeking by wanting a particular job or partner. In a strange way, you no longer even need them, because you already have them. But since the mirror of the world must reflect what's before it, you will see it there too, when you know you have it inside.

So grab the Un-Manifested Want Ads. They're free, and available to you at all times.

EN-JOYING YOURSELF

So often, we think that circumstances have to be a certain way for us to enjoy ourselves. But let's look at the word "enjoy". "En," means to put in, and "joy" means happiness.

So when we en-joy ourselves, we are putting happiness into ourselves. We would never say, "That movie really enjoyed me," or "This day is really enjoying me." When we understand that circumstances have nothing to do with our ability to put joy into ourselves, we can en-joy ourselves no matter what is going on.

GOD CAN'T APPEAR

Throughout the ages, people have asked, "If God is here, why must He remain invisible? Why doesn't He show himself so we can see him? Wouldn't that be proof positive that He exists?" (Or She, if that's the way you personally see God, but as I see it, God is actually neither a He or She, but English doesn't have a pronoun to express that.)

This is not meant to be a religious book, but since Thought Exchange began in Unity Church of New York, and thus was developed with people who were spiritually-minded and working with the concept of God, I had to be able to put Thought Exchange principles in spiritual terms and address the issue of God and how Thought Exchange relates to God.

In exploring this, I suddenly had a flash of understanding about why we can't see God, and never will. God can't show Himself (or Herself or Itself) to us because God is not physical. God is invisible. God is an experience.

As we discovered earlier in this book, we are an invisible conscious-ness experiencing invisible sensations and having invisible thoughts. And within these thoughts, everything is here, everything already ex-ists, everything has already been given, and everything is possible. All healing, all life situations, all disasters, all material possessions, all states of mind, are already here, within our consciousness, not outside of it. That's what it means when New Thought spiritual teachings say, "God is Within." It doesn't mean that I am God, controlling every-thing. It means that I can find God as an experience inside my own consciousness (which is not really my own, but rather simply Con-sciousness, which everyone shares.)

So in Thought Exchange terms, this Great Un-Manifested, this invisible, unlimited possibility IS God. God is available to us at all times, all of God's riches are available, but they are all invisible, Un-Manifested, because this is where the real world exists. The ONLY place it exists. In our experience.

So when the bible says, "Seek Ye First the Kingdom and All Else Shall Be Given," what it means is; "Go to God on the inside, in the world of experience, in the world where everything is. You will find everything you ever wanted there, and it MUST reflect on the outside.

And when the bible says, "Man is made in God's image," it doesn't mean that man looks like God. An image isn't physical. Where man is exactly like God is that man has, inside of himself, the same invisible consciousness and infinite possibility that God is.

You can never see God, yet you can contact God at any moment.

"Seek Ye First The Kingdom"
"Be Still and Know That I Am God."
"I am made in God's Image."
"God is Within"

All these biblical and spiritual statements that we've heard all our lives, make a new kind of sense when considered in the context of Thought Exchange. God becomes, more than ever, an ever-present, ever available omnipotence, easily contacted, easily relied on, easily lived in.

How Can God Let These "Bad" Things Happen?

When something happens that we regard as bad; a death, an illness, a loss of a job, The World Trade Center, Hitler, we generally hear people say, "How could God let that happen?"

Well, here's the thing. If everything we see is merely a mirror of our thoughts, all these events are doing is reflecting a thought we are having so that we can see it and exchange it. It's not that we're causing these events. There's nothing to cause. They're reflections.

So when some disturbing event happens, when we have some failure or some disappointment, we must go to the sensations it creates, since THE ONLY PURPOSE OF THE EVENT IS TO CREATE THE SENSATIONS IN US THAT WE'RE AFRAID OF, SO THAT WE CAN BE WITH THEM, MASTER THEM, AND RESTORE OURSELVES TO FREE CHOICE OF THOUGHT. The ability to be with the sensations produces healing. Free choice of thought produces free choice of what we see before us.

For example. A few days ago, I made a call asking if I could perform a song of mine at a large annual fundraising event. My song is performed by a Broadway star every year, and this year I wanted to do it myself. I was turned down. They had already offered it to one of the biggest stars on Broadway.

I felt a sensation. It was a sort of sinking feeling. My mind immediately went to all sorts of thoughts, "I'm nothing. If another, more famous composer had asked, they would have said yes. I don't get to have anything. My career is nowhere. Probably nothing will ever happen for me again. I should give up. Why go on? My life is over." It's amazing how quickly our thoughts will go to tragic lengths to get away from a sensation.

I observed my thoughts with interest for about twenty seconds. I knew they were just thoughts, but it was important to observe them. Why? Because the whole purpose of my being turned down was so that I could see the reflection of what I was thinking so that I could exchange it. So although it seems like this incident CAUSED my thoughts, in fact, this incident, simply REVEALED them. Through experiencing this incident I could see that it was I who had been thinking, "I'm nothing. If another composer had asked they would have said yes. I don't get to have anything. My career is nowhere. Probably nothing will ever happen for me again. I should give up. Why go on? My life is over."

And why had I been thinking that? To avoid the sensation that happens when I don't think that, when I "dare" to think that I can have something or do something or be something. So the first thing I did, after observing my thoughts for twenty seconds, was to say, "Whoa, go to the sensations." I simply sat with the sensations, and by doing so, I immediately reconnected with the fact that as long as I was willing to be with my sensations, I could think any thought I chose.

I looked at all the protective thoughts that this incident had revealed to me, and decided that the thought that might be most likely to appear in the world as what I wanted to see there was, "It's possible."

I woke up the next morning, and before I got out of bed, I went through all the things I desired, while simply holding the thought "It's possible" and experiencing any sensations that came up. That seemed easy enough, so I decided to do the same thing every morning.

After a few days, the stock market went way up, and we got an offer of a large amount of money for a Broadway show we wanted to do. I had the feeling that things were really beginning to move in my life.

But really, what had shifted was, I had shifted my thought. So that "bad" thing that had happened had been an opportunity, not to prove that I can't have anything, but to see what my thoughts were and exchange them.

When we get into bigger "disasters," it's often harder to see how this works, because the sensations can be so powerful and overwhelming that we don't want to stay with them. But if we can stay with them, we get the greatest healings. Big disasters are the ones that often lead to national or global healing, if we let them, rather than fighting them.

Often, when we're discussing how anything we see before us is simply a mirror for us to use to see ourselves, someone will play what my partner, Shawn Moninger, calls "The Hitler Card."

We were at a retreat, and were discussing the concept that every upsetting thing that happens is a reflection of our thoughts that can be used to heal us. In that context, I brought up the idea that even our experience of Hitler must be here to generate healing.

One Jewish woman stood up in a rage and said, "How can you say that? Hitler was a monster! He killed Six Million Jews! If God wanted to teach us a lesson, he could have done it in another way. I'm sorry, but there is NOTHING good about Hitler!"

After the session, I went up to her, and I said, "I agree that Hitler was a monster. I don't like Hitler. I often wish he had never lived. But let me ask you this. When you think of Hitler, what sensation do you feel?" She checked, and said, "I feel an extreme tightness in my chest." I asked her if that felt in any way familiar, and with a bit of surprise in her voice she said, "Yes. I get that sensation when I'm confronted with having to do something really scary to me, like performing or going out on a date." I asked her if that sensation ever stopped her from doing those things, and she had to admit that it often did.

So here's the thing. Hitler is dead. He's no longer reachable. We can think anything we want about him, wish he could be tortured as he had tortured others, spew venom, get angry, but it won't change a thing. But Hitler is useful to us in that the memory of him brings up our most powerful sensations that we've been afraid to feel our whole lives. If we can be with those sensations, our own personal bravery and ability to move through challenges that in certain ways, to us, feel like Hitler, will create tremendous growth and added power and potential to our lives.

And the paradox is, when we are able to experience those sensations, we won't need Hitlers to come into our lives to give us more opportunities to experience them. Resisting Hitler creates more Hitlers. Being with the thoughts and sensations that Hitler is reflecting for us, allows us to choose new thoughts that will no longer reflect as Hitlers.

So when things happen that you didn't want to have happen, they are not "bad" (though of course they may be painful) and God is not allowing things that "shouldn't" happen to happen. They are reflections (not caused by, but reflections of) our thoughts. No matter how painful, if you can allow yourself to see what you're thinking, and go right to the sensations, you will find, sometimes to your great surprise and amazement, that you can actually feel grateful for this incident, no matter what it is, as an opportunity for you to experience sensations you've been afraid of, master the ability to be with those sensations, and thus be able to choose new thoughts that will produce what you wish to see in your life as opposed to what you are currently seeing.

TALKING TO DEAD PEOPLE

Have you ever had a conversation in your mind with someone who is no longer living? Most people have. Some people do it all the time.

The question often arises, "Am I really talking to them, or am I just imagining that I am? Are they really there, or am I making this up?"

Well if we've learned anything in our study of Thought Exchange, we've learned that the ONLY place in which we talk to people, dead or alive, is in the Un-Manifested, because that's the only place in which we experience anything.

Remember, when you're talking to someone who is alive, you still don't know if you're even really talking to them. All you know is that you're experiencing talking to them inside of yourself. Maybe they're there. Maybe they're not. This can be a very difficult concept to wrap yourself around, because they certainly seem to be there. But all you know for sure that you experience them.

Since everything exists only in the world of experience, if you want to talk to someone who is dead, you can ALWAYS find them in the Great Un-Manifested, as this is the place where you can always find anything.

When someone in the Thought Exchange says, "I wish I could talk to my departed mother," I say, "Close your eyes. Can you see her?" They always can. "Now, ask her a question. Did she answer?" She always does. Or if she doesn't, it's because she's not answering.

That's talking to your departed mother.

This practice not only allows us to communicate with relatives and friends (or famous people, or anyone for that matter) who are no longer in physical bodies, but strengthens our willingness to have the experience of us all being in the Un-Manifested together. If you can talk to someone dead in the Un-Manifested, you can certainly find whatever else you're looking for in there.

HOLD THAT THOUGHT
(SENSATIONS AS THE KEY TO STAYING WITH THE THOUGHT WE WISH TO HOLD)

If you want to hold a thought and have it turn into a belief and appear in the mirror of the world as Manifestation, you must be willing to stay with the sensation that the thought produces. So when you take on a thought of something you want, immediately notice the sensation you're having and stay with it. If you notice a different thought come in, go back to your original thought and immediately notice the sensation again. Since the sensation is the reason we jump away from the thought, being with it is the anchor that causes the thought to stay put, become a belief, and manifest.

THE FOUR PRINCIPLES OF NON-RESISTANCE
(WHAT YOU RESIST PERSISTS)

It's a commonly known axiom of New Thought that What You Resist Persists. If we think through this, we realize that it must then be true that What You Don't Resist Doesn't Persist. Once we know this, we can stop resisting what we don't want, and it should disappear. But here's the catch. If we stop resisting it because we want or need it to disappear, we're resisting it. So it won't disappear. So in order to do real non-resistance, and thus have the problem disappear, here are the four steps we must go through.

If: What you resist persists,

Then: What you don't resist does not persist

But: If you are "not resisting" something so that it will disappear, you are resisting it

So: The only way to have something that's a problem disappear is to be WILLING TO HAVE IT FOREVER.

You might say, "Well, if I'm willing to have it forever, then I just might end up having it forever." This is true. But if you're not resisting it, it doesn't matter if you have it forever. It doesn't hamper you in any way. Since our life is experienced only on the inside, we have the capacity to be comfortable and happy no matter what is going on. Comfort and happiness are the ability to be with what is. Discomfort is being attached to conditions and having to have them be a certain way.

So when you're not resisting something, it may disappear, it may not, but either way, it completely ceases to be a problem.

Our Tactics for Avoiding Sensations

In one of our Thought Exchanges, we focused on all the ways in which we avoid sensations. It was an amazingly long list. Very often, thoughts, things and conditions that seem very real are just another way for us to avoid sensations. Once we know this, no matter what we see, no matter what we think, we can simply go back to the sensation and reopen the entire world of unlimited possibilities to ourselves.

The next time you meet a circumstance that you find uncomfortable, look at this list and see if you're doing any of these things to avoid your sensations.

The list includes:

- SAYING YOU'RE GUILTY

- SAYING YOU'RE ASHAMED

- SAYING YOU'RE NOT GOOD ENOUGH

- DECIDING THAT THIS SITUATION IS AN EXCEPTION, THAT WHAT YOU'RE SEEING IN THE MIRROR OF THE WORLD IS, IN THIS CASE, REAL.

- DECIDING THAT IF THIS CERTAIN THING HAPPENS IT'S "ALL OVER."

- TELLING YOURSELF YOU DON'T DESERVE TO HAVE THIS.

- DECIDING THAT THE SENSATION YOU'RE HAVING IS IM-POSSIBLE TO TOLERATE.

- DECIDING THAT YOU HAVE TO FIND OUT WHAT THE ORIGINAL DAMAGE WAS, AND "RELEASE" IT.

- DECIDING THAT SOMEONE ELSE IS TO BLAME OR THAT THEY HAVE TO DO SOMETHING DIFFERENT

- SAYING YOU HAVE TO "EXPRESS" YOUR ANGER OR YOUR SADNESS OR UPSET.

- SAYING THAT YOU'RE PARALYZED. (I can't tell you how many people easily get up and move while saying they're paralyzed.)

- SAYING THAT THIS SITUATION IS TRULY UPSETTING AND THE PERSON WHO'S IN IT HAS TO BE PITIED OR GIVEN SUPPORT FOR THE FACT THAT THE SITUATION IS REAL. (In this case, I'm not saying that it isn't painful, because it's extremely painful. Staying with these sensations may be the most difficult thing you ever do. But we must support people in staying with the sensation because that is where the healing is. To support the "realness" of their story only keeps them stuck. Rather, support the realness of their sensations and support them in having them.)

- SAYING SOMETHING SHOULDN'T HAVE HAPPENED.

- DWELLING ON WHAT HAPPENED TO US. (It's not what happened to us that's keeping us stuck. It's our current thought about it, a thought that we've taken on to stay away from the sensation that's associated with what happened. So what's keeping us stuck is our resistance to simply experiencing the sensation.

- SAYING WE CAN'T GO ON IF WE'RE GOING TO HAVE THAT SENSATION.

- TRYING TO GET RID OF THAT SENSATION.

- TRYING TO FEEL THAT SENSATION SO THAT WE CAN GET RID OF IT. (Just as a leg that's been amputated can never grow back, you may never get rid of the sensation, but you could still live a full life if you're willing to know your leg is gone, and experience what that feels like while doing anything you please.)

- PROFESSING NOT NOT TO HAVE ANY SENSATIONS.

- FOCUSING ON HOW YOU'RE SUPPOSED TO DO SOMETHING, OR ON HOW HAVING SENSATIONS IS GOING TO HELP IN ANY WAY (I refuse to have any sensations until I can know how I can use them to get what I want.)

- THINKING THAT THINGS HAVE TO TURN OUT A CERTAIN WAY TO GET WHAT YOU WANT.

I'm sure there are many more. But if you are in a challenging situation and you notice that you're doing any of these things, look for the sensation that underlies it, the sensation you're trying to get away from, and just sit with that. Do not interpret what the sensation means or what will happen if you stay with it. Do not judge the sensation. Just be with it. If you do this, you will notice an immediate opening of possibilities, with new thoughts and new ideas coming to you spontaneously and effortlessly. Before long, the problem is "nothing."

Try it. It's amazing.

WHAT'S REAL AND WHAT WE MAKE UP

I was doing a corporate event, and one of the attendees was telling me about her boyfriend breaking up with her. She said, "My boyfriend broke up with me and I was so humiliated. I felt like such an idiot, and knew that he was judging me and that he hated me."

I stopped her and asked, "What is the only thing you KNOW about this?" When she thought about it, all she knew was that her boyfriend had broken up with her and that she had a tightness in her chest. All the rest was made up to get away from that tightness.

The next time you have something disturbing happen and you notice your mind going off into fantasies and explanations, just ask yourself, "What does it feel like to physically go through this?" and stay with the sensations.

That's all. The event itself does not mean anything. It doesn't mean there will be a particular outcome; it doesn't mean that people do or don't think anything about you; it doesn't mean you're good or bad."

It's just a mirror to show you what you're thinking, and to direct you back to the sensations you've been avoiding. So use it for what it's there for, and you won't need to keep creating events like it.

WE ARE ALWAYS IN THE PERFECT CIRCUMSTANCE
(THOMAS MERTON)

Thomas Merton was a brilliant writer who spent the first part of his life in secular, intellectual pursuits, and the second part as a Trappist Monk, meditating and writing in silence. In Christian terms, it could be said that he decided to "Seek the Kingdom First" by going inward to find God. In Thought Exchange terms, we would say that he chose to realize that where he lives is in the Un-Manifested world of experience, rather than in the world of circumstances and events.

There are several quotes of his that I wanted to share here, as they have proven to be a powerful way to use the visible world to go toward the invisible, where all the real life and all the healing takes place.

Here are the Thomas Merton quotes.

"The situation I am in now has been given to me to change me, if I will only surrender completely to reality as it is given me by God and no longer seek in any way to evade it, even by interior reservations."

"God gives us the freedom to create our own lives, according to His will, that is to say in the circumstances in which he placed us. But we refuse to be content unless we realize in ourselves a "universal" standard, a happiness hypothetically prescribed and approved for all men of all time, not just our own happiness."

"I feel more sure than I ever have in my life that I am obeying the Lord and am on the way He wills for me, though at the same time I am struck and appalled (more than ever!) by the shoddiness of my response."

In Thought Exchange terms, these quotes can be interpreted to say that if every circumstance we see before us is simply a reflection of what we're thinking, then we must not only accept, but welcome the circumstance (since it gives us the opportunity to see what we're thinking) take on the thoughts we wish to take on, be with the sensations we've resisted, and come to the deep understanding that we have everything, there is nothing to want, nothing to need, nothing to lack.

It could be said that in Thought Exchange we think of God as The Great Un-Manifested, that place where everything already exists, where there is nothing lacking, and where we can go to know that we have everything. So let every circumstance lead you back to that invisible place.

Time and again, we see ourselves in the mirror of circumstance, and we try to fight off or alter the circumstances. But if they're a reflection of ourselves, they will have to keep reappearing, since a mirror can only reflect what's in front of it. So see what's there, experience the sensations, and then go to the only place where you have free choice and where those choices matter. Inside.

It's The "Positive" Thought That We're Afraid Of

When something upsetting happens, we think that we're having uncomfortable sensations because something upsetting has happened, and if only we could change the circumstance we would feel better.

As strange as it may seem, the exact opposite is true.

We take on thoughts of lack because somewhere in our past, a painful sensation is associated with the thought we wish to take on. If, as children, we took on the thought, "I can have this" and the thing we wanted was taken away from us, the thing that would bring back the painful memory would be the thought, "I can have this." All the other thoughts, the "I can't, it won't happen" thoughts, are designed to keep us away from the pain.

So when you really start going for something you want, expect to have sensations which may be uncomfortable, stay with them, and take them as a sign that you're on the right track, not as a sign that you're getting into danger.

A more subtle understanding of this concept reveals that it is not the upsetting thing that happens that directly causes us to have the sensations we're afraid of. When something upsetting happens, we immediately recognize it as something we don't want. Seeing that, we are instantly aware of what we do want, and it is that new thought (the thought of what we do want as opposed to the thought of what we don't want) that immediately brings us back to the sensation we're afraid of.

If we continue to be afraid of the sensation, we will immediately take on the protective thought that brought about the result we didn't want, and before we know it we'll be back to the result we didn't want, followed by the awareness of the thought of what we did want, followed by the sensation we're afraid of again.

Life Is Sensational

NO MATTER HOW YOU LOOK AT IT, LIFE IS SENSATIONAL. SO YOU MIGHT AS WELL JUST FEEL WHATEVER SENSATION YOU'RE AFRAID OF, BECAUSE IT WILL ONLY COME UP AGAIN AND AGAIN UNTIL YOU DO.

CHAPTER 29
WHEN YOU GET STUCK
DEALING WITH RESISTANCE AND QUESTIONS
THAT ARISE

In the course of teaching The Thought Exchange, I have found that certain questions and forms of resistance consistently arise. Some people question the basic premise. Some feel that because of religious beliefs, or because of the way the way they naturally work, think and feel, that they cannot apply The Thought Exchange to their lives. People from other disciplines, such as psychotherapy and body work, often question how Thought Exchange fits in with the important work they're doing. And some people simply get stuck, or find that even though they understand how it works and have seen the results, they just can't seem to get themselves to move forward.

As I have endeavored to answer these questions, I have discovered a number of underlying principles that, when applied, often help people to have a deeper understanding of what Thought Exchange is, and of how it actually works. This understanding can be very helpful in allowing people to get through those times when they are experiencing resistance to continuing. In this chapter, I explain some of these principles and how they might answer some of the questions you may have.

HOW THE THOUGHT EXCHANGE TIES
IN WITH OTHER DISCIPLINES

Professionals from other disciplines, such as psychotherapy, body, work and energy work, often ask if The Thought Exchange, with its emphasis on Thought as Cause, generates conflict with the emphasis of their work, which may be based on feelings, rational working with events, the body or energetic release.

This is a very important question, the exploration of which has led me to a deeper understanding of the valuable place Thought Exchange holds in conjunction with all of these other important and valuable disciplines.

The simplest way to explain this is to give an example of how I used Thought Exchange to allow myself to break through in my own psychotherapy.

Over the course of my personal spiritual and psychological journey, I have spent many years in therapy, and have explored many other healing disciplines. I have done psychoanalysis, bioenergetics, Inner-Child work, eye movement work, Somatic Experiencing, TMS work, Primal Scream, EST, The Forum, spiritual counseling, meditation, New Thought work, massage, Rolfing just to name a few. I got a great deal out of all of them, but there was always a basic breakthrough that eluded me. I would get to a certain point of progress, and then I would fall back and it would all seem to go away.

I was in my thirteenth year of working with a wonderful therapist, struggling with yet another one of those setbacks, and I was complaining that no matter what we did it never seemed to work. She postulated that, for some reason, I just did not seem to be willing to deeply commit to doing the particular modality of therapy we were working within.

It was clear that she was right, but the question was, of course, "Why? Why could I not deeply commit to the therapy? Why could I not allow the therapy to work? Why, whenever I went inside and asked my body what was at the root of my issues, did I hear a distinct voice saying, 'You'll never find out!'"

I had just begun to work with Thought Exchange, so I asked myself, "What am I thinking in regard to my therapy?" The answer came back loud and clear. I am thinking, "This cannot work. In fact, nothing can work."

So I was doing my whole therapy inside the thought "This can't work." Just as, at previous times in my life, I had held the thought "I can't get a date," while trying, unsuccessfully to date; or, "The Orchestra will not follow me," while trying, unsuccessfully, to conduct an orchestra, so I was now holding a thought inside of which no matter what I did, I would not get the therapeutic result I desired.

So I thought to myself, "What thought could I exchange this for that would allow the therapy to work?" I came up with the obvious and simple thought, "It is possible for the therapy to work."

This simple thought exchange made a tremendous difference in my ability to have a major breakthrough in my therapy, but there's a very important point that needs to be stressed. **That thought did not heal the wounds that needed to be healed! I still had to do the therapy.** That thought simply allowed me to do the therapy I needed to do. It opened the way. It created a context within which I could allow the therapy to work.

What the therapy then became about was handling the sensations that arose when I "dared" to take on the thought that I could actually have a successful therapy. What the thought exchange essentially did was open the wound that needed to be revealed so that it could be addressed and ultimately healed.

When one exchanges a thought from one of no possibility to one of possibility, the work still needs to be done. It could be said that it is the new thought that is causing the condition within which the work can be done. You still have to do the psychoanalysis, or the body work, or the energy release, perhaps for years.

So the Thought Exchange becomes a tool for therapists in any discipline to use when their patients seem to be inexplicably stuck or resistant to the work. When this happens, I would suggest stopping, looking at the underlying thought, exchanging it for a thought within which the therapy can proceed, and going on with the therapy.

Thought Exchange is not, in any way, a replacement for any of these other important disciplines, nor does it function in conflict with them. Used properly, it can be an adjunct and a strong support for the therapy at hand.

THOUGHT EXCHANGE

A SENSATIONAL ADDITION TO OTHER MODALITIES OF THERAPY AND SPIRITUAL WORK

Having participated in many wonderful and helpful modalities of therapy and spiritual work, here, in my opinion, is how each of those could have been catalyzed and supported, had I been aware of Thought Exchange principles at the time.

I want to be clear that this is not intended as a criticism of any of these ways of working, but rather as an adjunct to working with those modalities, based on misconceptions or difficulties that I had when I worked with them.

Each of these disciplines could just as easily offer suggestions as to how working with them could enhance and support Thought Exchange work.

As my partner, Rev. Shawn Moninger, learned in Seminary, "Always in addition to, never instead of."

PSYCHOTHERAPY

As I mentioned above, I was not able to make true progress in years and years of psychotherapy, even though I had many brilliant and helpful therapists, until I was able to realize that my underlying thought about the whole thing was, "It's impossible for me to heal." When you're in therapy, and you feel yourself getting stuck, examine your thoughts about the process itself, and see if you find one that says that you can't succeed. Then look in the Un-Manifested, where success MUST be one of the infinite possibilities, and notice the sensations that you experience when you take on the thought that it is possible to succeed. When you can stay with that thought, and the sensations it brings up, your therapy will progress.

Also, another challenge in therapy is that one of the goals of therapy is often to get you to remember old incidents in your childhood so you can "feel the feelings." Remember that the point is to experience the sensations, not to get rid of them. If you keep trying to "get over" something, you are avoiding the sensations. Only by developing your capacity to experience them will you be free of any stoppage the earlier incident has caused you.

If you find yourself repetitively going back to childhood incidents, even after you have worked through them deeply, it is often because the Inner Child is speaking and not the adult that you are now. Go to your own adult, and see how you might listen to the child and give it what it needs yourself, rather than thinking the therapist has to provide that. The therapist can hold the space for you to find your own strength, by being the good parent your child never had, but only you can ultimately provide the parenting that will grow the child up.

EMDR and Somatic Experiencing

EMDR and Somatic Experiencing are just two of a number of excellent and effective ways to deal with traumas and Traumatic Stress Syndrome. In both, one through eye movement, the other through a close attention to the sensations you're having, you gradually unravel the tightly-held trauma, and experience it. This is all excellent. Where I got tripped up was that I kept thinking that somewhere in the process I was supposed to "get rid of" or "get over" the experience. In fact, experiencing the sensations is the whole ball of wax. There is nothing more to do. By trying to get over them, I was subtly avoiding them, and thus the therapy never truly worked. So if you're doing this kind of work, simply do it with no goal, no aim, no need to fix anything, and it will do what it's supposed to do, automatically.

The Forum

One of the principles that is extremely useful in The Forum is the notion of changing your story so that you can see something different in the world. This is very important, but often doesn't work because a change of story means a change of thought, which means that whatever sensation is associated with that thought will arise. The only reason you originally took on the story you took on was to protect yourself from that sensation. So when you change your story, you will immediately feel the sensation you were afraid of. You MUST be with that sensation rather than running away from it, or you'll be back to your old story in two seconds.

ABRAHAM HICKS WORK

I have found Abraham Hicks work brilliant and helpful, but the one stumbling block for me was the notion that you'll know you're on the right track when you feel good. For myself, I found that confusing, because every time I would take on the thought that was clearly on the right track I felt uncomfortable sensations. I think the point is that once you are on the right track and willing to experience your sensations you will feel a deep sense of power and your life will begin to turn out. When doing this kind of work, make sure that you don't get discouraged or sidetracked when you experience the sometimes uncomfortable sensations that go with the thoughts you wish to hold.

THE "LAW OF ATTRACTION"

The "Law of Attraction" has become one of the most popular New Thought concepts in the past few years, because it promises that when you "vibrate" or think a certain way, you "attract" things to you that match your vibration and thought. The only problem I have with it is that it implies that there is something that is "outside" you to "attract." Given that our whole life takes place within, and all of our experience, and thus all possibilities also lie within, in the invisible, Un-Manifested world, in my understanding there is nothing to "attract." Everything is already here, right inside us. All we have to do is notice it. So I prefer to call it "The Law of Noticing."

When you notice that you already have whatever it is you desire, in the only place in which you ever can "have" anything (the invisible world of experience inside you) you automatically hold the thought that it exists, and thus, you are "vibrating" with it, and seeing its reflection when you look "outside." But all you're really seeing, since the "outside" is just a reflection, is what is already, and has always been, within. You haven't "attracted" anything. You've simply noticed that you already have it.

THE "SECRET"

A few years ago, the book "The Secret" took the world by storm, and introduced millions of people to the concept that when you change your thought you change your life. Everyone was talking about how simple life is. You just think something different and it happens.

But as time went on, many people began to be disappointed in "The Secret" because they found it "wasn't working."

The principles of the "Secret" are actually completely sound, but there's one part of the process that's left out. When you take on a new thought, it generates sensations, and they're often uncomfortable. If you can't stay with these sensations, you will immediately exchange the thought back for the protective thought that you were holding to stay away from sensations that were perceived as dangerous in your childhood.

So it wasn't that the new thoughts weren't working. It was that people couldn't stay with them, and before they knew it, found themselves back in the old thoughts. So in order to work the principles of the "Secret," you need to notice the sensations that arise, and be with them. Then you'll be able to stay with your new thought, and see it reflected in the mirror of the Manifested World.

That's the "Secret" behind the "Secret."

A COURSE IN MIRACLES

A Course in Miracles is one of the most popular and effective means of Truth study around. When understood, it is a complete system of getting to the basic truths of existence: That the physical world we're living in is an illusion. That "God" is not aware of itself, or of us. That there's no-one else out there. And that there are NO EXCEPTIONS to The Truth.

The one challenge I have found is that often people who are very steeped in Course in Miracles and very aware of the truths it puts forward, especially the principle that there are no exceptions, make exceptions to it anyway, in situations they find troubling. People who KNOW that none of this is real, will panic because, "This is about my kids," or "I'm going to lose my house." Or decide that some challenge is too much to take.

The only reason this happens is because people come across sensations that are frightening to them. So if you're studying Course in Miracles, and you find that you're thinking or doing something that seems to go against the principles you know to be true, go immediately to your sensations, experience them as harmless and meaningless, and you will find yourself immediately able to think and act in ways that reflect what you KNOW to be true.

12 STEP PROGRAMS

The other day, I was drawing the basic Thought Exchange Chart for a class, pointing out how when we take on the thought of something we want, if we can't allow ourselves to experience the sensation that comes with the thought, we will take on a "protective" thought to get away from that sensation. That protective thought will generate a sensation that's more tolerable, but will not only keep us from having what we want, but will eventually lead us right back to the sensation we've been trying to get away from.

One of our members pointed out that this is exactly the pattern of addiction. We don't want to feel a sensation, so we pick up a drug. As I've said earlier in this book, the "negative" thought can definitely be thought of as a drug, since a drug is something you take to avoid pain.

So the way in which Thought Exchange can be helpful in supporting Alcoholics Anonymous, Overeaters Anonymous, Al-Anon, Drugs Anonymous, Sexaholics Anonymous, Debtors Anonymous, or any other 12 step program, is that Thought Exchange emphasizes that when you stop taking the "drug of choice" you will not necessarily feel good, but rather, will come face to face with the sensations you've been trying to avoid.

People often naively think that if they can just stop drinking or eating or taking drugs, they'll feel fine. Nothing could be further from the truth. It's the sensations that arise when we stop the addiction, that are the reason we go back to it. So in order to stay off the drugs or alcohol, or whatever the addiction is, we must be willing to experience the sensations that arise when we STOP picking up the substance or behavior.

Only by being able to be with these sensations can we continue to choose and stay with the thought of staying sober. And as we know, the choosing of this thought will generate the manifestation of this thought.

As time goes on and we go through the 12 steps, it is the ability to stay with the sensations that arise when we DON'T drink, take drugs or act out in other ways, that will allow us to exchange our old protective thoughts for thoughts we truly want to hold, and see those thoughts begin to manifest in our lives as health, success and happiness.

Our member who had participated in AA for years, pointed out that just as in AA, where you must take a first step, in fact, several steps, before being able to begin exchanging thoughts, it might be helpful to have a "first step" in Thought Exchange.

What we came up with was:

"We admitted that we were powerless to get over, under or around our sensations, and that our lives had become unmanageable."

Taking this step causes us to move in the direction of letting go to experiencing our sensations. Once we can experience them, we will have no need for the protective thought or whatever substances or behaviors we've been abusing, since the only purpose of "picking them up" was to get us away from a sensation that we're now willing to feel. This "surrender" to sensations sets the stage for us to be able to take on and hold thoughts that will lead us on the path to true recovery.

POSITIVE THINKING

Positive Thinking is a very powerful tool, but where it can fall down is when people refuse to see or think or say anything "negative." Stuff like "cancel, cancel" or "I'm not going to let myself think that negative thought," rob us of the ability to see and take responsibility for what we're actually thinking at the moment. Only when we can really look in the mirror of the world, and see and take responsibility for the thought we're actually thinking that's causing the world to appear as it does, can we know which thought to exchange it for. In truth, we don't even have to exchange it. The moment we see the "negative" thought we're having as just a thought, it automatically exchanges. So in truth, the "negative" thought is more important for us to know about than the "positive" one. The positive one will automatically arise.

One more point about positive thinking. If you want to stay with the positive thought you've chosen, you MUST be able to stay with the sensations that thought produces, even if they're uncomfortable. Otherwise, you will exchange the thought back for the old one before you know it.

BODY WORK

Being someone who had a great tendency to get into my head and avoid my experience, I found body work very useful in helping me to work through issues. The one pitfall in body work, especially the deeper kinds like Rolfing or shiatsu, is that often we try to avoid pain and think that the object is to get away from pain. Since what you resist persists, it's crucial to, as much as possible, experience and go through the pain. This will not only help your muscles release, but will give you the ability to experience sensations that you've tried to avoid by tensing your body. In an even deeper way, more lifelong, unconscious holdings will come to the surface for you to experience them, not for you to avoid them. The more you do this, the more the world of infinite possibility re-opens to you.

ENERGY WORK

Working with the invisible forces of energy that flow through us and flow through the universe can be a very powerful tool to getting in touch with forces that are greater than those we can see. In Thought Exchange terms, things that are invisible; consciousness, sensations, thoughts, are all energy. Through a process that we don't understand, these get "translated" into what we see before us. It's important to ac-knowledge that the two are running parallel to each other and are not separate. Just as in the case of a light bulb, where electricity turns the bulb on, we must remember that energy is the source and the physi-cal world is the result. To put it another way, energy is cause, and the physical world is effect, not the other way around. When we know that things that happen in the physical world do not cause our energy, but rather that our energy causes us to perceive the physical world in a particular way, we can make great use of energy work. Blaming the "stress" of the physical world, or the way people treat us, for our energetic issues, is putting the cart before the horse. Anything we're seeing in the visible world can be nothing more than an exact reflec-tion of what's going on in our invisible world. So let what you see in the physical world be a clue as to what you're doing with your energy. Then work exclusively on your invisible world, and watch the visible world immediately change.

PSYCHIC WORK

It's often fun and interesting, and even helpful, to get a psychic read-ing, but it's important to understand what it is and what it is not.

Within Thought Exchange Principles, since anything and everything that "happens" in the world can be nothing more than an exact re-flection of our thoughts, it's not possible for something to "happen" or to be "going to happen in the future" without our thinking it first.

And since we always have unlimited choice, at every moment, as to what our thought is, it is not possible that there is some set, unchangeable future in store for us.

So what is a psychic reading? It is a mirror, and as such, becomes extremely useful in that you get to see what you're thinking. When you can see this, it gives you the opportunity to exchange the thought, experience the sensations that go with the new thought you're holding, and see a different outcome than the one that was predicted.

So have your psychic readings, go to your fortune-tellers, but know that what they're telling you is about your perfectly exchangeable thoughts in the PRESENT, not about some FUTURE that you're stuck with.

BUDDHISM

People sometimes get confused around Thought Exchange when they study Buddhism, because Buddhism states that thought is not real either, and that you must get beyond thought, to a place, as it were, of no thought, in order to be enlightened.

In truth, though Thought Exchange may seem to be in opposition to that, ultimately it isn't.

We exchange thoughts because we become aware that thoughts are causing the way we feel and causing what we see in the world to appear. Once we know this, we realize that what's preventing us from choosing the thoughts we want is that we can't stay with the sensations that they bring up. In truth, all that matters is that we stay with the sensations, with our experience as it were. Once we can simply stay with our experience, we have no need to choose thoughts. They choose themselves. It no longer matters what happens. We are always centered, because we are simply experiencing our life. We watch each thought simply arise and pass away. And our life, whatever happens, turns out as a reflection of the great peace and acceptance of "what IS" that we hold within. We have let go of the need to have things any certain way, let go of the notion that our happiness depends on outer circumstances, let go of the "illusion" that the physical world is real, and are living in the reality of experience and acceptance, which is the

Nirvana that Buddhism speaks of.

So Thought Exchange could be called "Buddhism for Westerners" in that it provides a rational and graspable gateway for people who are not steeped in Buddhist tradition and an eastern way of living and thinking, to go through the steps that eventually lead to not depending on thought at all.

SPIRITUAL WORK AND RELIGION

Thought Exchange work can often seem antithetical to many religions, because it defines God as The Great Un-Manifested, and it locates the infinite possibilities of the Universe within each of us. If we remember that no religion and no way of working can possibly be the Truth (since the Truth is unspeakable and unknowable) and that ALL religions and ALL ways of working are simply symbolic representations of the Truth, then we can know that the purpose of religion is to point us toward the Truth, not to be the Truth itself. Most religions and spiritual modalities will lead us there, if we can get past the dogma and understand the underlying principles. For instance, I may not understand how Catholicism works, or be interested in practicing it, but I certainly am moved and enlightened when Thomas Merton talks about it. What Thought Exchange tries to do, is work with the principles that underlie all religion. So if you are involved in a religious or spiritual practice, Thought Exchange can always be used in conjunction with it, and does not in any way exclude following your religious or spiritual path. I often think of Thought Exchange as a way to redefine or clarify religious teachings in ways that make sense to me personally, when the religious teaching, because of the particular terminology it uses or the particular ways in which it defines things, is confusing or doesn't make sense to me.

NEW THOUGHT

Since Thought Exchange came out of New Thought, it is of course very close to it. The issue I have found is that when New Thought churches talk about abundance and prosperity, people often mistakenly think that what they're referring to is "stuff." People sometimes practice New Thought in order to get a car, to find a boyfriend or to get rich. It must be understood that although these things may be the result of having a New Thought, all of the new thought principles make no sense if you're not aware that what they're talking about is the invisible world where we already have everything. We must use New Thought to go to the source, not to the result. This means the difference between always being in lack, want and desire, and always living in the fullness and contentment of knowing that we have all that we desire, no matter what the circumstances.

I think the reason for this misunderstanding (and actually, one of the main reasons I felt compelled to develop Thought Exchange) is that New Thought teachings often leave out two very crucial parts of the process: The importance of the "Negative" Thought, and Sensations. Often New Thought will say, "Don't be negative" or, "Don't focus on that." Although these are, in their own way, good pieces of advice, we MUST be aware of the "negative" thought in order to see what it is we're thinking, and connect with the knowledge that it is we who are creating what's in front of us. When we can do this, we can go a step further, and know that whatever is happening in front of us is intrinsically meaningless, since it is no more than a reflection of what we're thinking. Then the "positive" thought, and the matching "positive" manifestation (positive simply meaning what it is we prefer to see before us) will arrive spontaneously.

Of course, once the "positive" thought arises, the downfall of many New Thought methods is that people have trouble staying with it. They can try affirmation after affirmation, action after action, prayer after prayer, but if they can't be with the sensations that the thought generates, they'll never stay with it.

In short, whatever form of spiritual practice you are involved in, whether it's working beautifully for you or whether you have areas in which you're getting stuck, don't let it stop you from exploring the principles of Thought Exchange, or of any of the other modalities I've mentioned (or ones I haven't.) Each way of thinking and working has something to teach us. Each system, method, religion and spiritual practice has its unique ways of looking at the Truth that can add to our understanding, and compliment and clarify what we already know. If you truly believe that your practice is leading you to The Truth, nothing in other practices that are also leading there will undermine it, and questions and doubts will not disprove it. They will just enhance it.

In my Thought Exchange Workshops, I love it when people challenge me, when they bring up their doubts and questions. If our Truth is so easily thrown that we can't look at other things, it may very well be a sign that we need to re-examine the way we're thinking about it. Remember, the object is to know and experience the Truth, not to use dogma or a system to get away from uncomfortable sensations. Truth is Truth, it is unshakeable, and only the Truth will set us free.

YOU CAN ENTER THE THOUGHT EXCHANGE CIRCLE AT ANY POINT

When I teach Thought as Cause, I invariably encounter people who say, "I don't start with Thought, I start with Sensations" or "I start with Belief," or "I start with an event." These people often struggle with how to use the circle of Thought/Sensation/Belief and Manifestation, since their first awareness that something is going on in their life tends to come from something other than a thought.

The fact is, we can enter the Thought Exchange Circle at any point. Some people first notice a sensation. If you notice a sensation, the question to ask is, "What thought is causing this sensation?" To find that thought, you might have to go even further back in the circle to Manifestation and ask, "What event happened, about which I chose a thought that caused the sensation?" The important subtlety here is that the event did not cause the thought. The only thing that <u>causes</u> things is Thought.

Some people enter the wheel at event. They notice an event first, and only later experience their thoughts, sensations and beliefs. That's fine. We notice an event, notice the thought we have about it, remind ourselves that that is just one possible thought among infinite thoughts that are available, and that the event did not <u>cause</u> the thought. We can then exchange the thought for a thought that is more likely to produce the event we want to see.

Some people go the other way. They see an event, and they immediately go to their belief about it. (Or, it could be said, to the belief that preceded it, even though it doesn't look that way.) So, for instance, someone might fail at something and immediately say, "You see, I failed. That's because I always fail."

If this is the position in which you find yourself, notice the belief, then label it as a belief. As we know, a belief is nothing more than a thought we think is true, and thoughts are not "true," they are just thoughts. Obviously, you can't know whether you will fail every time you ever try anything in the future. Once you've labeled this as a belief, you can continue back around the circle, through your sensations related to this, and find the underlying thoughts. Thoughts, unlike beliefs, can be exchanged, so you can exchange the thought you're holding for a new thought. This new thought will generate new sensations and beliefs, the result being that a different manifestation will appear.

If you are contemplating some future event, and you come across a belief you have about the projected outcome, label it as a belief, and go back around the circle to the underlying thought, where you can make the exchange.

So you can do it your way. Enter the circle from wherever you happen to be; Thought, Sensation, Belief or Manifestation. Then move around the circle, in either direction, until you get to Thought, where you can make the exchange.

THE WHOLE WORLD HAPPENS INSIDE YOU

One of the most commonly asked questions is, "Are my thoughts <u>really</u> making the world out there happen? Did that event <u>really</u> happen because I thought it?

With all the magical thinking that goes on in religious and spiritual practices, and all the attempts to find ways to control the world so that we don't have to feel subjected to change, challenges and uncertainty, it's very important to understand what is actually happening when we exchange our thoughts. Do we cause things to happen "out there?" Do we actually bring things into existence that weren't there before?

In working with these questions over the years, I have found that the simple yet potentially perplexing answer is, "Yes, our thoughts are causing the events we see and experience in our lives," and "No, we are not creating those events and making them happen."

Do you realize that when you see someone "out there," what you're actually seeing is an image that is appearing on your own retina that is being perceived inside your own brain? The whole thing is happening inside your own head, even though it appears as though the person or thing you're looking at is outside of you. You have no way of actually knowing that there is something outside you. In fact, there may not be. All we have is an image inside our own head that looks like it's "out there."

In the same way, in terms of any event, all we have is our experience of that event. The event intrinsically has no "reality" to it. Each person experiences what they experience, and that becomes how their life is lived.

I remember being at a dinner party, and speaking with a woman who was going through a difficult divorce. She was complaining bitterly that her ex-husband had left her with "nothing." The only asset she'd received in the settlement was their apartment, and in order to maintain her lifestyle, she had to sell it. She described herself as "destitute," and wondered how she would be able to live.

Someone at the table happened to ask her what she was asking for the apartment. The selling price was $7.75 million dollars. This poor woman was down to her last $7.75 million dollars!

Now we may laugh, but the fact is, this woman was having the experience of poverty and destitution. For whatever reasons, related to the lifestyle to which she was accustomed or related to her internal sense of self, she was experiencing lack, poverty and fear.

I think it's easy to see that the adjustment that would need to be made here would be internal. But this brings up a very important question.

We do Thought Exchange because we want to see specific results in our lives. We don't do it so that we can settle for or become happier with what we don't have. We want what we want!

But what is it that this woman really wants? Is it that specific apartment? Is it a specific amount of money? Or is it what she thinks those things would bring her? Abundance. Peace of mind. A feeling of safety and joy and satisfaction.

If we understand that the manifested world is a reflection and not a cause of our thought, then we understand that what this woman sees in the world is a reflection of a thought she's having. And by her words about it, we can glean that the thought she's having has to do with there not being enough.

It doesn't matter that what is in the world for her would be considered, by most people, to be tremendously abundant. What matters is that when she looks at it, the thought that is revealed to her is, "There's not enough."

Our Thoughts Cause Our Experience of the World

So it could be said that rather than our thoughts causing the world, our thoughts cause our experience of the world. Everything is always here, every possibility, every situation. Unlimited amounts of money exist. Unlimited relationships, partners and friends exist, right now. So it's not like our thoughts create the stuff. The thought is reflected back to us by the stuff. We can look at the world, at

ANYTHING in the world, and it will reflect our thought back to us. When we then exchange the thought that we see reflected back to us by the mirror of the world, we will look in that same mirror (world) and see something different. Perhaps, based on whatever thought we're holding, we see different aspects of the same world. Health and sickness are both always here. Does our thought determine whether we see health or see sickness? Wealth and poverty are always here. Consider the possibility that our thought determines which part of the world we see.

In one of our Thought Exchange Workshops, Janet related an incident that illustrates this beautifully.

She was on the bus, headed to a church retreat, when the bus broke down. Janet immediately asked herself, "What was I thinking that caused the bus to break down?" The answer she came up with was, "There were several people who I'd hoped would be going to the retreat who weren't going, and I thought that perhaps my thought, 'I don't want to be on this retreat,' caused the bus to break down"

I asked her if she really believed that her thought had actually caused the bus to break down. We agreed that that was pretty farfetched. So what was the relationship of the thought to the incident? What happened was, when she looked at the incident as a mirror of her thoughts, she saw the thought, "I don't want to be on this retreat." That was the thought that was reflected to her by the incident.

At this point I turned to Luke, who had been on the same bus, and had experienced the same incident and asked, "What did you think when the bus broke down?" His response was, "I thought, 'Great. There was a funny smell on the bus, and now we'll get a new and better bus.'" Same incident, different thought reflected.

So this incident served as a mirror of both Janet's and Luke's thoughts. Luke's thought involved getting a better bus and getting to the retreat more comfortably, so he chose to keep that thought, and that's exactly what happened. Janet had a choice too. She could stay with the thought, "The bus broke down because I don't want to be on this retreat," in which case she might get on her cell phone, call a car service, and head for home. Or, she could notice that she was having that thought and exchange it for, say, "Regardless of who is on this retreat, there are many opportunities for growth and enjoyment for me here," wait for the bus to be changed, and have a wonderful retreat. That is, in fact, what she chose to do, and thus she was able to have the experience of a great retreat.

So it's not that we have to watch our every thought so that we make sure disaster doesn't happen, but rather that we have to look at the "mirror" of the world to see what our thought is, and exchange that thought if we want to see something different reflected in the world.

As we've seen above, a 7.75 million dollar apartment sale can reflect as abject poverty, and a bus breakdown can reflect as either the thought of not wanting to be at the destination or the thought of getting there more luxuriously. It all depends on the thought the person observing those sensations is thinking.

And lest you think that you have to give up what you want and just be content with what's "inside," remember that, if the world is a mirror, when you are content on the inside, you MUST see contentment on the outside. When you know you have everything on the inside, you MUST see that you have everything on the outside. So the outcome is the same, but your focus is inward instead of outward. Having this knowledge allows you to know that everything is available to you right here and now, no matter what the circumstance, and when you know this, circumstances will always appear to be just as you desire them to be.

In short, you become the projector rather than the screen.

RIGHT ACTION

When people hear that in The Thought Exchange we work on manifesting what we wish to see in the world simply by using our thoughts, one of the first questions they often ask is, "What about taking action? How can you have something manifest without DO-ING anything?

Sometimes, people who come to The Thought Exchange for the first time are disappointed, because they were hoping we would give them tasks, lists or ways to achieve things, and we never do that. In Thought Exchange, we focus on the thought within which our actions are being taken, and watch to see which actions naturally come out of the thoughts we choose. Our premise is that it is not the particular action taken that determines the outcome, but rather the thought within which it is taken. For instance, when a person who wants to get a date asks someone out, whether or not the person being asked says yes can be dependent on what thought the asker is holding. Two people might take the identical action, ask the same question, and get different outcomes, depending on what they're thinking. How often have we seen people who are gorgeous, kind and talented unable to meet someone, while people who we would regard as not as attractive or suitable seem to be dating all the time. The difference is in what they're thinking when they ask.

Often, when we have a situation where the outcome is uncertain or the path is unclear, we can simply hold a thought, and watch how that thought plays out in action.

For instance, this past year I hurt my back severely and had to go to the Emergency Room. In the Emergency Room, I was given anti-inflammatory drugs and muscle relaxants. These drugs made me seriously drowsy and gave me a bad case of reflux, so I had to stop them. A few days after the accident I suddenly went numb in the top part of my left leg. This was very frightening to me, so I immediately called my doctor and made an appointment to see him. On my way to the doctor, I noticed that I was having the thought that this was something dangerous and something that wouldn't go away. Realizing that that was actually a possibility, I also realized that that was just a thought, and that many other thoughts and possibilities also existed. I decided to exchange that thought for one within which I might not only find the most comfort, but which also allow the healing I was looking for. So I exchanged the thought for, "I know that there is already a way in place for this numbness to disappear." What I was saying was that whether it was a pinched nerve or something chemical or something else, whatever it was, there was a process that could occur by which it would heal—a process that was already known to nature, that had already been created, and that existed in the Great Un-Manifested. A nerve could un-pinch. A chemical could be released. If it was psychosomatic, it could go away. I just held the thought that the way was already in place for it to heal.

The doctor had no idea what was causing the numbness. He said it could be any number of things, and suggested I take a round of prednisone for the back pain. He also suggested a physical therapist. I left the office holding the thought, "There is a way already in place for this to heal," and inside of that thought, called the physical therapist. The physical therapist also didn't know what might be causing the numbness, but we got to work, not only working on the back injury, but doing a lot of important exercises to improve my general health and physical capability. The numbness got slightly better, but was still definitely there. During this time, from time to time, I would notice that, out of fear, I had taken on the thought, "This is serious, this is dangerous, this won't go away." When I would notice that, I would immediately exchange that thought for, "There is a way already in place for this to heal." Holding that thought, I was moved to call my own body-worker, who worked on the condition in her own way, again, helping it a bit but not getting rid of the numbness. Through all this, I just held the thought "There is a way already in place for this to heal." Inside that thought, I found that I was quite calm about the condition, not resisting it, not fighting it, not afraid of it, just being with it, knowing that there was a way for it to heal, and also knowing that since that way was already in place, I was not in any danger, and could simply tolerate the sensation of numbness I was having. I could also enjoy my life in each present moment, since knowing that the way was in place for the condition to heal, I didn't have to wait for it to actually heal to allow myself to feel comfortable.

The prednisone had made me very jumpy and bloated, as prednisone often does, so I was glad when I could get off it a week later. It had, in fact, helped the back pain, even if it hadn't gotten rid of the numbness.

I had occasion to travel to Tulsa Oklahoma to give a Thought Exchange seminar for the Oklahoma Women's Bar Association. Although I was on a very busy schedule, something told me to take the time to visit my favorite chiropractor, whom I had met the previous year when I was doing a show in Tulsa. I went to the office and he was closed for lunch, but something told me to come back later in the afternoon.

I came back, and he examined my back and said, "Boy, you're REAL-LY stuck in this one place." He put me on the table, gave me a couple of cracks, and my numbness was gone, never to return.

So in terms of Thought Exchange, I simply held the thought "There is a way already in place for this to heal." That's all I did. But inside that thought, I was moved to go to my doctor, take prednisone, find an excellent physical therapist, work with my body worker, and go to a chiropractor. A lot of stuff happened, I DID a lot, and those things were instrumental in my healing, but the point is that my holding the thought I held allowed me to spontaneously see the ways the universe had available to heal me, and to move toward making choices that supported that.

Had I taken on the thought, "I have this awful condition and it's permanent and there's no way for it to go away," or, "I have to fight this thing," I might have made different choices, chosen medications that would have masked it or upset my system, elected to have surgery that would have done permanent damage, not gone to the practitioners I went to, etc. So, as is always the case, the thought was the cause of many actions that led to the manifestation of the thought, which was healing. Action was taken, but what made me choose those specific actions, and what made those actions have the results they had, was the thought I was holding.

You Don't Have to DO Anything

Often, even though people understand how Thought Exchange works and have had good experiences with it, they find themselves not exchanging thoughts and resisting moving forward.

After running my first Thought Exchange Workshop for two years, I decided to ask four people who seemed particularly adept at working with the material, to do an Advanced Thought Exchange Workshop.

In this workshop, we picked one specific thing that we knew existed in the Un-Manifested that we were willing to see appear in the Manifested, and for a period of time, wrote down and exchanged EVERY thought we had that was related to that.

People began to make immediate progress, but at a certain point, for several people, the progress stopped. People stopped working on their thoughts, forgot to bring their books, got sidetracked....all sorts of forms of resistance began to appear.

One of the members of the workshop was working on getting herself to go to an audition for a Broadway show. Now this is something that should appear easily doable. You just go! Auditions happen all the time, she was a member of the union, it required nothing "outside" herself, nobody else's help or permission or cooperation, and yet she wasn't doing it.

When we explored what she was thinking, she immediately stated the core thought she had been working with, which was, "If I go to an audition I will get creamed!" We had talked about this thought a great deal, and she understood that her mother had let her know throughout her childhood, in overt and covert ways, that she was not to succeed, and that if she did she would experience disastrous retaliation. She knew all about this, knew it was not a FACT and was only a thought, and knew that it was exchangeable for thoughts like, "It's just an audition; It is possible for me to succeed without retaliation; I'm allowed to have what I want," or any number of other thoughts like that.

So why wasn't she doing the exchange?

The explanation came to us in a sudden flash of understanding. It's very clear, but perhaps a bit difficult to explain, so follow carefully.

If she is holding the thought, "If I go to an audition I will get creamed," then anything she does that might lead her to go to an audition will be thought of as dangerous. This includes exchanging that thought. Within her original thought ("I'll get creamed") she unconsciously thinks that if she exchanges that thought, she will <u>have to</u> go to an audition, which, within her original thought, means she will get creamed. Are you following the logic?

So her only choice, to avoid going to an audition and getting creamed, is to <u>not exchange the thought</u>. Even though it is that very exchange that would put her inside a new thought that would allow her to go to an audition happily, with excitement, or at least with safety, she can't get herself to make the exchange inside the old thought.

So what is the solution to this?

In discussing it, we realized that since what she fears is having to do something that within the old thought would be dangerous, if she takes out the "having to do it," she can simply have the new thought. Once she's in the new thought, doing it will not hold the same danger, and she will naturally do it. In fact, she will know she's taken on the new thought when she see herself doing the thing she's set out to do.

So she can allow herself to take on the thought "It's safe to go to an audition," without thinking that she will be in any way obligated to go to one. Once she has taken on the new thought, she most likely will just naturally go to the audition, which is, of course, exactly what happened.

THE IMPOSSIBLE DOUBLE BIND

As we began to explore our resistance to moving forward in our special workshop, we came across a phenomenon which seemed to be consistent and universal to everyone in the group. As each of us described our childhood histories, looking for parallels in our present issues and struggles, we found that in every case there was a basic, impossible double bind that we each had experienced. It was different for each of us, but in each case there was some painful and difficult situation in which strong feelings had been generated, and in which no solution was possible.

I'll give you some examples.

A parent beats his or her child periodically, for no reason that is apparent to the child. The reason the parent is beating the child is because the parent has sensations that the parent can't tolerate, but the parent can't know this, so the parent blames the child for some made up infraction that "requires" beating.

Since the beating is about the parent, there is nothing the child can do to stop the beating. If, as the parent is beating the child, the child pleads with him or her to stop, the parent keeps hitting harder, telling the child he deserves the punishment. If the child cries, the parent says, "Stop crying or I'll give you something to cry about." If the child fights back, the parent, who is much bigger and stronger than the child, beats the child even more forcefully and violently. And if the child decides to suck it up and just take the beating, the parent hits harder until the child has a reaction.

So the child experiences something extremely painful, that no reasoning, pleading, moving toward, moving away from, expressing emotion or not expressing emotion can do anything about. The result of this, is that the child is left with a murderous, un-expressable rage which he tries, for the rest of his life, to either suppress or act out, neither of which works.

In another example, a child takes on a project, like raising money for a bicycle he wants to buy. It's his birthday, and in a very mature way for a ten year old, he tells each of his relatives that if they were planning to give him a birthday present, he would prefer to have them give him money toward a bicycle. He collects enough to buy a bicycle, and puts it in his little toy bank for the summer, planning to buy the bicycle when he returns from camp.

He gets home from camp, goes to his bank (which is locked and requires a $10 deposit to open) and discovers that the bank is empty. When he asks his parents where the money is, they tell him, "We put it away for college." When he naturally gets extremely upset and says, "But I wanted it for a bike. You took my money," they say, "Don't be silly. We did you a favor. What do you think? We stole it? We've put it away for your college. We don't think you should have a bike." When the child gets more upset, they ridicule him and tell him he's foolish for being upset. So not only has the child had an extremely upsetting thing happen (he hasn't gotten the bike which he so badly wanted and for which he worked so hard to raise money) but his feelings are not recognized, he cannot use any reasoning or emotion to transmit to his parents what he wants and possibly have them give it to him (or at least understand how he might be deeply upset) and so his only choice is to stuff down his feelings, which remain there for life trying to either come out or stay hidden.

In another example, a child says he wants to go to camp and his parents sign him up in January for the following summer. During the next few months, the child begins to have personal issues and fears and decides he doesn't want to go to camp. The parents tell him that he has to go because he signed up, and add that if he can't stick this out he'll never stick out anything in his life again. The child tries to reason with them. When that doesn't work, he cries and throws a fit, and toward the end of his six-month-long campaign to be allowed to stay home he even tries to injure himself, but to no avail. On the day camp is to begin, he is left alone with his mother who is to drop him off at the bus. When he begs and pleads one more time to stay home, his mother says, "Fine. You can stay home, but we won't speak to you all summer."

This, of course, is intolerable to a child, so he agrees to go, but asks if he can come home if he doesn't like it. His mother tells him that if he tries it and is really unhappy, they'll take him home.

He tries camp for 2 weeks and is really unhappy, so he calls home and says, "I've tried it, I'm really unhappy, can you take me home?" To which his parents say, "No." They come up for visiting day, he rants, he raves, he cries, he even throws himself in front of a moving car, but they drive away, reiterating, "If you can't stick this out, you'll never stick anything out for the rest of your life."

He gives up and stops asking, stuffing the feelings, but still, of course, having the rage. Three weeks later, on the second visiting day, he says nothing and is just pleasant. His parents, happy to not have to deal with his emotions, say nothing, and at the end of the day, the head of the camp comes up to him and compliments him on the way he's come around and "grown up." He still knows he's enraged, but smiles and says nothing, since expressing anything is hopeless.

How The Double Bind
Plays Out in Later Life

Can you see how in each of these instances, there was nothing the child could do to get help, get what he wanted, or even to be seen and heard? All efforts at expression only made it worse, and efforts at no expression got no results. So the child was left with enormous sensations that had nowhere to go. Resolution of this conflict was impossible by either expression or suppression, so the question is, how do these situations and the sensations they generated get resolved?

The remarkable thing we discovered by looking at our own impossible double binds and how they played out later in our lives, is that we all, in one way or another, did the same things.

The first thing we did was take on a protective thought that would hopefully keep us away from ever being in a situation where the double bind could occur again.

In the case of the boy who was hit, he took on the thought "If you ask for anything you will be attacked." This caused him to avoid asking for things directly, or to try to find manipulative ways to get what he wanted while trying to circumvent the attack. In later life, this would either prevent him from asking for things he very much wanted (the more he wanted it, the less likely he would be to ask) or would cause him to ask for things in ways which would actually get him attacked, reflective of the thought he was holding.

In the case of the boy who didn't get the bike, he took on the thought "No matter how well I plan, everything will get taken away from me at the last minute." This caused him to either not try for things that were important to him, or to try in such a way that the thought manifested and things were actually taken away from him "at the last minute." In later life, this showed up as shocking losses of relationships that seemed secure or jobs that he thought he would get.

And in the case of the boy who was forced to go to camp, he took on the thought "You have to stick everything out, like it or not." This caused him to lose touch with whether or not he liked to do things, and to make choices that were disconnected from him. In later life, he would often find himself doing work he was unhappy with or constantly fulfilling obligations that meant nothing to him, while ignoring the things he really wanted to do.

The amazing thing is, that by taking on these "protective" thoughts, instead of being protected from the situations and sensations we were trying to avoid, we kept generating situation after situation in our lives that had the same double bind. Sound familiar? It seems that so many people have their own version of a problem or frustration that keeps appearing over and over again, and keeps not getting solved.

As we explored why we might be repeating these difficult situations, we realized that in some way, we were generating situations that would bring up the double bind so we could find a way to resolve it. The problem was, each time we brought up the double bind, we would complain about it, fear it, and try to resolve it by either expressing huge feeling to someone, or stuffing those feelings down and moving forward. In short, we kept running from the sensations, to the protective thoughts which were generating upsetting circumstances, which were not what we wanted. As soon as we would see these circumstances we would immediately remember, fleetingly, what we did want, and BAM! We would be thrown right back into the sensations we were trying to avoid.

These were the same tactics we had tried to use in order to escape our original double binds, and given the nature of the double bind, they can't work.

So the question became, what would resolve the double bind? Was there something that was neither expressing nor repressing, that we had not allowed ourselves, or been too afraid, to do? The answer, although it seems obvious, was one that had eluded most of us for most of our lives.

The answer was, FEEL IT. Experience the sensations that the double bind brings up, without trying to change the circumstances or get away from the sensations.

Feel what it felt like (as a sensation) to be beaten and not be able to stop it. Feel what it felt like (as a sensation) when the money you'd saved for a bicycle was taken away from you and you weren't allowed to express your upset. Feel what it felt like (as a sensation) to be forced to go to camp, and no matter how you expressed yourself, to be forced to stay there.

That seems simple, but the fact is that we could not have allowed ourselves to feel those sensations, as children, because our very life and survival depended on the people who were perpetrating the abuse, and there was no competent adult around to help and understand us. If we were to feel those sensations, we might have been afraid that we would either kill the people who were responsible for our care and feeding and well-being, or conversely, be too painfully aware that these people were not taking care of us. Either way, we would be left with associations to sensations that were intolerable for a child. In adulthood, we keep trying to find strategies for getting around these situations without ever having to feel them. If we could just get famous enough, find the right partner, have enough money, we would never have to be exposed to those sensations again. The trouble is, those sensations are always waiting there to be experienced

So it stands to reason that we are totally terrified to feel those sensations, but as long as we don't, we will keep bringing up the same situations, in different guises, in order to give ourselves the opportunity to experience them.

Once we do allow ourselves to experience them purely as sensations, an amazing thing happens. We no longer have to take on the protective thoughts that we misguidedly thought would keep us from the sensations. By being able to stay with the sensations, we become able to stay with the thoughts that generated them (thoughts of what we want, thoughts of success, thoughts of satisfaction.) And as we stay with those thoughts, they become beliefs, and begin to appear in our lives as what we want to see there.

Some Examples From The Present Day (Janet)

Janet, whose mother had repeatedly abused her, and then demanded that Janet love and respect her, was having lunch, as an adult, with her sister. Janet arrived at lunch, where her sister began the conversation by saying, "God, I had to have two drinks before I came, just so I could have lunch with you." Her sister then proceeded to criticize Janet, make fun of her, and be the usual antagonistic, unfriendly person that she always was to Janet.

I asked Janet what she did. She said, "Nothing." History had taught her that if she attacked her sister, her sister viewed her as hysterical and the criticism got worse, and if she said nothing she felt terrible.

I asked her how she felt at the lunch, and specifically what sensations she was experiencing. She said that her feet and her head were going numb. I asked her why that was happening, and she said that she had to block her feelings to prevent herself from hitting her sister. So the only two choices Janet saw were to either shut herself down or hit her sister. I asked her what would happen if she did neither, but just noticed how the situation felt in her body, and did nothing to express it or get rid of it. At first, she said, "My God. That would be impossible. I would explode." (That was the child in Janet speaking. The child who remembered the initial incidents with her mother, and was still living in fear of the sensations these incidents had caused.) I asked Janet if she would actually explode, and of course she knew that people don't really explode. I persisted in having her sit there and just feel the sensations. She twisted and turned a bit, expressed a lot of fear, but finally was able to just sit there and experience the sensations associated with the rage and anger and hurt that that situation, and so many others before, had caused her.

All of a sudden, she calmly turned to me and said, "You know what? I don't like my sister. And you know what else? She probably doesn't like me."

Now can you see that in her original household, she could never have allowed herself to know this? "I don't like my mother? I'm 6 years old? My mother is my sole provider of food and sustenance and I'm aware that I don't like her?" Impossible.

But in the present, as an adult, even though it was still very difficult and very threatening, she could tolerate just having the sensations and being aware of the thought.

Can you see, that as an adult, she could sit down with her sister and say, "You know what? I don't like you. And I don't think you like me." In which case her sister would either respond by discussing it with her, and they would come to the real root of what was going on with them and perhaps resolve it, or, if the sister was unwilling to talk and was still in the childhood dynamic, Janet and her sister would not be friends. This would be hurtful, but tolerable to the adult Janet, and she could begin to make friends who were more supportive to what she actually needed.

(JOSEPH)

Joseph's impossible double bind as a child was that he was teased, bullied, and told he was not good enough, while at the same time being expected to take care of everyone, even his parents. As an adult, he had two wildly conflicting dreams. To be (in his own words) "An international playboy billionaire philanthropist with my name on hospitals and several Ferrari's in the garage," and "A simple family man with children." When we explored why he wanted these things, he became clear that he wanted the billionaire life so that people would finally respect him, and the simple family life so that he could be happy without being overly (or underly) responsible.

The trouble was, that any time he went toward either of these, he was so filled with guilt and anxiety that he would thwart his efforts and end up failing at both marriage and at the acquisition of great wealth. He would give away money in great amounts, but feel empty and frustrated. He would help his relatives, but his help would be futile, their demands a bottomless pit with no gratitude, and the results frustrating and not what he desired.

When he looked at this, he realized that he was trying to achieve either of these dreams in order to avoid what it felt like to be in his original impossible double bind. But it didn't work, because each of these things, being part of the original double bind, brought on sensations that he translated into thoughts of futility and hopelessness. Even when he finally got behind the wheel of a Ferrari, all he felt was emptiness.

Gradually, he began to realize that these sensations came along with his efforts to go for these things, and he allowed himself to feel them. This enabled him to move forward and begin to have real, authentic success, and not lose himself in the process. The solution, as it always is, became not to get around those sensations, but to be able to experience and simply be with them, something he never could have done as a child.

Psychosomatic Symptoms

Psychosomatic symptoms are a very common way of diverting attention away from the core sensations related to the impossible double bind. They give us something to be upset about in the exact same way we would be upset about the double bind, except we don't have to experience the hopelessness that we experienced when we were first in the double bind.

In my own life, I have found that psychosomatic symptoms have consistently developed at points where I had successfully navigated some challenge and was now "in the clear." After a successful run of my own Off Broadway show, I was headed to Palm Beach for four days of absolute relaxation, when my left leg became so painful that I couldn't walk. After another successful production of the same show, I developed a severe pain in my right knee that kept me limping for a couple of months. I had signed up with a doctor to do a medical fast, which proved very debilitating and exhausting. Finally, I made it through and was off the fast, on my way to Florida for a vacation and then to work on a show I loved, when my retina spontaneously tore. I was moving the last box into place, ending a seven-month torturous renovation on my dream house, when I pulled a back muscle, became completely physically incapacitated for several days, and remained in pain for weeks. Years earlier, I had gotten married at the young age of twenty. I had looked to this marriage as the answer to all my problems, as the ultimate happiness. The day after we were married, I had a breakdown that ended up putting me in a mental hospital.

Years later, an excellent therapist made the observation that it seemed that, at all costs, I must avoid success and a feeling of joy and accomplishment. Why was that?

When I looked at it, I realized that my own impossible double bind had been designed to not allow for my success. In fact, it was essential to the person putting me in the double bind that I hold his thoughts and sensations of non-success for him, so that he could have the possibility of success for himself. Thus, for me to have thoughts of success would have forced him to look at his own thoughts and sensations, which would have been tantamount to my "killing" him. On the other side of the coin, had I been able to have power and success and autonomy at the time of the abuse, I might have actually wanted to kill him. So either way, success resulted in killing.

Somehow, even though, as an adult, I knew that this was not true, the child in me was still afraid to test it, so I always avoided success with psychosomatic symptoms. (What I was really avoiding were the sensations and thoughts that would come with success.) My constant task, as I recovered, became to look at the symptoms, notice what I thought about them, ask myself, "What do I actually think this way about?" and simply experience the sensations I had when I thought about that. Whenever I could successfully do this, the symptoms would immediately go away, to be replaced by tremendous anxiety, anger and fear. When I could tolerate those feelings (really what I was tolerating were the sensations under them) and know that, because of my past, they came part and parcel with success for me, I was able to experience the success I desired. Others often saw me as successful, but I could not allow myself to experience it until I was able to experience the sensations that came with it.

How The Double Bind
Appears in Thought Exchange Work

When you've had a double bind in your past, whenever you take on the thought that led you into that double bind, the double bind will come up.

So if, as a kid, you created a solid plan of action to get yourself a bike, and had it mysteriously and inexplicably taken away at the last minute, every time you generate the thought, "I can work for what I want and get it," the memory (often unconscious) of that double bind will come up. Usually, it will come up as a sensation that we interpret as fear and discomfort. As a reaction to that sensation, we will often take on a thought like, "It will never work" or "I can't have what I want," in order to protect ourselves from moving into a double bind situation like the one in our childhood. (Which will produce the sensation we're afraid of.)

Or, if you were beaten when you expressed autonomy or confidence or a strong opinion, every time you take on thoughts of strength, autonomy or strong opinion, you will feel like you're going to be beaten, and you will exchange that thought for thoughts that would have saved you from getting a beating. (Or, more accurately, from the sensations you experienced when you were beaten.)

Or, if as a child, you had taken on the protective device of developing psychosomatic symptoms to make sure you didn't think or act in a way that would get you hurt, when you take on thoughts that you can succeed or be strong or be independent, you may develop psychosomatic symptoms and exchange the thought for one that keeps you from doing what you want to do.

So how do we handle this? The way we work with this is to be clear that thoughts cause manifestation, so the object is to stay with, or at least get back to, the originating thought of what it is you want. So if you have a thought and notice a sensation which you associate with

411

anxiety or fear, make sure you don't exchange the thought away for one that will cause less anxiety but not get you the result you desire. If you see a result you don't want, you will know that you have exchanged the thought away. The moment you see that result, take on the thought of what you do want, and you will have yet another opportunity to be with the sensation you're afraid of.

As I've said before, this process involves developing an ability to tolerate and feel your sensations. It is within this ability to feel them, not to throw them off or suppress them, that the healing lies. This is what we were not able to do in our childhoods, because our lives actually depended on not knowing that certain people who were supposed to be reliable were not. But as adults, as painful and difficult as it may be, we have the ability to experience these sensations as sensations, and stick to the thoughts we take on in order to have what we desire in our lives appear before us.

Working with "Obstacles" as Signposts to Healing

As we have just seen, there are many obstacles that come up in the areas of sensation, belief and manifestation. But actually, if we don't consider them obstacles, but rather indications of where we are and where we need to go, we can always use them to get where we're going. Whenever you meet what you might consider an obstacle, ask yourself where in the circle the obstacle is occurring? Is it in the area of some sensation you don't want to experience? Is it in the area of a belief you've been unconsciously holding? Is it something that is manifesting that you don't want? Once you know what area it's in, just move around the circle, in either direction, until you get to thought. Remember, thought is the ONLY thing that can be exchanged. All issues can be resolved by exchanging the thought that's connected to them, but this may require experiencing sensations that are uncomfortable, exposing beliefs that you are not pleased to be having, and even possibly seeing manifestations that are not what you immediately desire. But as long as you remember that Thought Is Cause, you will know how to position yourself to bring about the manifestations you desire.

So when you decide to use Thought Exchange, really use Thought Exchange. Don't worry about the result. That will automatically appear as a reflection of the thought you take on. Exchange the thought, be willing to feel whatever sensations you feel, and do whatever you're moved to do next. And more importantly, don't do whatever you're not moved to do. Just keep exchanging thoughts.

When you're stuck, completely let go of the result, and simply exchange the thoughts. In that way, the process becomes simple, and you allow this Principle of the Universe to work, to manifest the results you desire.

"EXCHANGE THE THOUGHT, BE WILLING TO FEEL WHATEVER SENSATIONS YOU FEEL, AND DO WHATEVER YOU'RE MOVED TO DO NEXT"

CHAPTER 30
GETTING SPECIFIC
APPLYING THE THOUGHT EXCHANGE ®
TO A PARTICULAR ISSUE IN YOUR OWN LIFE

Now that you have a description of the how the process works, and examples of how people have used it, the question becomes, "How do you use it for yourself?" In this section, I'll summarize the steps involved in doing The Thought Exchange, and remind you of some of the principles.

1. Look at something in your life that you are dissatisfied with or that you want to change.

2. Ask yourself, "If I were seeing that in the mirror as a reflection of my thought, what thought would I be having that would reflect as that?"

3. Be brutally honest and identify the thought. Don't worry if it's really negative or embarrassing. It usually is. But remember, it's just a thought.

4. Ask yourself, "What thought might be likely to reflect in the mirror as what I want to see there?"

5. When you've come up with that thought, exchange the old thought for the new thought by simply thinking the new thought.

6. Notice what sensations you have when you think the new thought. Often they may be surprisingly painful or uncomfortable, but those sensations are the reason you haven't been able to stay with the thought.

7. Throughout the next period of time, keep returning to that thought and see what happens. Any time you see something that is not that thought before you, all you know is that you have exchanged away the

thought to get away from the sensations it generates. Go back to the thought.

8. LET THE NEW THOUGHT DO THE WORK. (Do whatever you're moved to do while holding the new thought.

Remember: Everything has already been created and exists in the Un-Manifested. Our question is: "What is it that reveals the particular situation we are interested in revealing? The hypothesis is that it is Thought that shines the light on whatever it is directed at.

There is no problem for which an answer has not already been created; no disease for which a cure has not already been created; nothing in the world we could want or think of that has not already been created. We only need shine the light of Thought on it.

CHAPTER 31
LIVING THE THOUGHT EXCHANGE

Life is like a wonderful store that carries everything and gives you the power to return anything, exchange anything, find anything— any time you want to. It's all there, always in stock, always available, and the currency is thought—something of which you have an unlimited supply— because every thought is available to everybody all the time. Know this, and you will know that you actually have an unlimited supply of everything available to you at all times.

So happy shopping.

THE THOUGHT EXCHANGE IS OPEN!!!!!

CHAPTER 32
LIFE IS SENSATIONAL
THE ONLY THING YOU NEED TO KNOW
(IN CASE YOU MISSED PAGE 154)

We've talked about how thought causes sensation which causes belief which causes manifestation. We've talked about how the avoidance of sensations associated with childhood trauma causes us to take on protective thoughts which manifest as things we don't want to see in the world. We've laid out the basic Thought Exchange Process. We've talked about how Thought Exchange can be applied to almost any area of life. We've talked about how our real lives are lived completely inside, in the world of experience, with the "outside" world being just a "mirror" of that experience. And we've looked at all sorts of examples, stories and ideas that elucidate the basic concept.

It can all seem pretty complicated, but in the end, it boils down to just one thing.

If we do this one thing, everything else happens by itself. We exchange protective thoughts for thoughts we wish to hold. We spontaneously and naturally take actions that support these new thoughts. We integrate the child parts of ourselves that we'd left behind. We become reacquainted with the awareness that the entire Un-Manifested world of infinite thoughts is always available to us. And ultimately, we heal and begin to live lives where we see our dreams consistently and easily appear before us.

If there is just one thing that you take from this book, take this.

When things get complicated, when you feel overwhelmed, when you don't know what to think, when you're caught up in circumstances, when you're frustrated, when life isn't working out as you desire, there is one simple thing to do that will fix the whole thing.

GO TO YOUR SENSATIONS!
BE WITH YOUR SENSATIONS!
EXPERIENCE YOUR SENSATIONS!

All our challenges, all our problems, boil down to one thing. The avoidance of being with the sensational experience we're having right now.

When you can't be with your sensations, you can only choose thoughts that get you away from them, thoughts like "I can't, It will never happen, I'm a loser," etc, and these thoughts MUST be reflected in the manifest world.

When you can simply have your sensations, without worrying about what you're thinking, what's happening, what's going to happen, when you can be with your sensations rather than avoiding them, THE ENTIRE WORLD OF UNLIMITED POSSIBILITIES AND CHOICES IMMEDIATELY OPENS TO YOU. You have free rein to think anything, experience the sensations that go with it, and see it manifest in the physical world.

GO TO YOUR SENSATIONS!
BE WITH YOUR SENSATIONS!
EXPERIENCE YOUR SENSATIONS!

SENSATIONS ARE THE GATEWAY TO THE GREAT UNMANIFESTED, WHERE UNLIMITED THOUGHTS, UNLIMITED POSSIBILITY AND UNLIMITED FREEDOM RESIDE.

That's it. That's all there is to it. This is the real secret to living a happy, fulfilled, unlimited life.

Welcome to your SENSATIONAL Life!

APPENDIX

APPENDIX A
GLOSSARY

There are numerous commonly used terms that have a different or specific meaning in Thought Exchange. Here is a list of terms used throughout the book that fall under this category.

Belief – A belief is a thought that we think is true. As such, a belief is a lie, because no thought is true. In a belief, we take a little slice out of the pie of infinite possibility and say that that's the only possibility that's true. Thus, in order to change a belief, all we have to do is recognize it as a thought and then exchange the thought for the thought we want. This will bring up sensations. When we have taken on a thought and stayed with the sensation that that thought produces, a belief emerges. Belief is thus the effect of thought and sensation combined. Beliefs reflect as Manifestation so that we can see before us what our thoughts actually are.

Consciousness – That invisible sense of "I Am" that each of us has. It doesn't even have our name on it, we're just aware that we exist. It's an experience, and as such is invisible. Nobody can see your consciousness, and you can't see yours or anyone else's consciousness. But it's there. It's not physical. It's not your body. But it is the context in which your whole experiential life happens, since your sensations and your thoughts are also invisible and happen within the context of consciousness.

Cause - Something that generates other things. Actually, Thought is the cause of everything. It causes Sensations which cause Beliefs which cause Manifestation. They're all an outgrowth of Thought. When we know this, we know where we really live, and know where to make the changes we need to make to know more deeply that we have it all.

Effect – Something that happens because of something else. Something that is not self-generating but simply appears and changes based on something else. Sensations are the effect of Thought, Belief is the effect of Thoughts and Sensations, and Manifestation is the effect of Thoughts, Sensations and Beliefs. So, in truth, they are all the effects of Thought. Always go to the thought, and know that it is causing (or more accurately, being reflected by) everything you see.

En-joy – In Thought Exchange, we break the word down into its component parts. En means in, and joy, of course, means joy. So when we En-joy ourselves, we put joy into ourselves. Things or circumstances don't en-joy us. They don't put joy into us, we put it into ourselves. This means that we can en-joy ourselves, if we so choose, NO MATTER WHAT IS GOING ON.

Feeling – A feeling is a thought which is an interpretation of a sensation. When someone says, "I'm angry" or "I'm sad," I ask them, "How do you know?" And they will answer, "Because my throat is tight" or, "My stomach is in a knot" or, "My chest is burning." Those sensations do not necessarily mean that they're angry or sad. Each of those "feelings" is just one interpretation among many possible interpretations. Most people have butterflies before they go on stage. Some call them fear. Some call them excitement.

God - In Thought Exchange, we translate God as The Great Un-Manifested, the invisible world where infinite possibility, infinite thoughts and infinite abundance always exist and cannot be taken away. God is inside, experienced within our Consciousness. Because God is infinite possibility, anything can happen, and happen instantly, in God. (In the Great Un-Manifested.) God is always with us, and cannot not be with us. All of these things describe the Great Un-Manifested, where we live in experience, and where infinite possibility is ALWAYS present.

God could also be said to be the impartial Observer or Noticer within us. We do not live in the "outside" world, and we are not our sensations and thoughts. We are the One who is observing all this, without comment, without judgment, without fear and without limitation, seeing everything, knowing everything, accepting everything just as it is, wanting or missing nothing. The impartial observer cannot be hurt or changed or limited by anything in the world of experience or the physical world. This is who we REALLY are, and this is God. One and the same.

Manifestation – Manifestation is what we see in the physical world. Since our experience of Manifestation takes place on the inside, in the invisible world of experience, it could be said that Manifestation is simply the mirror of what we're thinking, sitting out in front of us so that we can see it. Many people mistakenly think that Manifestation is the goal, rather than the mirror directing us back to our invisible inner selves where all the work, all the healing and in fact, all the living is done. To think Manifestation is the goal, is tantamount to thinking that the reason you're wearing a dress is so that it can appear in the mirror.

Mirror of the World – In Thought Exchange, we look at everything that happens in the world as merely a mirror of what we're thinking. It seems like what happens in the world causes us to think certain things, but in fact, the thought comes first, and we just see whatever we're thinking in the world. When you look in the mirror and see yourself, if you've got a few pounds on, you might notice that you're overweight. But the mirror didn't cause you to be overweight. It just reflected your overweight-ness so you could see it and do something about it, in the only place something can be done. On you. When we begin to see everything in the physical world as merely a mirror of our own thoughts, our lives change radically

Imag-in-ation – In Thought Exchange we break this word into its component parts. Image-in-ation. We image in, which means we go to the Great Un-Manifested and see what it is we want on the inside, where it already exists. We just hold that image and have whatever sensations arise with it, and the image MUST appear reflected in the outside world.

Noticer/Observer - (see God)

Sensation – By sensation, we mean physical sensation. Hotness, coldness, tingling, tightness, shaking, upset stomach, pounding heart. These are experiences, as opposed to feelings, such as anger, sadness, love, which are actually thoughts that are interpretations of physical sensations. Sensations can also be "energetic" experiences such as sinking, emptiness, fullness, or a "rushing" sensation.

Source of All Possible Thoughts – This is actually the same as the Great Un-Manifested. It is the invisible place you go to, to know that every thought is there, and every thought is possible.

The Great Un-Manifested – The Great Un-Manifested is that invisible place, always accessible to us in our thoughts, where every possibility exists, eternally. The physical world is always temporary, but in the invisible world, no possibility can ever be taken away. It is ALWAYS possible for anything to happen, no matter what is happening now. We can also instantly find any thing or situation or outcome in the Great Un-Manifested, simply by thinking of it and "seeing" it there, in the infinite, invisible world where EVERYTHING always exists. By knowing that where we live is in the Great Un-Manifested, we begin to project our lives out from that infinite, fulfilled place, rather than thinking that things on the outside are separate from us and causative in any way.

Thought – A thought is the taking on in the mind of one of the infinite possibilities in the universe that are available to us at all times. It takes place in the invisible, Un-Manifested world. A thought, by nature, isn't true, and can be exchanged for any other thought. The original thought is still here, just as pepper is always in the kitchen, whether you're using it or not. Thought is also "cause," in that our thoughts generate sensations which generate beliefs which generate Manifestation.

Thought Exchange Circle – The Thought Exchange Circle is the basic Thought Exchange chart that says that Thoughts cause Sensations which result in Beliefs which reflect as Manifestation. The chart can be found in chapter 6. The Thought Exchange Circle also refers to way we usually do Thought Exchange Workshops, sitting in a circle so that everyone can see each other.

<u>Thought Exchange Thought</u> – A thought that states a Truth that exists in the unlimited world of The Great Un-Manifested. A thought about thoughts, not things. This differs from an Affirmation, which sometimes can express a wish and sometimes can express a desired outcome in the "outside" world. Thought Exchange Thoughts are always only about the invisible, inside world of experience, where we really live.

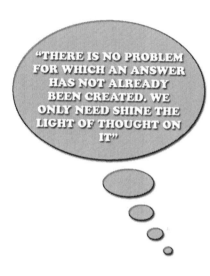

APPENDIX B
SAMPLE THOUGHTS FROM ACTUAL THOUGHT EXCHANGE® WORKSHOPS

Although many Thought Exchange thoughts are also Affirmations, and many Affirmations are also Thought Exchange thoughts, there is a specific requirement which a thought must meet in order to be considered a true Thought Exchange thought.

The reason I first began to explore the principles that eventually led to The Thought Exchange® is that many of the Affirmations I heard people doing seemed more like wishing and hoping than statements of the Truth.

The intrinsic distinction that I was finally able to make between a Thought Exchange and an affirmation, is that Thought Exchanges ALWAYS deal exclusively with the place where everything is truly unlimited and always here and available to us. The Un-Manifested.

Affirmations often state things that we wish were true, or things that we hope are true in the Manifested world (where, in fact, nothing is true.) When we misguidedly think that the object is to see something manifest, or to have something, or get somewhere in the physical world (as opposed to knowing that we already have it in the Un-Manifested) we sometimes create an affirmation that says that that's what we have or that's where we are, or that's what has happened. This may or may not be true.

Statements like, "My cancer is gone; I have only pleasant sensations; I have a million dollars in the bank by Friday; I meet the love of my life on this trip," refer to the Manifested world and as such, may or may not happen.

Statements like, "Wellness is always available to me; I am willing to be with my sensations and know that they are meaningless; All the money in the universe is available to me at all times; The love of my life exists and is available to me," refer to a knowledge of things that we already have in the unlimited world of the Un-Manifested. They don't depend on anything happening, or on us getting anywhere, and as such, are statements of Truth.

The following are examples of thoughts, that we have come up with in the various Thfought Exchange® workshops. They all pertain to what already exists in the Great Un-Manifested, and because of this, each thought pertains to and is available to all of us. Notice the wide range of thoughts, subjects, metaphors and images that people come up with, and know that there is an unlimited array of thoughts available at all times to choose from. Some of the thoughts are simple, straightforward and direct. Some have double meanings that stimulate the mind and heart on many levels....thoughts like "I am <u>in</u> Love," "This is <u>for</u> good," "I could care <u>less</u>," or "<u>Enough</u> already!" Some are things we might say, as our adult self, to our inner child.

Whenever you feel you need to be empowered, simply read through the list, and remember that every possible thought is available to every human being. If you find a thought on the list that helps you to open the space for what you want to know is here for you, use it. It's yours for the taking. If the perfect thought for you is not on this list, choose one from the infinite thoughts that are always available in the Great Un-Manifested.

The following page contains some of the thoughts we chose in Thought Exchange Groups:

I am good.

It's safe for me to feel successful.

A person of my talent and education can have a wildly successful business.

The opportunity to have the success I desire already exists and is right here now.

As a professional, I can allow the process to unfold as it does.

It's my responsibility to be creative.

I know who I am, I love my family, and neither of those are dependent on how they act.

I can have security and creativity in my life at the same time.

I am worthwhile in every "Now."

I am in God's hands. When I Let Go and Let God, I am prosperous, successful, healthy and well, no matter what the circumstance.

I don't give a shit.

I can do that.

I don't know and I don't have to know. Thank God.

I think I'll have the Peter Luger steak today, and gnocchi with walnut sauce.

My value is inherent. It is not dependent on other people.

I am Big Time!

No matter what happens, I am loved and I am safe, EVEN when I make a lot of money.

Every comment, every piece of feedback that I get, is a gift that moves me one step closer to excellence.

I am an Oscar-winning person.

OK God. Let's go!

It's possible for me to make money doing what I love.

So explode!!!

It is possible for me to have my sensations and do whatever I want.

There are many, many jobs available to me, and all I need is one.

I can see my business attracting new and prosperous clients.

My life is manageable.

I surrender to prosperity.

A fabulous life is here for me right now!

Joy without punishment is all around me.

It's safe to expand on diverse levels.

I am spirit creating a CD.

It is possible for me to win auditions.

I can have it, now.

I can have a boyfriend who is both intellectually stimulating and sexually attractive to me.

I am willing to have it all.

I am good enough.

I belong.

It is possible for me to be an artist, support myself and leave it to God to make it happen.

I'm lovable.

It is possible for me to have help.

It is possible for me to be with my depression.

It's safe for me to be out in the world.

By being successful, I offer myself and my family the opportunity to heal and grow.

It can happen for me.

What I love is within my reach and is inevitable.

I can heal.

It is possible for me to have steady, consistent, artistically fulfilling work.

My life is mine and I am taken care of.

I am worthy of all that I desire.

I am completely acceptable and I don't have to change a thing.

Success and integrity walk hand-in-hand together for me.

My singing can heal my mother.

I channel spirit through my work.

My perfect healing is here now.

My spirit is alive and wealthy.

I am divinely inspired.

I can accomplish everything with God.

I can write a book.

I can have the Technicolor, digital, flat screen, big creative life that I desire.

You know I can do it.

My healing already exists and I am grateful.

I am seen.

I am more than enough.

I am the best singer in the room.

Without my having to do a thing, very creative collaborations can come to me.

My financial security and my artistic self-expression go hand in hand.

All parts of me come together as one.

My body knows how to heal itself, and it's safe to let it do so.

I am worthy. Thank you God.

Because of my age, talent and experience, I have something useful and wonderful to offer the world.

I am so good!!!

It is possible for me to heal.

It is totally possible for EVERYTHING to heal.

This incident can be the source of my healing and my contribution.

It is possible for me to live in grace and deep faith.

It's safe for me to make a commitment.

Real love is possible.

I can have a happy family without doing anything.

I know, finally and clearly, that other people are not the source of my self-esteem—that the divine within me is the source of my self-esteem.

My worth is of tremendous value, and is a gift from God and a gift to all who encounter it.

I am divinely guided and inspired.

I can do ANYTHING I want!!!

I am entitled to tremendous amounts of money.

The moment I Let Go and Let God, my deepest dreams and desires manifest.

I call the shots.

I deserve infinite happiness and success.

I can hold my own hand.

I am free to be exactly who I am.

I am the light.

Who I am manifests all the joy and abundance I need.

Anything I can think about is already here.

I can make money acting.

I have my own ideas, I can do my own thing, and money is here for me.

I am worthy to have abundance and financial success as an actor.

Everything I do is healing and brings me love and abundance.

The world needs exactly who I am.

I rock for God.

I am at peace knowing I am in the hands of God.

I am gifted and fabulous and have so much to give to the world.

I am having the artistic life I've always wanted—NOW.

My acting is for good—I cannot get in the way of my prosperity.

I am in God's hands, and there is nothing I have to do.

Everything I experience brings me to my wholeness Now.

My neediness and greediness are the key to my success.

Who I am is the real thing.

We are Spirit perfectly expressing.

My personal shopper in the Un-Manifested knows what I need, understands me, and leads me to everything I want.

I have to lose everything.

I AM Diva!!!

I dare.

F*#! You! I can too!

I'm OK just the way I am.

I have everything right now.

I AM the juice.

It's NEVER over.

Oh, Please! Stop it already!

I am gifted and fabulous and have so much to give to the world.

I am having the artistic life I've always wanted—NOW.

My acting is for good—I cannot get in the way of my prosperity.

I am in God's hands, and there is nothing I have to do.

Everything I experience brings me to my wholeness Now.

My neediness and greediness are the key to my success.

Who I am is the real thing.

We are Spirit perfectly expressing.

My perfect love exists.

I have a lot to contribute.

The people who desire me are already here.

I can support myself doing what I want to do.

Spirit writes songs through me.

I have something worth saying.

I have something worth saying.

Thank God I'm not in control.

An overflowing audience already exists.

More people are way more fun.

I get it from God and I give it to God!!

I am willing to see God in the giving and the getting.

God gives it through me, God gives it to me.

The baby is healing.

I can have anything I want.

I am nothing.

Everybody loves the baby at work.

It is possible to get what I want.

They're dead already. My success can't kill them.

I Am.

My family is not my source, God's unlimited possibility is.

IT'S POSSIBLE!

I'm a part of everyone else.

I am like everyone and everyone is like me.

To be love able is to see love able.

God only knows what I should do next.

I have a lot to contribute.

I can succeed.

Success "R" Me.

I am made to be taken care of.

I am part of everyone else.

I belong.

I am entitled to all the goodness there is.

If something happened to someone close to me I could handle it.

I can have what I want.

I am worthy of someone who is worthy of me.

There are many possibilities for a wonderful outcome.

It is safe for me to be seen and to be intimate.

I can participate in the fullness of a relationship.

I am allowed to have what I want and keep it.

Money is here all the time.

It's easy. We can do it.

I'm on the right track.

My dreams are perfectly reasonable.

My future is unlimited.

No matter what, I get paid.

The bigger I am, the more support I receive.

I'm going public with the good stuff.

I am acceptable as I am.

The solution exists already.

It's safe not to know.

I can lean into my fear.

"But y'are Blanche!"

It is possible for me to have a lucrative career doing what I love.

There's ALWAYS enough for me.

I am God.

I see me.

It's just a thought

I am worthy.

It's OK to be neat. It's OK to be messy.

It's OK to work and it's OK not to work.

My life is an all-expense-paid vacation.

I am completely forgivable.

My success as an artist improves the lives of EVERYONE around me.

There's a way!

It is possible to be angry (not charming) successful and happy.

My healing is here at every moment.

I am a healer, and everything I need is here now.

This is for me.

I can't do it. Thank God I don't have to.

I can dress myself.

I am no thing.

I have value.

I am complete.

It's safe to heal.

I can have the result I want, and it can be easy.

Other people are like me.

I am a success.

Success is already here.

It always comes through.

Only good can come from this.

When I play, I'm taken care of.

I have what people want.

My family is not my source, Thank God!

Enough, already!

I could care less.

I am _in_ Love.

It's possible for me to completely be taken care of.

It's safe in here.

Life is full of green lights.

I am allowed to have what I want.

It's safe to be seen, to be heard and to be intimate.

It's not possible for me to make a mistake.

Give Up.

I'm OK.

My Life _depends_ on my being successful and happy.

It's crucial that I feel whatever I feel.

I heal when I feel.

I can do that.

By gosh, I can do that.

Of course I feel panicky, and I can do this.

My feelings are not as dangerous as I thought.

There are limitless possibilities for me.

I can do whatever I want. I'm valuable.

I am willing to be wealthy.

I give up.

A successful relationship is here for me now.

It is possible for me to have discipline and enough food.

I can be proud of my sexuality.

I am a desirable employee.

I can be excellent at whatever task is at hand.

I can be a good wife, mother, housekeeper, employee, and still get my education.

I can be good at what I'm doing and still get what I want.

I can be anxious and still talk to people however I want.

My partner is already here.

It's OK no matter what.

Failure is the beginning.

I am a success.

Every failure is a step toward success.

I am worthy of all that I desire.

My success is inside me.

I am part of the human race.

My success is helpful to others.

Good things are here.

It is possible that I am acceptable.

I have what they have.

It is possible for my relationship with my mother to remain exactly the same.

My imperfection is part of my perfection.

I have everything to give, and I deserve to receive everything.

Anger is safe.

It is impossible to fail God.

It is safe to not know.

I can.

I can be accepted now!

I am frickin' lucky. (not the real word used, but after all, this is supposed to be a spiritual book.)

It is possible for me to be financially secure doing the work I love to do.

It is possible for the person who is right for me to come into my life.

It is possible for me to have an exclusive relationship and freedom at the same time.

It is possible for me to belong to a church that supports its minister and supports good people.

Some people want me to be happy.

It is possible for my family to accept me.

It is possible for me to get a job that will pay me enough money to have the life I want.

Everything is possible.

Nothing is in the way of me manifesting right now.

It's never too late to be who I was meant to be.

I can take my own advice.

I can say no to what I don't want, and have what I do want.

It is possible to be successful and creative at the same time.

I can be in a relationship and have freedom.

There is another way to be seen.

If I am human, I am and will be supported.

It is possible to get what I want.

Who says I'm too old?!

Thank you God.

Money is <u>always</u> here beyond my wildest dreams.

Deals are everywhere! (no matter what my mother thinks)

I am whole and complete as I am.

No one is opposing me.

Money is limitless.

I tithe BECAUSE I have abundance.

I am organized.

I have what I need to get what I want.

I am allowed to do anything I damn please.

I can have what I want.

I'm allowed to have what I want.

I can be heard, and get what I want.

I can handle my feelings.

When I fail, I am human.

It's safe to receive love.

I am acceptable.

Prosperity even works for me.

The whole world wins when I have an agent.

I can publish a fabulous, successful book.

If I fully express myself, people will be inspired.

When I follow my dreams, others are encouraged to follow theirs.

I am good enough.

God is my source, no matter how I'm feeling.

It is possible to be a bitch, too much, and wildly successful.

I can be anxious and powerfully effective at the same time.

It is possible to be nice, happy and earn lots of money.

There are many solutions available to me, and I don't have to know what they are.

If not this, something else.

I am willing to experience ALL of the sensations that go with sustainable joy.

I am willing to experience ALL of the sensations that go with being right.

My feelings are worth being taken care of.

It is possible for me to tolerate the sensations that are generated by the thought, "I'll be killed for wanting something."

The way to get everything is to be able to tolerate the sensations generated by the thought, "I'm going to lose everything."

I can withstand the sensations that are generated when I hold the thought "I can do it."

It is possible for me to complete my work.

I can withstand the sensations that arise as I move toward completing my work.

I have something to offer.

It is possible to do what I love, and prosper.

OK God, show me.

It DOES happen for me.

It is possible to do my art and have enough money to live.

I can do anything while feeling anything.

It's here and I'm present for the journey.

I can have what I want.

I can feel this.

Everything is already here.

I can have what I want.

It's absolutely possible for me to get paid to have fun.

I have the right to use the power I have, and I have the ability to accept the consequences of using that power.

I have the power to manifest around me the community that is already there.

Money can help me change things in a positive way.

I can support myself and manifest my dreams.

I am able to support myself.

It is possible to love and be loved.

I don't have anything to be ashamed of.

I am what they want.

It is possible to have fun, express my creativity, have a flexible schedule, meet people, be immersed in something that really excites me, live in a world of adventure, and be financially secure and free to do that without worrying.

Look at that! I'm anxious.

It is possible for me to withstand the sensations that are generated by the thought, "I have what I want."

It is possible that my physical pain is nothing more than rage.

I have something to offer.

It is safe for me to have and enjoy the things that I love.

I am the source of my own peace.

I can do things right. I'm OK.

It is possible for me to think clearly.

I have something to offer.

I Am already everything I want to be, right now.

It is possible to make peace with anger.

I am IN security.

The world is showing me my thoughts.

I can have something good.

Hard is easy, easy is easy.

I am human.

I can let it be.

It's OK to relax.

I am willing to accept all the money in the world.

I am good enough.

I am want-able.

There's no limit to how happy I can be.

My joy is my livelihood.

My vulnerability is my ace in the hole.

I am my constant companion.

I can fulfill my dad by being fulfilled myself.

I matter, and I am the source of my own happiness.

I have something special to share that can help other people.

If I fulfill my dreams, I fulfill other people's dreams.

I am allowed to have what I want without retaliation.

I am allowed to have what I want and enjoy it.

It is possible for this relationship to heal.

Success is in my hand.

Money is all ways available.

As I let go of having, I AM.

I am allowed to want what I want.

It is possible for this to happen right away, for the price I'm asking.

I am not an apology. I am prosperity.

Fear is just fear!

I can be extremely anxious and care about people close to me.

I can experience "no" and live "yes."

I am complete.

My flaws are assets.

I am special......like everyone else.

I am visible.

There are unlimited opportunities in me.

Contentment is available to me right now.

Every experience is an opportunity for me to know Love.

Believe it or not, I have something great to offer.

What I think of me is my only business.

I think I'm a whore. So what!

No matter what, I can give my all.

My work is my joy!

I am the real thing.

I am Source.

My success is good.

I can do anything.

It is possible for me to have it all, powerfully and easily.

It's my world.

The world says Yes to my power.

Success is possible for me.

I am allowed to be an A-List success at what I was born to do.

I recognize that the life I desire is here for me now.

What I'm seeing and hearing in the world cannot be ANYTHING but a reflection of my thought.

I can be seen and heard and provided for abundantly.

Success is getting it published, not getting it perfect.

It is possible for me to know what to do and where to be.

I'm listening to me.

I'm good enough to lead, the way I am.

God is my source.

It's not my project, it's God's.

It's not my life, it's God's.

Nothing happens to me, it happens from me.

There's unlimited money around me and available to me at all times.

I get paid plenty for just being me.

There's nowhere to get.

I am willing to feel all the sensations that come with success.

My success is moving and "sensational"

I can't be captured.

I am good enough. I am smart enough.

I am lovable. I am valuable.

It's all taken care of.

I choose joy.

I am acceptable as I am.

It is possible for me to have a trusting relationship.

I deserve to look and feel good too.

I could be the first one.

I assume people are sincere.

It is possible that people can take care of themselves <u>and</u> hear me.

It is possible for me to publish a book.

To err is human.

I am good no matter what.

I have what I need.

I honor my feelings.

I can feel my rage and move forward.

I'm just here.

It is possible to have anything I want and tolerate the sensations that go with it.

Feeling the sensations sets me free.

Experiencing my sensations frees me to have my good.

Life is SENSATIONAL

My success is SENSATIONAL

Love is SENSATIONAL

I am not on a roller coaster. I AM the roller coaster

I am the adult. The pain is the child.

Tell me. I want to know.

Thank you for reminding me to fall apart.

Neither fear nor scattered-ness nor dyslexia nor misplacement can keep me from my source.

I am successful.

I am unstoppable.

I am a player.

Saying no to them is saying yes to me.

I <u>do</u> my career.

My feelings are non-negotiable.

I can <u>with stand</u> all that comes with success.

I can <u>with stand</u> all that comes with the joy of living my dreams.

I can feel this forever.

I can do this no matter how I feel.

The healing is <u>IN</u> the pain.

I can endorse myself.

I am self-validating.

I'm a treat.

I can be of great service to you.

I am Good & Plenty.

It is possible for me to be in a romantic relationship where I am loved as much as I love.

I am uncomfortably good and everything is OK.

I can be with big sensations and big success.

Same event, same sensations, new thoughts.

I don't have to do anything to show anybody anything.

It is not possible for me to be taken advantage of, except by myself.

I love you enough to want everything for you that I want for me. (to the inner child)

I'm listening. (to the inner child)

It's OK sweetheart. You're safe. I'm here. (to the inner child)

You are not alone. I'm here and I know. (to the inner child)

You've got my attention. (to the inner child)

The best way to parent is to sit with my sensations.

The sensations I feel when I'm attracted to someone encourage me to say hello.

When I have success and love, I feel sensations.

I am allowed to think whatever the F#*! I think.

I give myself permission to have unlimited thoughts and sensations.

I am willing to experience relationship inside myself.

I'm curious to experience the sensations that go with doing well.

Sensations happen and don't mean anything.

I am a sensationally successful _____ (fill in the blank)

It's safe for me to take care of myself and for everyone else to take care of themselves.

My full time job is to be with my sensations. Get back to work!

I can have peace inside of me, whatever the circumstance.

I can experience my anger and not kill anybody.

No matter how talented, gifted, qualified and interested I am, I can manifest no job. I am that powerful!

Speaking up is sensational.

The solution is the sensation.

My only goal is to experience the sensations that come with knowing it's all resolved.

I have it easy. In fact, I have it sensational.

Thanks for the choice to feel the sensations.

Thank you sensations, for helping me to be more whole.

This is all going on in the invisible, inside of me.

I am normal. The world is normal. I am part of the world.

No matter what I see before me, there is a way, and I don't have to know what that is. Why not live in the possibility?

I'm loving the movie.

This circumstance has no reality. Go to the sensations.

Dream big and experience the sensations.

I'm allowed to enjoy myself. This sensation doesn't mean that I can't.

I can do this while having the sensations.

That sensation means, "Go to the gym."

All the solutions lie within the sensations.

I can hold the thought, "There is a way out."

I'm whole just the way I am.

There's a sensation at the bottom of this.

The whole purpose of this is for me to experience my sensations.

That "punch in the stomach" sensation means I'm on the right track.

My business is sensational. The story is none of my business.

I can practice being with the sensations that arise when I take on the thought, "Unlimited money is available to me."

I can go beyond my family messages, and live from the inside out.

I am in the perfect place to heal.

I can go to bed in the middle of the day.

Every story is running from a sensation.

I'm great. Sensational in fact.

Every time I can be with those sensations, I'm healing my past.

The ability to experience hunger will heal me.

I should feel like this because I do feel like this.

If I'm willing to have the sensations, I can keep doing what I'm doing, no matter what.

I can be supported and independent at the same time.

I don't have to be "on" inside for anybody.

I'm too much, and that's OK.

Nothing can be taken away from me in here, where it counts.

Thank you mirror.

I'm enough just the way I am.

Ahh. Bring it on. Thank you. I needed that.

Sh*! Happens. It's OK.

Go to work! It's sensational!

Dealing with my coworkers is sensational.

Go to the sensations, and the sensations only.

Hey! I just avoided a sensation with that thought.

What I want is inside right now.

When I start to self-attack, go back to the sensations.

This is an opportunity to experience my sensations.

I'm seeing a reflection of my thoughts.

It's sensational to be looked at.

It is possible for me to be whole without struggling.

I am allowed to live.

Me and my heavy heart have unlimited possibilities.

It's not dangerous. It's sensational.

The "unbearable" pressure is bearable.

Living in the sensation is the solution.

I am not a child doing business with my family of origin.

It's possible, at every moment, for me to tap into my essence.

What I want is only to be found in the Un-Manifested.

Experiencing my sensations sets me free.

I have a job inside.

My husband is already inside.

My mortgage payment is already inside.

I am OK, my kids are OK, and I have a hot sensation in my stomach.

Sensations are my Gateway to God.

My sensational money is here now.

Turn into the skid.

Sensations. Sensations. Sensations.

I already have that.

I live in the "I" of the storm, where the wind is calm and the sky is clear.

There's nothing at stake here.

That hat's already on the peg.

I am the perfect boss for the perfect person to work for me.

The healing is in the sensations. I'm making a sensational recovery.

All the good I see, I already have inside.

All the good I see is a reflection of my thoughts.

What sensation am I feeling right now?

I have fortified myself to protect myself against things that have already happened. (and which I have already lived through)

I am not a child. I can experience my sensations and thrive.

Sensational, powerful people feel these sensations.

I'm looking at all the perfect job listings in the Un-Manifested.

Inside, where I really live, it's always safe.

When I have that sensation, take the next step and communicate.

The world is helping me to experience the sensations I need to heal.

Shake my sensations up, baby!

I am able to sit here and feel a sensation.

This sensation is here to heal me.

All of this is here to heal me.

The mirror is directing me to know it's all inside.

This sensation is the key to my success.

This sensation is the key to my liberation.

I'm fine exactly the way I am, and that's sensational.

That sensation comes with unlimited possibility.

Being with the sensation reveals that I have all I need.

Telling stories dis-empowers me.

I can choose to be dis-empowered any time I want to.

Being with my sensations make my life whole right now.

Completing things I want to complete is sensational for me.

Of course I can have that!

What sensation am I having? What sensation am I having? What sensation am I having?

The sensations mean NOTHING. Period!

Feeling the emptiness opens up everything.

It is impossible for anyone or anything to attack me.

I can have it all ONLY when I can have that sensation.

I have the power to ask for help.

The deals are inside. Period!

At this moment, "I am a success" comes with back and neck pain.

At this moment, "I won and it's sensational" comes with a frozen sensation.

At this moment, "I have what I want" comes with a tight chest.

The moment I feel the sensation I am powerful and I can do it.

I am buzzing through life.

Hurt is not the only game in town.

I can take credit and give credit.

Nothing matters.

I bless this disaster.

I can do whatever my heart desires and acknowledge my discomfort.

It is not possible for me to get ripped off.

Sensation is my salvation.

I ALWAYS make the right choice.

Whenever I feel a disturbance of any kind, go to the sensations.

That's a protective thought. What sensation am I protecting myself from?

I already live in a perfect world.

I see you. Thank you for reflecting back to me what I am thinking so I can see it.

It is here right now!

My interpretation is my interpretation.

I can experience sensations without being compelled to take actions.

My career is here.

I have unlimited resources.

It's safe to say yes to myself.

I can do what's best for me.

It's good to be the Queen!

There are unlimited resources available to me right now.

I am worthy of success.

I honor my feelings.

Bring it on!

Problems don't prevent me from having a fulfilling life.

I AM the spotlight.

It is possible to tolerate anxiety and frustration.

This sensation does not require a response.

I can choose whatever I want.

Choosing what's best for me is the responsible thing to do.

It costs too much to not be my authentic self.

I have it all.

My career can be easy, lucrative, fun and successful.

I empower myself by giving my boss what he wants.

Nothing terrible is happening here.

I am not despicable. Something despicable happened to me.

The world is safe.

I am the Mama!

I have and deserve all my good.

I am precious as me.

I am precious for no reason.

I am worth holding no matter what I feel.

My source is inside no matter what.

I have the happy gene.

I can "stomach" this.

I can be with my feelings.

Sensations are the antidote to the poison.

Success is natural no matter what they say.

I can do it.

I can relax and have joy without my life falling apart.

I can see the joy through the crap.

It is entirely possible that trouble I'm seeing in my life is a reflection of my anger at my parents.

It is possible that I can handle what comes up when I let myself be great.

It is possible that this pain could go away in ways I don't know about.

The answers to my prayers are outside of what I know.

I am willing to be willing to experience the support that is always available to me.

This makes me thrive

I am a success because of my experience.

Good things come from unexpected places.

There is no outside!

No matter where I go, the mirror people are there to help me.

This is all happening inside me.

The only purpose of what I see is for me to experience my sensations.

This can be resolved.

I am in the perfect place in my story.

The basics are doable by me.

It's never too late to be who I was meant to be.

My joy is my livelihood.

It's easy.

Wow! I'm creating this.

I love this!

There's lots of work with my name on it.

There is unlimited flow.

I am <u>NOT</u> bad, I <u>AM</u> good.

Wholeness is here.

APPENDIX C
OTHER RELATED BOOKS

This is just a partial list of books I have read in the course of developing The Thought Exchange® that I have found to be helpful, supportive and enlightening.

THE POWER OF NOW
Eckhart Tolle

THE MENTAL EQUIVALENT
Emmet Fox

PROSPERITY
Charles Fillmore

RADICAL FORGIVENESS
Colin Tipping

THE FOUR SPIRITUAL LAWS OF PROSPERITY
Edwene Gaines

THE ISAIAH EFFECT
Decoding The Lost Science of Prayer and Prophecy
Gregg Braden

FROM ATOMS TO ANGELS
WHERE DO YOU FIT IN?
Paul Walsh-Roberts

TRANSFORMING STRESS
Doc Chidre & Deborah Rozman, Ph.D.

THE LOST SECRETS OF PRAYER
Guy Finley

HOPE AND HELP FOR YOUR NERVES
Dr. Claire Weekes

FACING CODEPENDENCE
Pia Mellody with Andrea Wells Miller and J. Keith Miller

HOW TO STUBBORNLY REFUSE TO MAKE YOURSELF MIS-
ERABLE ABOUT ANYTHING
Albert Ellis

EXCUSE ME YOUR LIFE IS WAITING
Lynn Grabhorn

GETTING TO WHERE YOU ARE
Steven Harrison

DOING NOTHING
Steven Harrison

BUSTING LOOSE FROM THE MONEY GAME
Robert Scheinfeld

SEEDS OF CONTEMPLATION
Thomas Merton

A YEAR WITH THOMAS MERTON
Selected and Edited by Jonathan Montaldo

CHOOSING TO LOVE THE WORLD
On Contemplation
Thomas Merton

ABOUT THE AUTHOR
DAVID FRIEDMAN – CAREER HIGHLIGHTS

With multi-platinum recordings, Broadway shows, Disney Animated Films, Television scores and a teaching and lecturing career that spans the nation, David Friedman is truly someone who has made a major mark in all areas of show business.

From *We Can Be Kind to Listen to My Heart, Help is on the Way, We Live on Borrowed Time, Trust The Wind* and *I'll Be Here With You,* David has written songs of inspiration, love and hope that take on new emotional meaning in these challenging times.

After spending several years conducting musicals on Broadway, including *Grease, Joseph & The Amazing Technicolor Dreamcoat,* and *Song and Dance,* David went to Hollywood where he was the Conductor and Vocal Arranger on such Disney animated classic films as *Beauty & The Beast, Aladdin, Pocahontas* and *The Hunchback of Notre Dame.* This led to David's writing music and lyrics for Disney's *Aladdin and the King of Thieves,* scoring three animated television series (*Happy Ness, Sky Dancers & Dragon Flyz*) and the film *Trick,* and a 13 year stint as Music Supervisor and Vocal Arranger of Broadway's *Beauty & The Beast.*

Most recently, David has been writing musicals for Broadway. His show *Chasing Nicolette,* written with Peter Kellogg, has had three highly successful productions, at The Westport Country Playhouse in Connecticut, The Prince Theater in Philadelphia and the Village Theatre in Seattle, and won the Barrymore Award in Philadelphia for best music.

After a critically acclaimed production in Seattle, David's show *Stunt Girl,* about the life of Nellie Bly, also written with Peter Kellogg, was most recently presented at a staged reading in New York.

A new Kellogg/Friedman show, *Lincoln in Love*, about the early life of Abraham Lincoln, written for the Bi-Centennial of Lincoln's birth, had its first reading at Ford's Theater in Washington, D.C. and is currently being developed at the Village Theatre in Seattle.

And a fourth show by the Kellogg/Friedman team, *Desperate Measures*, a country and western version of Shakespeare's Measure For Measure, was an award winner at the New York Musical Theater Festival, and has been successfully produced in theaters around the country.

David's Christmas Oratorio, *King Island Christmas*, written with Deborah Brevoort, has had over 40 productions around the world, and continues to be a Christmas staple in community, regional and professional theaters across the country.

As a record producer, David started his own company, MIDDER Music Records, and wrote for and produced all of the late, great Nancy LaMott's CD's, including the recently released *Nancy LaMott - Live at Tavern on the Green.* A new Nancy LaMott double CD entitled *Ask Me Again*, hit the Top 20 Billboard Jazz Chart, and a new DVD of 25 of Nancy's performances has also become a best-seller. Most recently, MIDDER released a 4-DVD set of Nancy's live cabaret performances, and both a movie and a book on her life are in development.

David's songs have been sung and recorded by luminaries such as Diana Ross (*Your Love* - Quadruple Platinum) Barry Manilow (*We LIve on Borrowed Time* and *You're There* — featured on Barry's Two Nights live CD) Allison Krauss, Petula Clark, Laura Branigan, Kathie Lee Gifford, Jason Alexander, Lucie Arnaz, Laurie Beechman, Lainie Kazan, Leslie Uggams, and many others.

David's multi-platinum-selling song *Open Your Eyes To Love* was featured on the soundtrack of *The Lizzie McGuire Movie,* and he wrote the opening song for Disney's sequel to *Bambi* (sung by Allison Krauss) which was recently released to record-breaking sales.

David is a regular guest on the Today Show on NBC, writing a new song each month based on stories submitted by viewers, for the *Everyone Has a Story* series. David has written hundreds of songs with Kathie Lee Gifford, and they have co-written and co-produced two Children's CDs. One of them has just become a Children's Musical called Party Animals, produced at the Tampa Bay Center for the Performing Arts. David also co-wrote the score to the Broadway-bound musical, "Saving Aimee" with Kathie Lee and David Pomeranz.

David's songs have been used to raise money for charitable organizations ranging from Duke Children's Hospital to Broadway Cares/Equity Fights AIDS and Birmingham's Summerfest School for the Performing Arts. His song "Help Is On The Way" has been the theme song of the Equity Fights AIDS Easter Bonnet Competition for the past 15 years.

In 2003, David completed an Off-Broadway run of his revue, entitled *Listen To My Heart-The Songs of David Friedman*, featuring David and 5 of Broadways finest singers performing 27 of his songs. The cast CD containing a live performance of the entire show is released on MIDDER Records. The show has now been performed in 10 American cities as well as in London, Ireland, Germany and Australia. Recently it had a highly successful production in Tampa, and plans are in the works for this production to be reprised in Tampa and brought back into New York in 2011.

Having published his songbook, containing 63 of his best known songs, David is hard at work on three solo CDs, and as many as 10 new posthumous Nancy LaMott CDs.

DAVID FRIEDMAN – THE THOUGHT EXCHANGE ®

In an effort to give back and pass on the knowledge he has accumulated in his multi-faceted career, David has created a metaphysical method called The Thought Exchange.®

Originally developed by David in The Artist's Support Group at Unity Church of New York City as a way to empower artists and help them achieve their goals, The Thought Exchange® has taken on a life of its own as David travels the country bringing this easily graspable yet life-changing technology to people in all walks of life.

Through his association with Unity Churches, David first began expanding his Thought Exchange work by doing workshops at Unity Center for Practical Spirituality in Norwalk, CT, The Sacred Center in New York City, Trinity Retreat Center in West Cornwall CT, Unity of Clearwater, Florida, The Unity Convention Cruise in Alaska, The International New Thought Association Convention in Scottsdale, AZ, Unity of Tulsa, OK and Unity of Wichita, KS.

In recent years, David has added Unity of Dallas, Unity of Chicago, Unity of Phoenix, Unity of Pittsburgh, Unity of Laguna Hills, Fellowship for Today in East Lansing, MI, Unity of Hartford, CT, Unity in the Foothills in Torrington, CT, Unity in the City in Boston, MA, Unity by the River in Amesbury, MA, Unity of Central Massachusetts in Worcester, MA, Unity of North Houston, Unity of Tampa, Unity of St. Petersburg, Unity of Palm Harbor, Unity of the Gold Country, CA, Unity of Seattle, Unity of Bellevue, WA, Unity of Yakima, WA and Unity of Portland to the list of places where he has lectured and/or presented Thought Exchange® Workshops.

When David's Off Broadway show began to travel the country, David began doing Thought Exchange Workshops for theater companies in Milwaukee, WI, Tulsa OK, Eureka, CA, The Florida Chautauqua Festival and Birmingham AL, where one of the workshops included both teenagers and senior citizens. In Tulsa, David expanded the areas in which he did his workshops, offering them to a school for disturbed teenagers, students at Tulsa University, Oklahoma City University (a school famous for turning out numerous well-known Broadway stars) and the Oklahoma Women's Bar Association.

WORKSHOPS

David offers workshops on Thought Exchange and Inner Voice on a regular basis in New York City and in Norwalk, Connecticut.

The workshops are done on a Love Offering basis with a requested minimum donation of $20. Nobody will be turned away for lack of funds.

See the next two pages for blurbs on each workshop.

FINDING YOUR INNER VOICE
A BREAKTHROUGH SINGING AND ACTING WORKSHOP
WITH DAVID FRIEDMAN

Want to hit a high note you've never been able to hit before? Want to belt? Want to sing soprano? Want to overcome nerves onstage? Want to act a song truthfully? In fact, want to sing, act and LIVE as you've always longed to?

Let David Friedman show you how to let your voice show you how to do these things. Just as your body knows how to digest food, regulate your heart, keep your body temperature normal (and it's a good thing it does, since you don't) your voice knows how to sing. All it needs is for you to tell it what you want it to do (by simply hearing, inside your mind, the sound you want to make) and GET OUT OF THE WAY so your voice can show you how to do it.

With his unique approach of looking at the voice as a mirror of our minds, David teaches you to put your voice at your command rather than your being at its command.

The ramifications of this are much more far-reaching than singing. In this workshop, you will be given the opportunity to have a first-hand experience of how a change in your thought causes an immediate and matching change in what appears in the physical world. And when you can do this, not only is your voice at your command, everything in your LIFE is at your command as well.

Bring a song you want to work on, and change your life forever.

You don't have to be a professional singer to do this. David will work with you at whatever level you're at.

Given in New York City, every Tuesday evening from 8-10 PM at 853 Studios, at 853 Seventh Avenue (Between 54th and 55th Street) in the studios at the rear of the lobby.

THE THOUGHT EXCHANGE®
OVERCOMING OUR RESISTANCE TO LIVING A *SENSATIONAL* LIFE
A WORKSHOP WITH <u>DAVID FRIEDMAN</u>

"Our thoughts create our reality. What we think appears before us in the world. Change your thoughts and you change your life."

We know this. Why don't we do it? In this participatory workshop, we explore The Thought Exchange® a revolutionary new method that teaches us not only how to choose a new thought, but how to move through any resistance that comes up to staying with that new thought.

We begin with a meditation in which we remember that everything we could ever want and every possibility we could ever think of exists right here, right now, in the invisible world that we call "The Great Un-Manifested."

Knowing this, we ask whomever would like to speak (nobody has to speak, you get as much out of this whether you speak or not) to talk about a "problem" they've been having, something they want, something they think they lack. Then, looking at the physical world as an exact mirror of our thoughts, rather than as the cause of them, we ask the question, "If I'm seeing this problem in the mirror, what MUST I be thinking?" And we uncover thoughts we didn't know we were holding, or at least don't care to be holding, thoughts like; "I'm no good, I can't have anything, I'll never win, I'll always be alone." We think we've been sabotaging ourselves with these thoughts, but in fact, we've been protecting ourselves from the sensations that come up when we take on those thoughts, because of things that have happened in the past.

We then look for a thought that would reflect as what we wish to see in the world, and exchange our old thought for our new thought. But then, and this is the most important part, we stop and notice the sensations we have when we take on that thought, and instead of running from them or taking on a new thought to get rid of them, we simply stay with them and experience them as sensations. Simple but not easy, but the results in our lives are amazing. We get to break through to things we have never broken through before, and finally have the tools to not only choose a new thought, but to stay with it and see it manifest.

Join us in this intimate, safe environment, and change your life.

Given in New York City, every Wednesday evening from 7:30-9:30 PM at 124 W. 60th Street (between Columbus & Amsterdam) Apt. 41L.

If you're interesting in attending this class, please contact David at MIDDER2000@aol.com to make sure the class is happening that week and to check on availability of space.

To book a Thought Exchange Workshop,
Corporate or Private Coaching, or a Speaking Engagement
in your area,

or

For more information about
The Thought Exchange
please contact:

David Friedman
c/o The Thought Exchange
1 Meeting Grove Lane
Norwalk, CT 06850 -2205
(203) 899-0473

TheThoughtExchange.com

ALSO BY DAVID FRIEDMAN:

PAMPHLETS

Is Tithing For Me?
Is Forgiveness For Me?
Is Contributing For Me?
Is Prosperity For Me?

MUSIC

Listen To My Heart – The Songs of David Friedman - songbook
Listen To My Heart – The Songs of David Friedman – cast CD
A Different Light – David Friedman Sings His Own Songs – CD
Let Me Fly – David Friedman Sings More of His Own Songs – CD
Unity – David Friedman Sing Songs He Wrote for Unity

VISIT
WWW.THETHOUGHTEXCHANGE.COM

Made in the USA
Charleston, SC
28 September 2011